The OTTOMANS
Empire of Faith

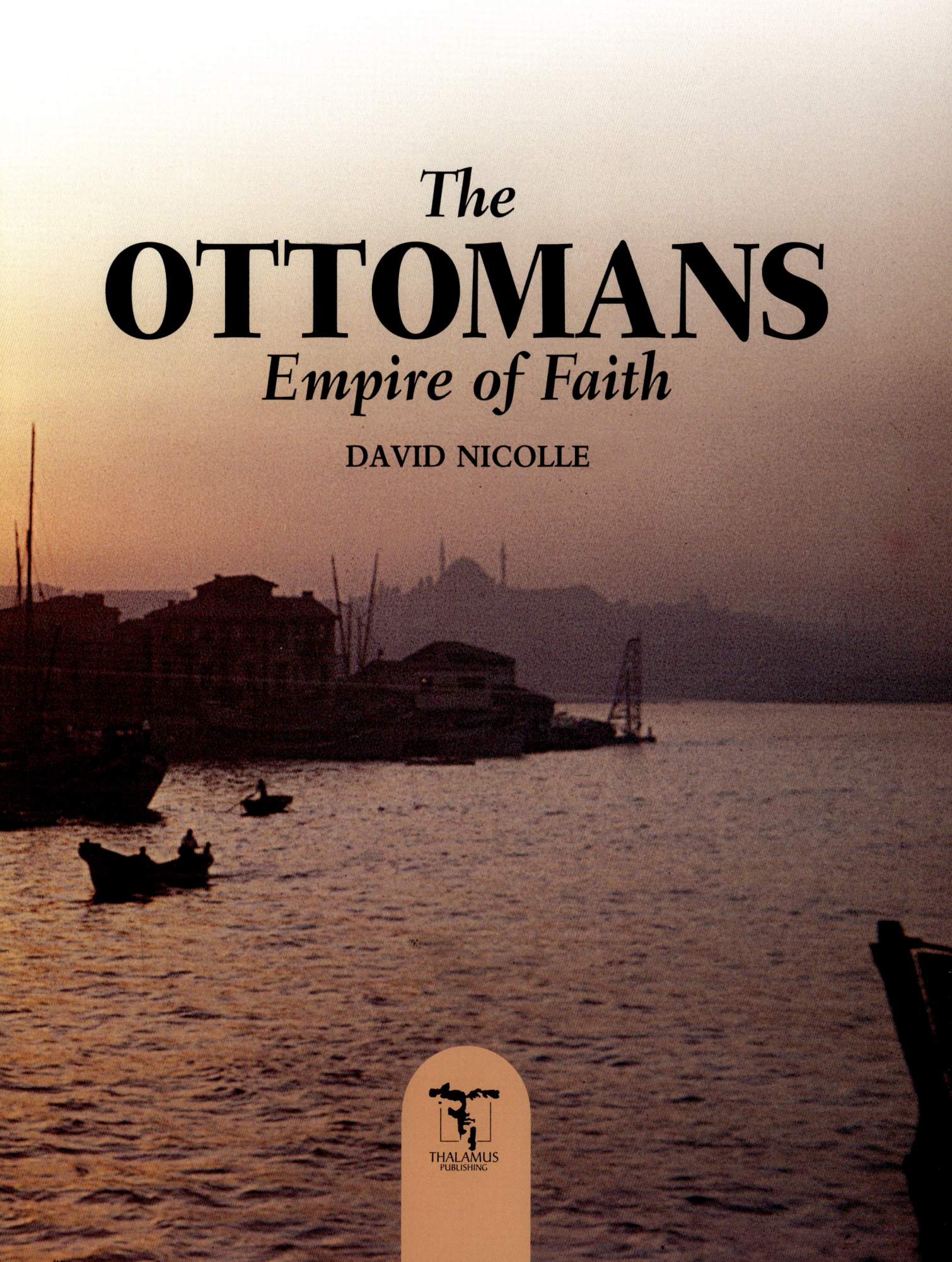

The OTTOMANS
Empire of Faith

DAVID NICOLLE

THALAMUS PUBLISHING

THE OTTOMANS –
EMPIRE OF FAITH

Copyright © 2008 by Thalamus Publishing

No part of this book may be reproduced or utilised in any form or by any means, electronic or mechanical, including photocopying, recording, or by any information storage or retrieval systems, without permission in writing from the publisher. For information contact:

Thalamus Publishing
4 Attorney's Walk, Bull Ring, LUDLOW
Shropshire SY8 1AA, England
(+44) 1584 874977
You can find Thalamus Publishing at:
www.thalamus-books.com

For Thalamus Publishing
Project editor: Warren Lapworth
Maps and design: Roger Kean
Reprographics: Thalamus Studios

Printed and bound in China

ISBN: 978-1-902886-11-4

10 9 8 7 6 5 4 3 2 1
This book is printed on acid-free paper

PICTURE CREDITS
All pictures by David Nicolle except for:
Archivo Iconografica/Corbis: 114, 124, 149 (above); Arte & Immagini srl/Corbis: 65 (right); Yan Arthus-Bertrand /Corbis: 4–5, 38, 45, 81, 113 (above); Askeri Museum, Istanbul: 74 (both), 150 (left below), 159 (below); Bettman/Corbis: 21, 22, 168, 173, 179, 185 (above), 148 (above); British Museum: 79 (below); Christies Images/Corbis: 82 (below); Corbis: 12, 174 (right), 176; Freer Gallery, NY: 24; Chris Hellier /Corbis: 88, 154; Hermitage Museum: 54; Hulton-Deutsch Collection /Corbis: 169 (above), 172, 178, 182; Istanbul Umar Library: 86; Wolfgang Kaehler /Corbis: 29; Oliver Frey/Thalamus Studios: 97 (above): Roger Kean/Thalamus Studios: 165; Louvre, Paris: 79 (right above); Ian Meigh 94: (below); Ali Meyer/Corbis: 111; Musée de l'Armée, Paris: 150 (above), 150 (below right); Musée Fabre, Montpelier: 153 (below); Museum of Islamic Art, Cairo: 132 (below); Müye Müdürlügu, Konya: 26 (right); Fred Nicolle: 36 (below), 134 (above left); Palazzo Mocenigo, Venice: 128; Pierpoint Morgan Library: 90; Royal Engineeers Museum, Chatham: 157; Rykoff Collection/Corbis: 161; Faith Saribas/Reuters/Corbis: 64; Stapleton Collection/Corbis: 155; Murat Taner/Zefa/Corbis: 127; Topkapi Library: 36 (left), 51 (above), 62, 64 (left), 71, 91 (below), 107, 109, 115, 118, 126, 130 (both), 131 (right), 132, 137, 140; Topkapi Museum: 134; Vanni Archive/Corbis: 32 (above); Vienna Kunst Historische Museum: 108; Roger Woods/Corbis: 89; Adam Woolfitt/Corbis: 20 (below); Adam Woolfitt/Corbis: 35 (below); Thalamus Publishing: 54, 66 (above), 77, 80, 82 (above), 83, 85, 94 (above), 96, 104, 110, 120, 121, 122–123, 143, 149 above), 183.

Contents

INTRODUCTION AND INDEX OF MAPS	6
CHAPTER ONE Turkey Before the Ottomans Turks living with Byzantines	8
CHAPTER TWO Origins of the Ottoman State Reaching out to the Sea of Marmara	24
CHAPTER THREE Across the Straits Pushing beyond the Byzantine frontier	38
CHAPTER FOUR The Invasion of Europe United against the fragmenting Balkans	52
CHAPTER FIVE Survival and Expansion Tamerlane, civil war, and European crusades	70
CHAPTER SIX Ottomans in the East From Istanbul to Egypt, Persia, and Arabia	86
CHAPTER SEVEN The Golden Age To the sultanate's greatest extent…before Vienna	106
CHAPTER EIGHT The Tulip Period Artistic flowering, music, and the legal system	126
CHAPTER NINE Restoration or Reform? Fragmentation and dissolution during the 19th century	140
CHAPTER TEN Striving for Modernization From the Hamidian Age to the skies	154
CHAPTER ELEVEN Fall of the Ottomans Disaster and redemption in the early 20th century	168
TABLES OF RULERS	186
INDEX	189

Aerial view of the Süleymaniye, Istanbul's grandest religious complex, overlooking the Golden Horn.

Introduction
The Turks in history

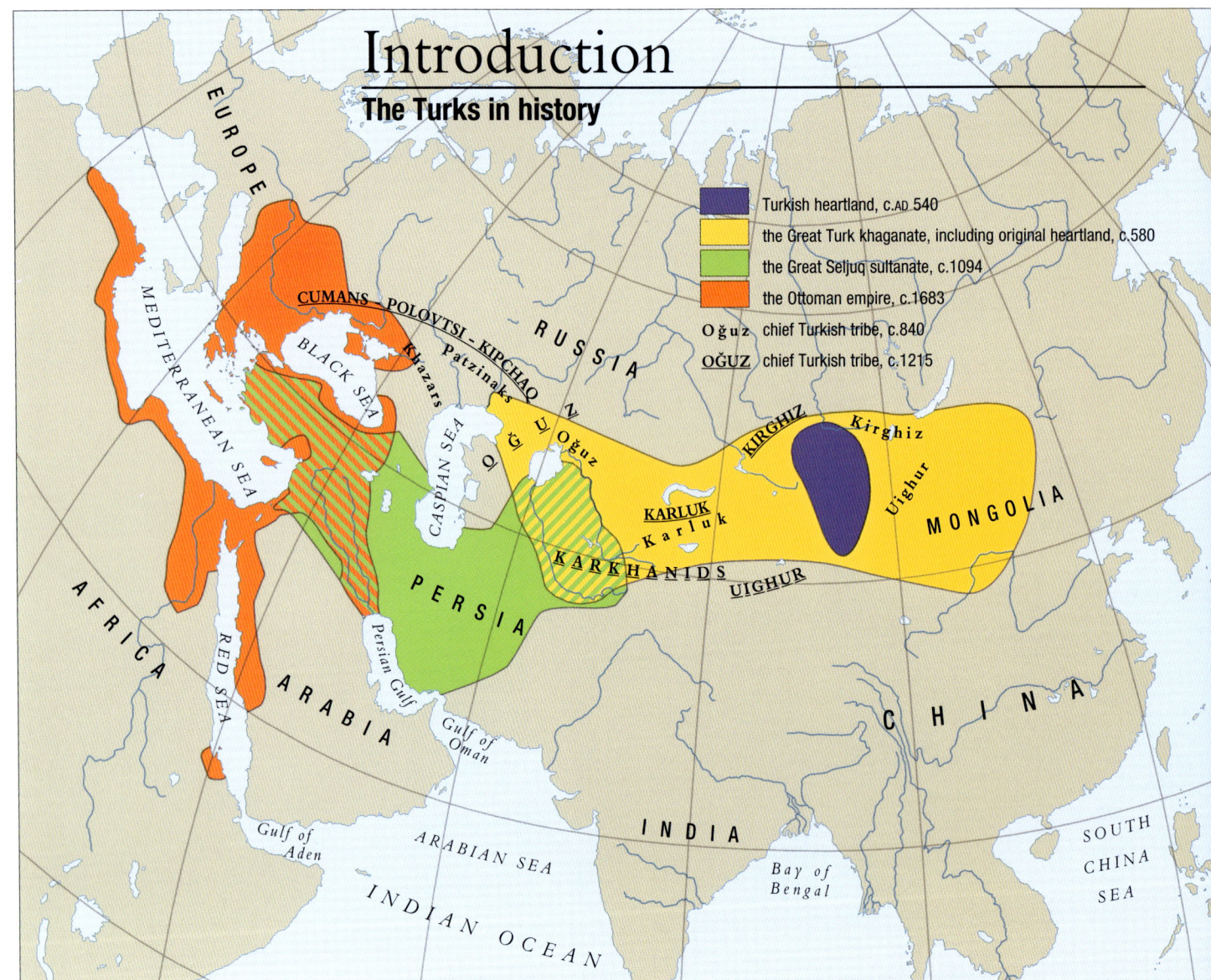

At its apogee, the Ottoman sultanate covered an area similar to that of the medieval Byzantine empire in its heyday, encompassing the Balkan peninsula, Asia Minor, Greece, and parts of North Africa. Many Christians as well as Muslims came to see the sultan as the "new emperor," a legitimate successor to his Orthodox Christian predecessors. In fact Turks and Byzantines had a long historical relationship stretching back at least to the fall of the Roman empire. This major event in European history is, of course, misnamed, since the Roman empire as a whole did not fall in the last quarter of the fifth century AD; only its western half collapsed as a result of internal decay and external invasion. The eastern Roman empire survived as the Romano-Byzantine or simply the Byzantine empire, its citizens continuing to refer to themselves as Romans, while the first Turks to conquer and settle Anatolia, now the heartland of modern Turkey, were known as the Seljuqs of Rum – of the "Roman land." In time, Rum became a vassal of the Il-Khans and Anatolia became a patchwork of small Turkish states. One of them was destined to become the most powerful of all the Turkish nations—the Ottomans.

CHAPTER ONE: TURKEY BEFORE THE OTTOMANS

Index of maps

6	The Turks in history
8	The Romano-Byzantine empire at the death of Justin II, AD 578
11	The Byzantine empire at the death of Basil II, 1025
13	Byzantium and the Turks, c.940
14	Battle of Manzikert, August 1071
15	The Great Seljuq sultanate and the conquest of Anatolia, c.1090
16	The Seljuqs of Rum, c.1182
19	Seljuq caravanserais and trade routes, c.1240
23	The Mongol invasion of Anatolia, 1243
25	The Mongol Il-Khanate, mid-13th century
26	Migration of the Qayï to Anatolia
30	Anatolian beyliks, c.1271
33	Ertuğrul's legacy
37	The Ottoman state with Bursa as capital
39	The Ottomans approach Constantinople, c.1340
41	A foothold in Europe, 1352–60
42	A glance back – the division of the Byzantine empire after the Crusader sack of Constantinople in 1204
44	Christian allies and enemies, c.1360
47	Sufi-dervish centres in Anatolia
50	The Ottomans and the Turkish beyliks
53	The Catalan Company raids, 1305–11; the Balkans, c.1328; Turkish naval raiding
56	The conquest of Didimotikhon and Adrianople, c.1362
59	The Serbian empire, c.1360
61	The Uç 'fronts' in the Blakans and Ottoman expansion, c.1389
66	The Nicopolis campaign, 1396
72	Bayezit's conquests and Timur-i Lenk's invasion
75	Ottoman civil war and revival, early 15th century
76	Ottomans reconquer Anatolia, 1413–83
78	The Ottoman empire and the Hungarian crusades, 1440s
81	Plan of Rumeli Hisarı
84	The conquest of Constantinople, 1453
87	Chalcidice and Mount Athos
93	The Ottoman conquest of the Black Sea after 1453
95	The Krim Khanate
96	The Portuguese threat, early 16th century
98	Selim's approach to Cairo, 1517
99	Overthrow of the Mamluk sultanate; the battle of Raydaniyah, 1517
101	Main Shi'a and 'Red Cap' uprisings
103	Ottoman Damascus
108	The Ottoman Golden Age: central regions and Balkans, 16th to mid-17th centuries
112	The empire's northwest frontier in the 1570s
116	Provinces of the Ottoman empire in 1609
119	Naval power in the Indian Ocean, 1524–89
120	Corsair power in the Mediterranean, 16th century
122	The Ottoman empire's last push, 1683
129	Istanbul in the 16th century
135	The Topkapı Palace
139	The sancaks of the European and western Anatolian provinces, mid-17th century
140	The Ottoman empire and the Napoleonic Wars
144	The Russian advance, 18th century
147	Egypt's bid for supremacy
151	The fragmenting Balkans
152	Losses and gains in North Africa
157	A new Egyptian empire in the 19th century
160	The First and Second Balkan Wars, 1910–13
163	Ottoman railway system
167	The Istanbul to Alexandria flight, 1914
170	The Ottoman empire during the First World War
175	The Gallipoli campaign
180	The post-war fate of the Arabian provinces
184	From sultanate-caliphate to republic

CHAPTER ONE

Turkey Before the Ottomans

Turks living with the Byzantines

By the mid-fifth century CE, the territory of ancient Rome had shrunk in the face of a series of devastating invasions, not least of which was that of the Huns. Their ethnic and even linguistic identity remains a mystery, and by the time that their most famous warlord, Attila, led raids across western Europe, the Huns seem to have been a confederation of peoples including Germans, Iranians, Mongols, and Turks. The Turks themselves emerged into history far to the east. By the mid-sixth century the T'u-kiu or T'u-chüeh, as they were known to Chinese sources, lived in and around what is now western Mongolia. Paradoxically, most of this original heartland is now inhabited by Mongols who are members of a different linguistic group, though vast lands to the west remain Turkish.

Of all the peoples who stemmed from Central Asia, none made a greater impact

- Byzantine empire
- Lombard kingdom
- Lombard duchies
- Sassanian empire
- Avar khanate
- Khazar khanate
- expansion of Khazars
- migration of Slavic people
- Byzantine enclave

The Romano-Byzantine empire at the death of Justin II, CE 578

than the Turks. Their name may have meant "helmet" and they initially seem to have been a minor group specializing in metal-working in the iron-rich Altai mountains. Their origins were mixed but in the sixth century, after defeating the Mongol-speaking Juan-Juan—a Mongol tribe related to the Avars who later invaded Europe—the Turks unified most of the nomadic peoples of East-Central Asia. This vast state was called the Gök (blue or celestial) khaganate, but around CE 583 it divided into the often competing eastern and western Turkish khaganates.

Echoes of almost forgotten wars between Gök Turks and Sassanian Persians are heard in the great Iranian national poem, the *Shahnamah*. The Turks were particularly well organized and disciplined—a characteristic that later foes far to the west would record with some awe—and their tactics were based on mounted archers. While eastern Turks settled down to agriculture and urban life, many of the western Turks clung to their nomadic ways and it was they who bore the brunt of the first Arab-Islamic thrusts into Central Asia, as well as attacks by the T'ang Chinese. As a result, the western Turkish khaganate collapsed in 740. Thereafter, the western Turks were better known as the Oğuz, from whom the Seljuqs and Ottomans would claim descent. While some Oğuz tribes infiltrated the eastern provinces of the Islamic caliphate and soon became Muslim, others migrated further west to settle in Byzantine Anatolia in the eighth century and in time were absorbed into Byzantine society and culture. Yet other tribes later played a major role in the history of what became southern Russia and the Ukraine.

Among the Turco-Hunnish tribes who had remained on the broad steppe lands of southeastern Europe after the collapse of Attila's empire (c.406–53) were the Onogurs (*On Oqur* or people of the Ten Arrows). Soon better known as the Bulgars (mixed people), they established a series of

The Amenian church of Aghtama stands on a promonotory above Lake Van in eastern Anatolia.

states, the most long-lasting of which were Bulgaria in the southern Balkans that adopted Christianity, and the Islamic Volga Bulgar khanate in what is now central Russia. The history of these peoples and regions is complex, but the Byzantine empire was often on the receiving end of their raids, while also recruiting soldiers from their ranks. The Khazars, another Turkish tribal people, established a more permanent state after seizing the steppe regions north of the Black Sea in the 670s. Their ruling elite eventually adopted Judaism. Even before the Muslim Arabs appeared on their southern frontiers, the Khazars had allied with the Byzantine empire against Rome's ancient rival, the Persian Sassanians of Iran. This friendship continued long after the Sassanian empire fell to the Arabs in 651, with the Khazars usually remaining allies of Byzantium.

Weakened by Russian attacks, the Khazars gave way to what is sometimes called the Third Wave of Turkish nomadic migration in the early 11th century. The Pechenegs had emerged from their ancestral grazing grounds between the Volga river and the southern Ural mountains in the ninth century, gradually occupying the Black Sea steppes and penetrating the Balkan peninsula. They were even more mixed than most tribal groups, and although the

majority spoke Turkish, the Pechenegs also included Finno-Ugrian and Iranian nomads. Despite clashes between Pecheneg and Byzantine forces, the Byzantine emperors encouraged some clans to settle along the Danube frontier as *foederati* or resident allies. Elsewhere, the Pechenegs gradually merged with other peoples, including Turkish fellow nomads such as the Torks and latterly the Kipchaqs. It has even been suggested that the Christian Turks who still inhabit the Dobruja region of eastern Romania are descended from Pechenegs and Kipchaqs rather than later Ottoman settlers.

A section of the Oğuz Turkish tribal federation, the Uzes, were next pushed westward, briefly taking the western steppes from the Pechenegs before being scattered by the Kipchaq Turks who followed close on their heels. Though their history in eastern Europe was brief, the Oğuz, or Ghuzz as they are called in Islamic sources, had a distinctive culture and their epic national poem, *The Book of Dede Korkut*, survives in a 14th-century form as a jewel of early Turkish literature. Oğuz warriors served in Byzantine armies from the ninth century, in Middle Eastern Islamic armies from the 11th century and were even recorded as far west as Morocco and Spain.

The Kipchaq Turks took over the European steppes at roughly the time that the Seljuq Turks, a subdivision of the Oğuz, took control of the eastern provinces of the Islamic world. In Russia they were known as Polovtsi, in Byzantium as Chomanoi or Sauromates, and in central Europe as Coumans (Cumans, Kumans, or Kun). They drove the Oğuz from the southern Russian steppes, which they then dominated until the arrival of Genghis Khan's Mongols in the 13th century.

Far to the east, events had already taken place which would have an ultimately fatal

Turcic ethnic memories of an oriental, mountainous past—carving of a lion preying on a cow, from the Great Mosque, Diyarbakir.

CHAPTER ONE: TURKEY BEFORE THE OTTOMANS

The Byzantine empire at the death of Basil II, 1025
Under Basil the "Bulgar Slayer" the Byzantine empire regained much territory lost in the previous decades, as the map of 85 years earlier on the following spread indicates.

impact on the Byzantine empire. The Karakhanids were Turks who had emerged from the Qarluk tribal confederation in the ninth century, converted to Islam and established a powerful khanate on both sides of the Tien Shan mountains. Under their rule, the previously Iranian-speaking province of Transoxania gradually adopted Turkish culture. The Karakhanids also created the first truly Islamic Turkish state, though their own civilization incorporated numerous Buddhist and Manichaean elements. Echoes of this mixed heritage would survive among subsequent Seljuq and Ottoman Turks—still identifiable in some aspects of modern Turkish-Islamic as distinct from Arab or Iranian Islamic civilization. The Karakhanid realm consisted of a series of autonomous military fiefs with only a loose government. To their south lay the Ghaznavids, descendants of Turkish slave-recruited soldiers who had served the previous Iranian Samanid rulers (819–999), to the west the Oğuz.

Some time in the late tenth century a Muslim convert and leader named Seljuq emerged. Having quarrelled with his immediate superior, Seljuq led his extended family and their retainers to new territory next to the Syr Darya river. For several generations their descendants fought for more powerful leaders, who were in turn competing for domination of the northeasternmost provinces of the Islamic world. Not until the mid-11th century did the Seljuq Turks, as they were by then known, strike out on their own. But within a few years they had altered the entire political spectrum not only of the Islamic world, but also of the Byzantine empire.

The Coming of the Turks

The Byzantine empire's defeat by Seljuq Turks at the battle of Manzikert in 1071 and its subsequent loss of Anatolia came as a huge shock to Christendom. Even today, many Western historians regard Manzikert as a catastrophe. Some see the roots of this supposed disaster in the rise of Islam, back in the seventh century AD. Others focus on a sequence of events beginning with the Byzantine empire's reconquest of eastern Anatolia and northern Syria from the Muslims in the tenth century, regions substantially Islamic for about 300 years previously. However, it was as much down to the arrogance of Byzantium as to the spread of Turkish culture, which was only beginning to cast off its tribal origins. The emperor's imposition of military rule on fellow-Christian Armenia in the mid-11th century unwittingly weakened the empire's eastern frontier, permitting a Turkish breakthrough only a few decades later. Byzantium's annexation of Armenia had major repercussions on both sides of the existing frontier. The Armenian kingdom ruled by Gagik II was placed under the Byzantine *dux* or military governor of Iberia, a territory already taken from fellow-Christian Georgia. Part of the old Armenian elite migrated to take prominent military roles in independent Georgia, while others moved into Byzantine Cappadocia or into Islamic Syria and Egypt.

The Seljuq conquest of most of the eastern and central Islamic world during the 11th century was equally significant. This broke the existing Shi'a political domination and led to a revival of Sunni Islam. It also brought predatory and only superficially Islamic Turkish tribes to the eastern frontier of the Byzantine empire. Widely known as Turcomans—to distinguish them from more settled, civilized and urbanized Turks—these largely nomadic tribesmen were troublesome neighbors.

The Seljuqs had been a clan or extended family within the broader Oğuz or Ghuzz tribal confederation. Their tradition shared power within the family rather than concentrating it in the hands of one senior man, and the system continued within the Great Seljuq sultanate, which they and their followers created in Iran, Iraq (roughly equivalent to ancient Mesopotamia), northern Syria, and some neighboring regions. Though regarded as near barbarians by Turks already living within the Islamic world, the Seljuqs' central Asian heritage enabled them to draw on well established traditions of state-building. But as the Seljuqs took over Persia, they became increasingly Persian in culture and outlook, while adopting a somewhat mystical and almost "folk" form of Islam often significantly different from the "book learned" Islam characteristic of the Arab provinces.

The Seljuqs and those who followed in their wake found the frontiers of Byzantium poorly defended. Many Turcoman raiders and even entire nomadic communities penetrated deep inside Anatolia several years before the climactic battle of Manzikert. Some were fighting as *gazis*, or religiously motivated volunteers,

Detail of a Byzantine mosaic showing Constantine IX (1042–55) sitting at Christ's right hand. The emperor lost Byzantium's Italian possessions and at the same time failed to check the new eastern threat from the Seljuq Turks, who overran Anatolia only 16 years after his death.

CHAPTER ONE: TURKEY BEFORE THE OTTOMANS

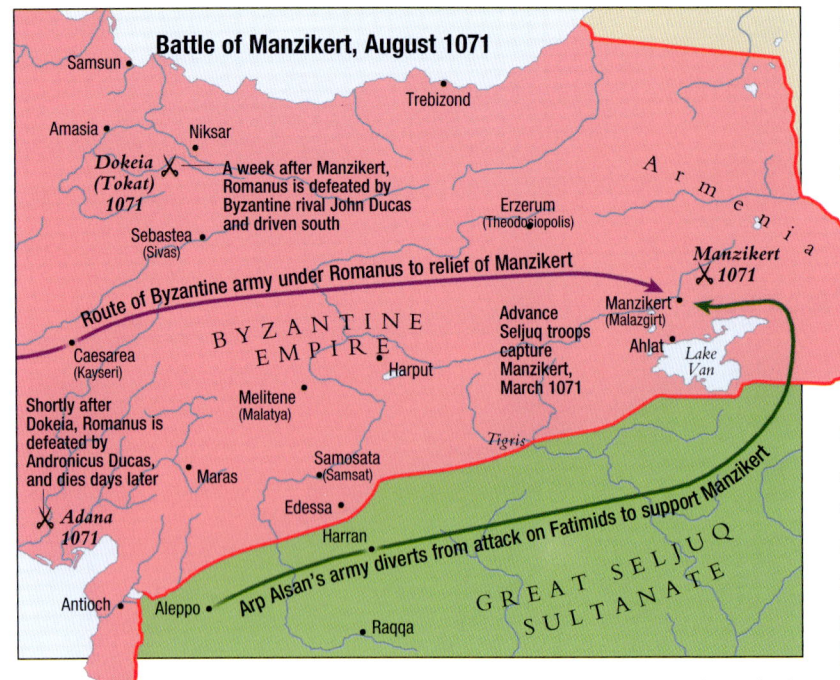

seeking to regain territory lost to the Byzantines a century earlier. Others were simply freebooters. However, a major assault on the powerful and ancient Byzantine empire—the "Rome" of Middle Eastern tradition—was not official Seljuq policy. It was the Byzantine emperor Romanus IV who initiated the anti-Seljuq campaign that resulted in his defeat by the Seljuqs' sultan, Alp Arslan, at Manzikert. A prolonged series of Byzantine civil wars and the gradual collapse of imperial authority across Anatolia followed. Many isolated garrisons clung to fortified strongholds in the hope of eventual relief, while losing control of the surrounding countryside. It was neither a wholesale Turkish conquest nor a complete Byzantine withdrawal. Some claimants to the throne offered groups of Turkish warriors a city or region in return for their military support. For example, Süleyman Ibn Qutalmïsh, the founder of the Seljuq sultanate of Rum, was invited to hold Nicaea by aspiring Alexius Comnenus. As Alexius I (1081–1118) he subsequently called for military help from western Europe to eject the Turks. This resulted in the First Crusade of 1095–99, during which Franks and Normans seized Jerusalem and established the Crusader States, the Counties of Edessa and Tripoli, the Principality of Antioch, and the Kingdom of Jerusalem, which had nominal sovereignty over them all.

After Süleyman died, Great Seljuq sultan, Malik Shah, took his son Qïlïch Arslan as a princely hostage, fearing that the Seljuqs of Rum would prove difficult to control. When Qïlïch Arslan was released and returned to Anatolia, he had great difficulty reasserting his authority because other, even less amenable, Turkish powers had arisen in the area, the most formidable of whom were the Danishmandids.

The Seljuq sultanate of Rum

From the 1070s to the arrival of the First Crusade at the close of the 11th century, several Armenian leaders established principalities in south-central Anatolia and northern Syria. Elsewhere, elements of the old Armenian military aristocracy, along with descendants of both Greek and western European soldiers in Byzantine service, accepted Turkish rule. They gradually adopted aspects of Turkish culture and language, and some converted to Islam. Other families remained Christian for several generations while still serving the new Turkish rulers in both civil and military capacities. The Christian Armenians similarly remained a distinct and highly significant group within what would become the Seljuq sultanate of Rum. The new Turkish states established in conquered Byzantine territory in the late 11th century survived the passage of the First Crusade on its march through Anatolia to Syria and Jerusalem. However, Rum was reduced to little more than the region around the city of Iconium—simplified by the Turks to Konya—which became its capital.

Having lost much less land to Byzantine reconquest, the Danishmandids came to

CHAPTER ONE: TURKEY BEFORE THE OTTOMANS

represent the leading Islamic military power in Anatolia during the early years of the 12th century. In fact, they swallowed up an entire Christian army which marched on the heels of the successful First Crusade in the summer of 1101. So disastrous was this debacle that history has not even dignified the crusade with a number. Two lines of Danishmandid emirs or rulers had emerged by the mid-12th century, one based at Sivas, the other at Malatya and Elbistan. Though their history remains obscure, they feature more prominently in Turkish folk legends and literature such as the epic *Danishmandname*. During the 1170s the Seljuqs of Rum recovered from their early setbacks and absorbed both Danishmandid states.

While generally maintaining good relations with the still-powerful Byzantine empire, the Seljuqs steadily gained territory from Armenian Cilicia and the Crusader County of Edessa to their south, as well as from the Danishmandids to the east. In 1176, between two campaigns that overthrew the Danishmandids, the Seljuqs inflicted a crushing defeat on an invading Byzantine army led by ambitious Manuel I Comnenus. For the Byzantines the battle of Myriokephalon was almost as great a catastrophe as Manzikert had been in 1071. Although the Seljuqs of Rum did not immediately follow up their success by invading neighboring provinces, Byzantine military power never fully recovered.

The first half of the 13th century marked the highpoint of Seljuq civilization in what is now Turkey. It was also under Seljuq patronage that a distinctive new style

15

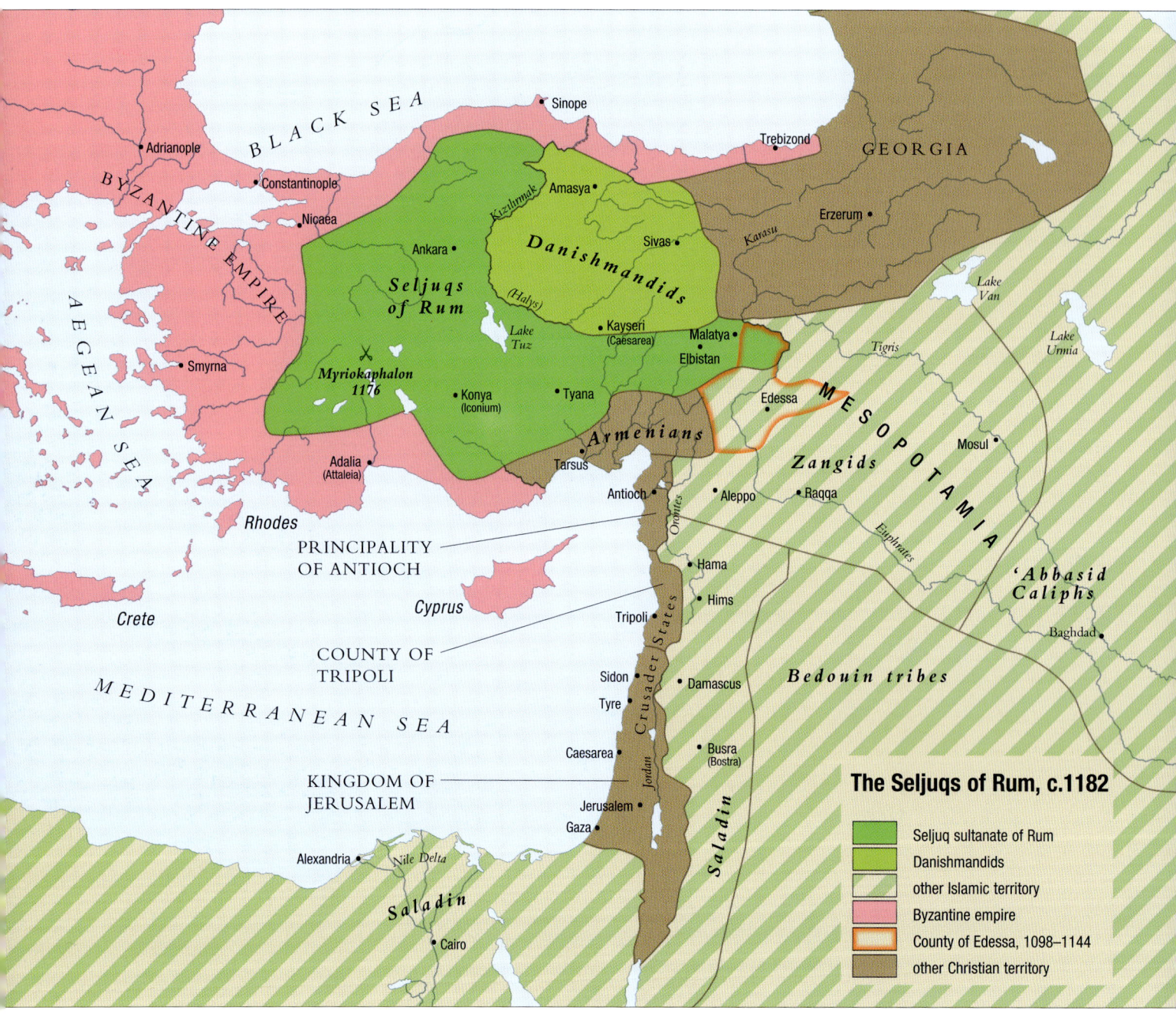

of Anatolian Islamic art and architecture emerged. Most of the many magnificent Seljuq buildings that survive date from these decades. The same is true of most surviving Seljuq textiles, stucco-work, ceramics, woodcarving, and metalwork. The strongest cultural influence came from neighboring Islamic Iran and the Turks' own central Asian heritage. But the influence of Christian Byzantine and Christian Armenian cultures can also be identified. Seljuq Anatolian art, architecture, and literature would provide the foundations for the Ottoman civilization which followed.

Most of the main cities in Turkish-ruled Anatolia had existed for hundreds if not thousands of years, and their Romano-Byzantine plans, fortifications, and other facilities did not disappear under Turkish rule; on the contrary, they were often restored and considerably improved by the Seljuqs. In contrast, the new towns they

CHAPTER ONE: TURKEY BEFORE THE OTTOMANS

Left: Entrance to the Karatay Madrasa, 1252, Konya

Below: Doner Gumbat, 1276, Kayseri

established in conquered Byzantine territory had many Central Asian characteristics, while reflecting Romano-Byzantine urban traditions. These tended to be more spread out than older towns, with scattered market-gardens, orchards, markets, running water, and numerous public fountains. The Turks also greatly increased the numbers of *hamams* or public bathhouses. These differed from Romano-Byzantine public baths, lacking a large immersion or swimming pool in favor of constant running hot and cold water, which flowed into several smaller basins. The Seljuqs, like their Ottoman successors, also changed the public faces of the ex-Byzantine cities by building numerous mosques and *madrasa* Islamic schools or "teaching mosques," along with hospitals for both physical and mental disorders.

Another characteristic form of new public building was the *imaret* soup kitchen and accommodation, provided virtually free of charge for the poor. Many of these charitable foundations were financed and administered by the *vakıf* (Arabic *waqf*) system, which itself depended on a rapidly increasing number of revenue-providing properties given in perpetuity for such purposes. Although religious foundations of all faiths were exempt from taxation in the Islamic world, users of vakıf land paid taxes to administrators who then passed these revenues to vakıf charities such as soup kitchens. Similarly, the urban population paid taxes to authorities, just as military fief-holders paid taxes to superior officers and freehold landowners paid taxes to the state treasury. Unmarried men often had to pay an additional levy until they found a wife.

As in other traditional Islamic cities, special areas outside the city walls or perimeter were reserved for animals who had been brought to market for slaughter as food. Similarly, most pungent or otherwise unwholesome industries were obliged to locate just inside or preferably outside the city limits. The more valuable or prestigious the goods involved in a specific trade, the closer to the center of a town that

Courtyard of the Madrasa at Erzerum in northeastern Anatolia, **above**, and the interior of Karatay Madrasa, Konya.

trade would be located. As a result, goldsmiths and book sellers tended to cluster around the main mosque in the heart of a city.

There were no officially recognized guilds in Turkish cities but, as in other parts of the Islamic world, each *esnaf* or craft association was supervised by a man recognized by the authorities. By the Ottoman period the esnaf was used by the government as a means of gathering taxes from the urban artisan class. Each trade tended to develop a shared identity, often attending the same mosque for prayers and in some cases forming militia units to defend the city walls. Characteristic of all Islamic cities, slaves were rarely employed in industry or agriculture, since slavery was seen primarily as a source of trained domestic servants or elite professional soldiers. Indeed, the title *kul* or slave would become a source of pride, adopted even by free men, during the Ottoman period.

Outside Turkish-speaking countries, Turkish literature has rarely been allowed the same status as that of Arabic or Persian. Nevertheless, the Seljuq sultanate of Rum and its immediate successors provided fertile ground for the further development of forms of literature which could trace their origins back to Central Asia, as well as to some new forms. These included exciting if rather unsophisticated war-like tales and perhaps the funniest stories in Islamic literature. Those concerning the escapades of Nasruddin Hoca were typically Turkish and remain very popular to this day. Often rude and disrespectful of authority, they nevertheless remain deeply moral and even mystical, having close links with the Sufi or dervish brotherhoods that were largely responsible for the survival of Turkish literary culture during the disastrous Mongol occupation of the 13th century. Thereafter, Turkish literature would flourish in its own right, though it never entirely emerged from the shadows of more prestigious Arab and Persian writings.

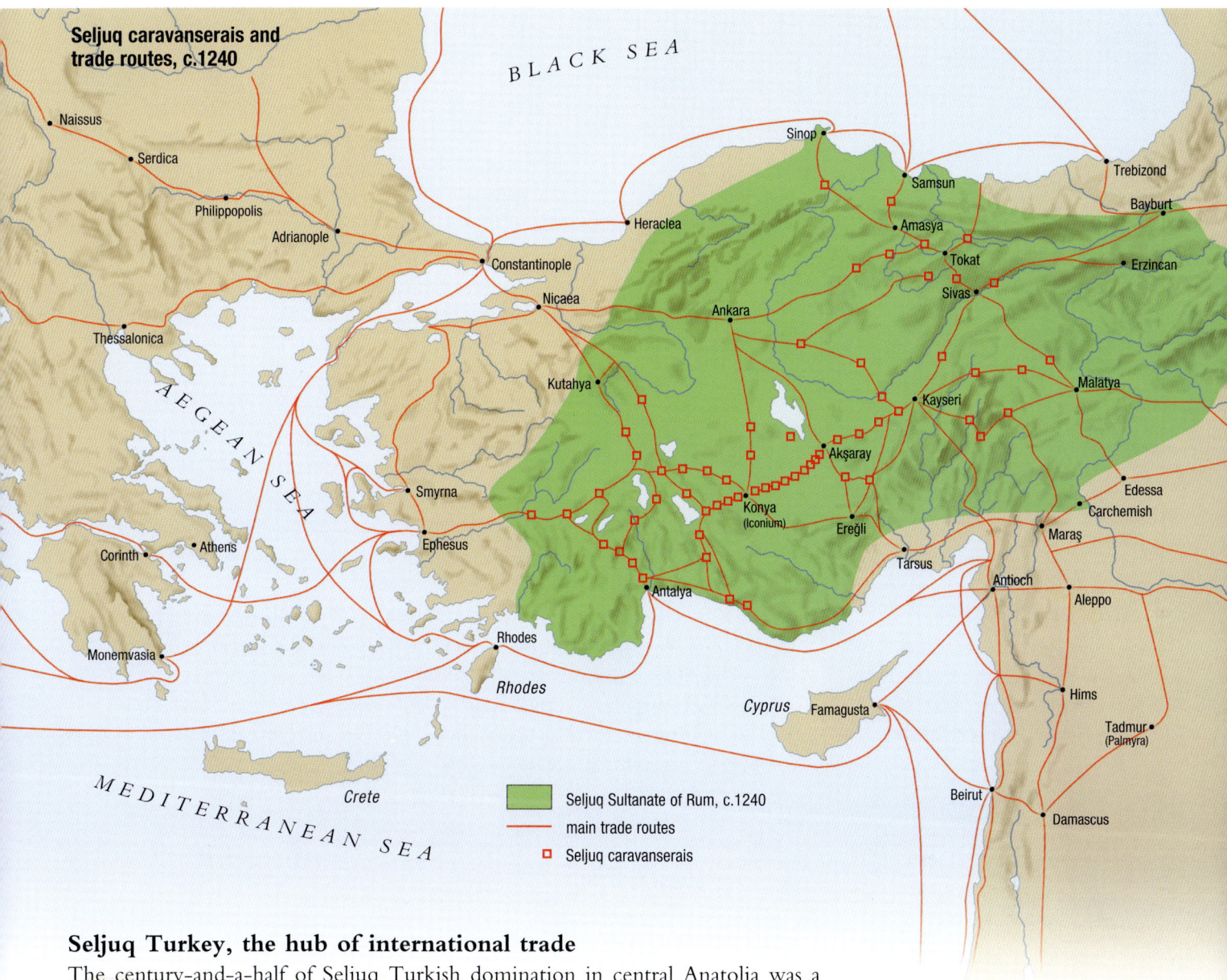

Seljuq Turkey, the hub of international trade

The century-and-a-half of Seljuq Turkish domination in central Anatolia was a period of striking economic progress, especially in long-distance trade. Adaptable tradesmen used new methods to match fine goods from the East, and a dedicated transport network spread their wares to much of the known world. Technology and the industries of the 12th century Islamic world, particularly in the Middle Eastern heartland, were in some respects very advanced. Several of these technologies were introduced into the economically expanding and increasingly wealthy Seljuq sultanate of Rum. Ceramics and textile manufacture flourished in some cities, with constant attempts by Muslim potters to compete with highly regarded but very expensive imported ceramics from China. Metalworking and woodwork also found ready markets, with Islamic civilization's scientific approach to metallurgy making it easy for Muslim smiths to adopt new steel and other techniques introduced from China and India.

The relatively rapid long-distance communication and trade links by both land and sea helped the spread of such technologies and the sale of resulting high-quality

Covered medieval galley docks at Alanya. The main Mediterranean ports—vital to Byzantine trade and customs duties— were great Seljuq prizes. Many older bridges were repaired and new ones built. The multi-arched bridge crossing the Köprü near Aspendos shows the skill of medieval Seljuq engineers.

manufactured goods. The Seljuqs of Rum took prompt advantage of their prime geographical location at the heart of several flourishing trade networks to buy, sell and transport goods across virtually the entire known world. By the 13th century this "known" trading world encompassed all of Europe, most of Asia as far as China, Japan, Korea and much of Indonesia, and a substantial part of Africa. Sometimes it seems as if the only continents whose goods did not pass through Seljuq markets were those from the Americas and Australasia! Small wonder that western European merchants, especially those of Italy, worked hard to establish friendly trading links with the merchants of Seljuq cities.

Transport was simple but effective. Each town had areas outside its gates where pack animals were loaded with goods, while the main markets within the cities often had large, secure warehouses. Routes which had fallen into decay under Byzantine rule were revived and many bridges were repaired or built from new, along with a remarkable network of *hans (khans)* or *caravanserais*. These were like fortified motels in which merchants and their goods could find shelter from brigands and from Anatolia's often harsh climate. Surviving or identifiable examples of han tend to be around 18 miles apart, representing about nine hours' walking time for loaded pack animals— a day's march. The grandest of them had an enclosed courtyard with a raised *musalah* or prayer room in the center, plus a hall, a hamam or public bath, workshops, private chambers, stables for baggage animals, and storage rooms for goods. Not all were as well equipped, but the concept was within a long-established tradition of eastern trade facilities which could be seen in Iran, Transoxania, and along some stretches of the Silk Road routes to China.

As yet, the Mediterranean and Black Seas were dominated by Christian fleets, largely Italian though the Byzantines were still active in the Black Sea, while Islamic vessels had not disappeared from the eastern Mediterranean. Once the Seljuqs and their Turkish successors reached the Mediterranean and Black Sea coasts, they once again took to the sea as both merchants and corsairs, just as their ancestors had done in the late 11th century. Sometimes the port facilities they built were remarkably sophisticated, ranging from slipways carved from the rock to entirely covered docks for galleys. Most of these more elaborate structures seem to have been intended for warships rather than merchant vessels, but trade was supported along every step of the Turkish sea lanes.

The Mongols invade Anatolia

The conquest of the Byzantine capital of Constantinople (later Istanbul) in 1204 during the Fourth Crusade and its occupation by western "Latin" forces until 1261 sapped what remained of Byzantine power in the region. The remanants in Asia Minor were the tiny and isolated "Empire" of Trebizond and the larger "Empire" of Niceaea. Since the latter's primary concern was with Constantinople's recapture from the Latins, the Seljuqs of Rum took the opportunity to expand again, reaching the Mediterranean in the south and the Black Sea in the north. Possession of even short lengths of suitable coastline brought even greater trading wealth, which in turn paid for increased military power and fueled territorial ambitions. Much of this ambition was eastward, toward the ancient heartlands of Islamic civilization.

The Seljuqs of Rum had several powerful eastern and southeastern neighbors. The Ayyubids, descendants of Saladin, the Kurdish general who defeated the crusaders

A Mongol illumination of c.1330 depicts Alexander the Great battling a dragon. As they made their westward migration, the Mongols absorbed many legends of those they conquered.

at Hattin in 1187 and retook Jerusalem, dominated Syria and northern Mesopotamia. The 'Abbasid caliphs of Baghdad had revived as a substantial power in central and southern Mesopotamia, as well as much of western Persia. Georgia was a major power in the Caucasus and the current Seljuq sultan, Keykhüsrev II (or Kay Khusraw), had taken Russudana, daughter of famed Georgian Queen Tamara, as his second wife. His first marriage, to the daughter of the Ayyubid ruler of Aleppo in northern Syria, had been a political move.

Mounted Mongol warriors fighting; painting from the 16th-century Persian school.

The Khwarazm-Shahs from eastern Persia and Transoxania also had ambitions in these regions. Though the Khwarazm-Shah 'Ala'al-Din had been defeated by Genghis Khan (c.1167–1227) and his Mongol horde, his son Jalal al-Din and much of his army had fled westward not simply as refugees, but as a powerful military force. In addition to clashing with the 'Abbasid caliph and some of the Ayyubids, the supposedly defeated Khwarazmians invaded newly acquired Seljuq territory in eastern Anatolia. Although Keykhüsrev defeated them, a far greater threat lay over the horizon. Panic-stricken refugees were already crossing into Seljuq territory, spreading news of the horrific cruelties committed by Genghis Khan's pagan troops as they swept aside all resistance in Transoxania and Iran. This led to religious hysteria against all non-Muslims and rebellions against the Seljuq ruler's authority. This may have forced the sultan to use more western European mercenaries than ever before.

For several years the Mongols targeted Persia, Georgia, and southern Russia. In 1221 the sultan of Rum even tried to take advantage of the situation by sending a naval expedition to impose his suzerainty on the Genoese trading outpost of Sudak (Soldaia) in the Crimea. The defenders of Sudak, probably with Seljuq assistance, repulsed a combined Russian and Kipchaq Turkish attempt to take control a few months later. But in 1222 the Russians and Kipchaqs were utterly defeated by Mongols in the epic battle of the River Kalka in what is now eastern Ukraine. The following year the Mongol commanders Sübodei, Jebei Noyan, and Jochi, Genghis Khan's eldest son, were ordered to return to the east and rejoin the main army. It may have seemed that the Mongol threat to the Seljuqs had faded.

Almost 20 years passed before the Mongols turned their attention to the Seljuqs. Genghis Khan had died and since 1241 the Mongol empire had been ruled under

CHAPTER ONE: TURKEY BEFORE THE OTTOMANS

The Mongol invasion of Anatolia, 1243

- Seljuq sultanate of Rum, c.1182
- expansion of Rum, 1182–1243
- Seljuq vassal, 1243
- temporary Seljuq vassal
- other Islamic territory
- rival Byzantine empires of Nicaea and Trebizond
- other Christian territory
- Mongol invasion under Baidu, 1242–43
- march of Seljuq Sultan Keykhüsrev II, 1243
- battle between Seljuqs of Rum and Mongols
- other major battle

the regency of Töregene Khatun, widow of his son Ögedey. The Mongols' string of conquests had slowed down and some of the Islamic regions they had conquered were threatening to slip out of Mongol control. Soon after Ögedey's death, a Mongol army besieged and took the eastern Anatolian city of Erzerum. Keykhüsrev realised that he was now a target, so he assembled a substantial army under the command of Georgian Prince Shervashidze. The Mongol invaders, under Baydu, also included Georgian and Armenian troops.

The battle at Köse Dağ on June 26, 1242, resulted in a devastating Seljuq defeat. It is particularly interesting for military historians because Keykhüsrev's army fought in an almost European manner, depending to a great extent on heavily armored, close-combat cavalry supported by infantry, and included large numbers of western European mercenaries, plus others from the disintegrating Crusader States in Syria. The Mongols relied on much the same central Asian horse-archery and dispersal tactics that the Seljuqs' own ancestors had found successful some 200 years earlier.

As Seljuq authority collapsed, various nomadic and semi-nomadic Turcoman tribes increased power and gained independence. The scene was set for the *beylik* phase of Turkish history.

CHAPTER TWO

Origins of the Ottoman State

Reaching out to the Sea of Marmara

For the last few decades of its existence, the enfeebled and crumbling Seljuq sultanate of Rum was a vassal of the huge Mongol Il-Khanate. After 1277, Mongol governors seized direct control, though nominal Seljuq rulers remained until the first years of the 14th century, the dynasty conclusively coming to an end in 1307. At that point Turkish Anatolia theoretically became part of the Il-Khanate, but many areas were already ruled by *beys*—local rulers of small Turkish states or *beyliks* —some acknowledging a distant Il-Khanid suzerainty, others becoming a focus of Turkish resistance to Mongol domination. The Il-Khans were themselves only one of several Mongol khanates that, in the later 13th and early 14th centuries, ruled most of the known world from the coasts of China to the Polish frontier. The havoc that Genghis Khan's Mongol armies wrought across the eastern and central lands of the Islamic world seemed to suggest that the Mongols had a particular hatred of Islamic civilization. Yet Genghis Khan's kindly treatment of Muslims in Central Asia before he attacked the Khwarazm-Shah, the leading Islamic power in this

Mounted Turkish warriors and infantry smite their enemies and make a busy decoration on this "battle plate."

region, suggests otherwise, as did the presence of Muslim Turks within his armies. Instead, the Mongol invasions' devastation resulted from political and military considerations, rather than religious rivalry.

It was Genghis Khan's grandson, Hülegü (1217–65), who took Mongol conquests to their greatest extent in the Islamic Middle East and established what became the Il-Khanate, a successor state centred on Iran and Mesopotamia. Only a few decades later, the Il-Khans converted to Islam, after which their huge but relatively short-lived realm played a significant role in reshaping the history, culture and art of the Middle East. Its existence did much to reestablish a sense of Iranian

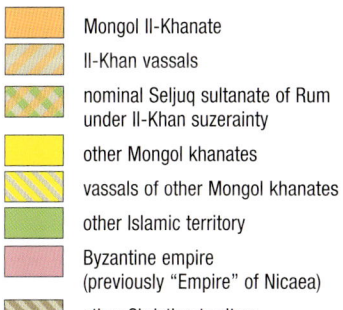

The Mongol Il-Khanate, c.1270

- Mongol Il-Khanate
- Il-Khan vassals
- nominal Seljuq sultanate of Rum under Il-Khan suzerainty
- other Mongol khanates
- vassals of other Mongol khanates
- other Islamic territory
- Byzantine empire (previously "Empire" of Nicaea)
- other Christian territory

national identity, previously dominated by Arabs and then by Turks. The Il-Khanate also served a channel through which ideas, technological development and artistic styles flowed between China and the Middle East. While Hülegü consolidated Mongol control over Iran, Mesopotamia, Anatolia and the lands north of the Euphrates, the Seljuqs of Rum seemingly resigned themselves to their new status as vassals. The Mamluk sultans on the other side of the river would occasionally try to replace Mongol domination of this area with their own, but they never succeeded. Paradoxically, the feeble and fragmenting Seljuq sultanate of Rum entered a sort of golden sunset in terms of art, architecture, and culture. This may have been an unconscious effort to maintain their Turkish and Islamic cultural identity in the face of what was, at first, the Mongols' partly pagan, partly Buddhist and partly eastern Christian domination. The Turkish language was, for the first time in the Islamic Middle East, given official recognition and began to be used for serious, high-status literary purposes.

Hülegü had shown great favor to the Christians, as did his successors Abaqa (1265–82) and Arghun (1284–91). This was often to the detriment of the Muslim majority and further fueled the resentment that would eventually do so much damage to eastern Christianity. Meanwhile, the Christians of Iran, Mesopotamia, northeastern Syria, and Anatolia flourished. The Nestorian Christians, whose communities were found across the Mongol empire, enjoyed particularly high status. During previous centuries they had got on well with the dominant Muslims—better than did most other Christians sects—largely because of their belief that Jesus Christ was a divinely-inspired man rather than a son of God, an interpretation very close to the Islamic view of Jesus.

Immediately to the south of the vassal Seljuq sultanate of Rum, the Armenian Christian kingdom of Cilicia was much more enthusiastic in its loyalty to the Mongol Il-Khan rulers. It suffered at the hands of various Mamluk invasions as a result of this ill-founded allegiance, but the Armenians regained some territory previously lost to the Seljuqs and earned great wealth through trade because their port of Ayas was the Mongols' best outlet into the Mediterranean. But as the Il-Khans declined, the Mongols gave the Armenians less and less support against Mamluk raids and encroachment by nomadic Turcomans from central Anatolia. The pendulum was swinging back in favor of the Muslim Turks, and although the Christian Armenians would be the losers, neither would the Seljuqs of Rum be the winners.

Ottoman myths and origins

The first Ottomans may have been one of many nomadic Turcoman groups or warrior bands, rather than a true tribe that moved west to the Byzantine frontier following the Mongol invasion of Anatolia in the mid-13th century. Traditional origins are grounded in myth, until the deeds of Ertuğrul. The most popular myth

Migration of the Qayï to Anatolia

CHAPTER TWO: ORIGINS OF THE OTTOMAN STATE

that the Ottomans had concerning their origins stated that a young warrior named Osman fell in love with Malkhatun, daughter of the saintly Shaykh Edebali, who may himself have been the leader of a local *ahi* or religiously-based urban militia force. Being poor, Osman's only hope of winning Malkhatun's hand lay in gaining military fame. This he did, yet it was said to have been only when the young warrior told the shaykh about a strange dream that Osman was allowed to be betrothed to his daughter.

In this dream Osman saw the moon, symbolizing the fair Malkhatun, rising from Shaykh Edebali's chest and setting in the young man's own. Thereupon a mighty tree sprouted from Osman's heart and soon spread across the entire sky. From its roots four great rivers flowed; the Tigris, Euphrates, Nile, and Danube. Such a dream drew heavily on symbolism popular among the Turks since their pagan past in Central Asia. However, the saintly shaykh is said to have interpreted the dream as a prophecy of imperial expansion, so he was happy to allow his daughter to marry the future conqueror.

Other more historical, but still perhaps partly legendary, accounts claim that the Ottomans—Osmanlis or Othmanlis, as they called themselves—stemmed from the noble Qayï clan of the Oğuz Turks. Their forebears had supposedly roamed a region of fertile steppe land around the town of Mahan on the northeastern frontier of Iran in the late 12th century. At the time of Genghis Khan's invasion, the leader of this Qayï clan was said to be a man named Süleymanşah (Shah).

Süleymanşah and his people fled from the advancing Mongols, as huge numbers of nomadic Turcoman tribes are known to have done, along with the herds of animals on which they depended. Süleymanşah and his followers made their way across Persia, into Mesopotamia and eventually into what is now northeastern Syria. Near the great brick-built castle of Qala'at Jabar, overlooking the Euphrates, the band of refugees tried to cross the river but Süleyman was drowned. Given the historical circumstances, the Turcomans would have been trying to get from the north bank to the south; from what eventually became Il-Khanid territory into that of the Ayyubid sultans or their Mamluk successors. In fact this part of the Euphrates would remain a war-ravaged frontier between Mamluks and Mongols for centuries. Süleymanşah's traditional tomb was, however, on the north bank, just a few hundred metres from Qala'at Jabar. Until the construction of the Tabka High Dam and the creation of Lake Assad in 1973, this little tomb was guarded by soldiers from the Turkish army, despite being deep inside Syria—an interesting example of cooperation between these two sometimes-tense neighbors. Today the site lies deep beneath the waters of the lake.

According to these traditional tales, Süleymanşah's sons disagreed on what to do next. Two sons took their followers back into Mongol territory, eastward to Khurasan where they supposedly entered Mongol service. The third son, Ertuğrul, took a smaller number of people northward to Erzerum. This might indicate that he

The entrance archway of the beautiful Il-Khanid Jumaa Mosque at Natanz, Iran.

Horses graze under the 11th-century Islamic castle of Qala'at Jabar, where the proto-Ottomans arrived in the region. Once guardian of a vital Euphrates crossing, its ruins stand on an outcrop of rock (**below**) above the river, now the dammed Lake Assad.

had abandoned the idea of crossing the great river into free Islamic territory. Instead they followed the river upstream, westward and then north into Anatolia. Some time later Ertuğrul and his people are said to have been living near Ankara, perhaps on part of the Anatolian high plains where they could pasture their flocks. It is reasonably certain that Ertuğrul's 400 warriors were then entrusted with the defense, and perhaps the extension, of a small frontier region further west. This was at a time when the power of the last Seljuq sultans of Rum was at best nominal.

For many years, a large number of European historians claimed that Ertuğrul never existed, but archaeologists have now found some coins bearing his name, apparently dating from the 1270s. Ertuğrul's tiny fiefdom was in the mountains around Söğüt and soon included the battlefield of Dorylaeum—Turkish Eskişehir—where the First Crusade had defeated the Seljuq Turks back in 1097. From these humble beginnings the Ottomans steadily expanded until they were knocking on the gates of Vienna in the west and sending powerful naval fleets into the Indian Ocean in the east.

The Anatolian beyliks

A consequence of the Mongol conquest of the eastern and central Islamic world was a notable increase in nomadism and a decline in agriculture. The revival of nomadism was also seen in Turkish Anatolia, with Turcoman forces taking advantage of the chaos that came in the wake of Mongol imperial aspirations. Turcoman tribes also provided the military and political foundations of an array of tiny states or beyliks which emerged from the declining Seljuq sultanate of Rum.

Following their crushing defeat by the Mongols at Köse Dağ in 1243, the military as well as the political power of the Seljuqs declined steadily, but it did not disappear overnight, since the Seljuqs remained significant vassals of the huge Mongol Il-Khan state in neighboring Mesopotamia and Iran. The Seljuq army initially remained much as it had before, though there were changes in the relative importance of its constituent parts. Slave-recruited *ghulams* or *mamluks*, though now fewer in number, remained the elite core of what was called the Old Army.

However, the traditional Turco-Islamic system of *iqta* fiefs collapsed. It would eventually reappear in a modified form as the

CHAPTER TWO: ORIGINS OF THE OTTOMAN STATE

Ottoman system of *timar* fiefs, but in the meantime it was replaced by a more strictly feudal system. As in most of 13th-century western Europe, land was usually owned by military families rather than merely held at the ruler's pleasure. It could therefore be passed from father to son.

Turcoman auxiliaries were rarely mentioned, but *jira-khvar* mercenaries of Turcoman origin became increasingly important. The New Army was largely tribal, many contingents coming from the powerful Germiyan tribe that soon controlled large parts of west-central Anatolia. Foreign mercenaries, including Europeans, were still used but vassal contingents disappeared after 1256. The role of the Germiyan was key to the emergence of the western Anatolian beyliks. Their state was based on Kütahya and founded in 1286. It rapidly attracted considerable support as a center of resistance to Mongol domination, and Germiyan beys also sent raiders down the western valleys to take over Byzantine territory. Several commanders of such forces established their own beyliks, which eventually stretched as far as the Aegean coast. This was the origin of Aydın and Saruhan, which soon became substantial sea powers, and Karasi which, despite eventually covering a large area facing the Byzantines across the Dardanelles, lacked a formidable navy. The first little Ottoman beylik also seems to have emerged as an offshoot of the Germiyan.

A new force was meanwhile appearing on the scene, one that was to play a vital role in the earliest days of the subsequent Ottoman state. It was given various names —*fityan* in Arabic, *ikvan* in Turkish, or *javan* in Persian—that meant "brothers" or "brotherhoods." They seem to have been based on a loose code of religious, civil, and military ethics known in Arabic as *futuwa*. Most were foot soldiers and almost all were based on towns where they supplemented or even supplanted existing urban militias. In the confusion of the Seljuq decline, these men often found themselves defending their cities against the surrounding and now barely controlled Turcoman tribes.

The Turcomans had already been urged, or even forced, by the Seljuq sultans of Rum into what was, in effect, a broad no-man's-land between the provinces controlled by Seljuq and Byzantine rulers. Here the Turcomans considerably expanded

A valley below the Taurus Mountains in the central Anatolian countryside.

- Turkish beyliks (nominally under Seljuq/Il-Khan suzerainty)
- disputed territory
- Byzantine, 1258–61
- Il-Khanate, including nominal Seljuq sultanate of Rum
- other Islamic state
- Byzantine empire
- other Christian state

Islamic territory during the late 13th century, at first by dominating the countryside while leaving the Byzantine-held towns and castles like islands, isolated from the main centers of imperial power. If these outposts remained unsupported by the Byzantine central government, they eventually came to terms with the Seljuq sultan or, in later decades, one of the emerging Turkish beyliks.

Benefiting from the Mongols' victories, some Turcoman tribes used the same tactics against towns which were nominally part of the Seljuq sultanate, forcing them to accept Turcoman overlordship. Meanwhile, much of the old gazi class of religiously motivated frontier warriors deserted the Seljuqs for the rising power of the Turcoman beyliks. The same was true of the many refugees who flooded into Anatolia from the east to escape Mongol oppression. These included Muslim religious teachers, less orthodox dervishes and huge columns of dispossessed peasants, as well as professional soldiers seeking employment but unwilling to fight for the Mongols.

Neglected by the empire

Other Turkish tribes, some superficially converted to Christianity but others still pagan, had been invited from the steppes of southern Russia and Ukraine into the Byzantine empire, resurrected under the leadership of Michael VIII (1259–82) of the Palaeologus dynasty. These Turks were also fleeing the Mongols, and after this Byzantine "Empire" of Nicaea regained the ancient capital of Constantinople from its crusader occupiers in 1261, many of them were sent to bolster Byzantine defenses in western Anatolia. Despite reinforcements, the government tended to neglect its remaining Anatolian provinces and focus on rebuilding its strength on the European side of the straits. The level of neglect eventually became so bad that some frontier governors and even entire garrisons, as well as the abandoned peas-

CHAPTER TWO: ORIGINS OF THE OTTOMAN STATE

antry, transferred their allegiances to the new beylik or gazi Turco-Islamic states.

Some of the new beyliks that emerged from the wreckage of the Seljuq sultanate of Rum were rich and cultured as well as locally powerful. They naturally used booty from their conquests to strengthen their positions, but this entailed cultural as well as military expenditure because Islamic rulers were expected to be patrons of religion, literature, art, architecture, and trade. As a result, many of the towns and cities of what is now Turkey boast fine mosques and other buildings which date from the second half of the 13th and the 14th centuries, when they were the capitals or provincial centers in one of the beyliks. It is interesting to note how many decorative and even naturalistic features were included in architectural decoration during this and to extent the preceding Seljuq periods. Some elements were drawn from the Turks' pagan past in Central Asia, some seem to reflect Chinese influence, perhaps via the Mongols, while Byzantine or European features can also be found. Much of it seems almost alien to the traditions and spirit of classical Islamic art and architecture.

Early 13th-century Turkish stucco work from a palace near Konya.

Selçuk (Greek Ephesus, medieval Turkish Ayasoluk) is an example of how the Turcoman conquerors announced their cultural presence in newly conquered ex-Byzantine territory. Now a relatively small market town, though a major tourist

destination, it was important under the beyliks of Sasan and then of Aydın, and was briefly regained by Christians in 1365. In addition to the extensive ruins of ancient Ephesus, the relics of the huge early Christian basilica of St John and a large part-Byzantine, part-Turkish castle, Selçuk boasts the superb mosque of Īsa Ibn Muhammad Bey. It was built in 1375 for the last of the ruling Aydın Oğullari dynasty, in an effort to outshine the famous basilica. The *muqarnas* or multiple stalactite decoration above the main entrance is in a late Seljuq style. Inside, a beautiful courtyard contains a graceful lawn around which the tall walls once supported the roof of a colonnaded portico, now largely lost. To one side the prayer hall is divided by four huge pink granite columns, which held up two domes. These columns, like so much other material used in the building of Īsa Ibn Muhammad Bey's mosque, were taken from the ruins of ancient Ephesus. This was not merely a cultural and religious statement. It was a way of saying that a new civilization had arrived, and that those which had existed before were now history.

In some regions the lives of Turcoman nomads has hardly changed: Yurts near a lake next to Ayay Kala in Uzbekistan, **left**, and encamped nomads near Niğde in central Turkey.

CHAPTER TWO: ORIGINS OF THE OTTOMAN STATE

The first Ottoman state

The scholar and geographical historian Donald Pitcher offered the most satisfactory account of what he described as the *probable* early years of the Ottoman state: "The original cradleland of the future emirate was the pastureland stretching from the northeast slopes of the Domaniç Dağ [Domaniç Hills] east-northeast to the curve of the Sangarios [Sakarya river]." Ertuğrul, the Ottoman leader whose existence and achievements are obscured by legend, died around 1280; his son and successor Osman Gazi almost certainly ascended the throne in 1281, and from this point the early history of the Ottomans becomes gradually clearer. Osman I Gazi reigned until 1324, and during his period the Ottoman state developed from a tiny and rather obscure Turkish beylik into a significant, though still small, frontier state, its aggressive actions important enough to be recorded in Byzantine annals. One such raid won Osman his first victory over a small Byzantine field army at Koyunhisar (Bapheus), traditionally dated to 1301. The last years of Osman's reign focused on the lengthy siege of Prousa (renamed Bursa by the Turks), which fell to Osman's son Orhan, shortly before the old man's death in 1326.

Being located on the frontier with the fast weakening Byzantium, the Ottoman beylik also seems to have attracted more than its share of gazi warriors dedicated to the defense of Islam. Though originally intended to be only defensive, the concept of the gazi and *jihad* had taken on an expansionist character in many parts of the Islamic world, not least in Turkish Anatolia. On the other hand, it seems that many clashes between the beyliks and Byzantine frontier forces were a result of traditional Turcoman raiding and the nomads' constant search for better pastures for their flocks, rather than official aggression sanctioned by the rulers of either side.

Motivations may have been mixed, but the results were obvious as the Ottomans, like the other frontier beyliks, took control of more and more Byzantine territory. As elsewhere, they sometimes avoided or ignored fortified towns, leaving them isolated. If such outposts were not relieved by the Byzantine army, their governors and garrisons usually submitted to Ottoman rule—though sometimes only after years of blockade. It sometimes seemed that the Byzantine emperor was unwilling, as well as unable, even to try to come to their aid.

One interpretation of these events maintains that many ex-Byzantine Christian troops and their officers entered Islamic-Turkish service. Most were Greek-speaking, but among their number were Armenians and western European mercenaries, eventually including Catalans from far away Spain. Before turning on the emperor, the Catalans under the command of the greedy Roger de Flor (*see also page 51*), are said to have driven the Ottomans out of Lefke in 1305. One such ex-Byzantine commander even featured in the legend of Osman, Shaykh Edebali and his daughter Malkhatun. According to this story, the young warrior-leader Osman captured the Byzantine lord of Khirmencik castle during his efforts to win fame

Opposite: The Byzantine-Turkish fortifications of Ayasoluk castle at Ephesus (Selçuk) stand on the citadel, with the Īsa Ibn Muhammad Bey Mosque in the foreground. Its facade (**left below**) has late Seljuq *muqarnas* decoration above the entrance. Beside it, decorative detail from the entrance to the Hatuniye Madrasa in Karaman betrays multi-cultural influences.

- traditional fief of Ertuğrul
- traditional conquests of Osman before 1300
- Germiyan domination, c.1310
- other Turkish territory
- disputed between Byzantines and Turks, c.1308–20
- Byzantine empire, c.1320

Seljuq Turkish dynasties

Great Seljuq rulers
1037–63	Tuğrıl I
1063–73	Alp Arslan *(victor of Manzikert, 1071)*
1073–92	Malik Şah I
1092–94	Mahmud I
1094-1105	Barkiyaruq
1105	Malik Şah II
1105-1118	Muhammad I Tapar
1118–57	Ahmed Sanjar

Seljuq rulers of Kirman (south Iran)
1048–73	Ahmad Qawurd
1073–74	Kirman Şah
1074–85	Sultan Şah
1085–97	Turan Şah I
1097-1101	Iran Şah
1101–42	Arslan Shah I
1142–56	Muhammad I
1156–70	Toğrül Şah
1170–70	Bahram Şah
1170–71	Arslan Şah II
1171–72	Bahram Şah *(second time)*
1172–77	Arslan Şah II *(second time)*
1177–83	Turan Şah II
1183–87	Muhammad II

(Kirman as a separate state was conquered in 1187, probably by Ghuzz tribes)

Seljuk rulers in Syria
1078–95	Tutush I
1095-1113	Ridwan
1113–14	Alp Arslan al-Akhras
1114–23	Sultan Şah

(sultans/emirs of Damascus)
1076–78	Abaq al-Khwarazmi
1078–95	Tutush I (of Syria)
1095-1104	Duqaq
1104	Tutush II

---

and thus the hand of the fair Malkhatun. Osman and his captive, Köse Mihal ("beardless Michael"), became friends and went on to fight as allies. This was an ancient theme in Turkish folklore, going far back into the Turks' pagan past in Central Asia. The family of the Mihaloğlu (sons of Mihal) became a politically and militarily important Ottoman family by the end of the 14th century.

Many ex-Byzantine soldiers seem to have converted to Islam very quickly, but in other cases they and their descendants remained Christian for several generations while still serving the new Muslim Turkish rulers. Such absorption of previous military and aristocratic elites was to remain a feature of Ottoman expansion, both in Anatolia and in Europe. This had a profound impact on the personnel, organization, tactics, weaponry, and costume of Ottoman armies, as well as on the structure of the Ottoman state. Similar fusions of new and old, Islamic and Christian, Turkish and Greek or Balkan Slav would subsequently be seen in Ottoman art, architecture, and other aspects of culture.

The glory of Bursa

Of only limited importance to Byzantium, Prousa-Bursa became the Ottoman capital. Today it is one of the most beautiful cities in western Turkey, boasting some of the finest examples of early Ottoman buildings anywhere. As the new capital, Bursa benefited from Ottomans' innovative developments in mosque architecture. The city's impact and its classical architecture were the result of centuries of development. The earliest Ottoman monumental buildings, mosques, madrasas, and tombs were linked to the Seljuq architectural traditions of Anatolia, but they soon began to betray strong Byzantine and even Italian influences.

The most obvious contribution of Ottoman designers and builders to the history of Islamic architecture is undoubtedly the domed mosque. Today the domed mosque plan is so widespread across the Islamic world and beyond that the fact that it is essentially an Ottoman invention is usually forgotten. Earlier mosques had been developments of the first Islamic prayer building, the Prophet Muhammad's house in Medina, Arabia, and as such basically consisted of an enclosed courtyard with a covered area to one side. The covered part of what had originally been a simple Arabian house became the prayer hall of the first mosques. Features added over the years included domes and multiple domes, decorated monumental entrances, minarets, and so on. Nevertheless the basic concept remained and dominated from Andalusia in the west, through the Middle East and Iran, to Islamic northern India in the east—even being found in Indonesia.

However, it was Ottoman architects who, by adopting some of the main design elements of the great Byzantine domed churches, developed a form of mosque which consisted of a rectangular prayer hall covered with one large dome, with the courtyard reduced to a subsidiary architectural feature leading the visitor into the main structure. Partial or smaller domes covered the rest of the prayer hall but also led the viewer's eye up toward the great dome. Outside, minarets were brought close to the dome, unifying the design and emphasising its upward thrust. But it is inside that the greatest achievement of Ottoman builders is evident through their removal of the numerous columns or arches that had been needed to support the roofs or multiple domes of earlier buildings. Mosques could now enclose one huge, undivided, uncluttered space, achieving a sense of unity which reflected the concept

CHAPTER TWO: ORIGINS OF THE OTTOMAN STATE

of Divine Unity at the very core of the Islamic faith. This process took time, of course, and the earliest surviving Ottoman buildings in Bursa date from after the Ottomans had transferred their capital to Adrianople (Turkish Edirne) in Europe. They include the Hüdavandigar mosque dating from the second half of the 14th century, designed for use by dervishes, with contemplation or study rooms on each side of a central pool.

The Hüdavandigar's central dome remains modest, and the building still has the impressive arched portico which characterises the earliest Ottoman mosques. Above this portico there is, however, a beautiful loggia or open gallery, which, while similar to that at the slightly later Karaman madrasa at Niğde in Anatolia, has more surprising parallels in the earliest Italian-style palaces in Dalmatia on the Adriatic coast, and with the extraordinary facade of the church of Hagia Sophia at Ohrid, Macedonia. Such a mixture of influences from so far afield was a sign of things to come in Ottoman architecture.

In 1333, about seven years after Orhan Bey's troops entered the city of Bursa, the famous Moroccan traveller Ibn Battuta visited the Ottomans' new capital. He wrote that Orhan was "the greatest of the Turcoman rulers, the richest in wealth, lands and military forces, possessing nearly a hundred fortresses." Ibn Battuta had visited all the Turkish beyliks and was writing as an independent observer with no allegiances in the area, so his description of the power of the early Ottoman state comes as a surprise—almost all the other evidence suggests that the Ottomans were still relatively minor players in the confused politics of Anatolia.

The primary focus of Ottoman expansion in the early 14th century was to the north, taking over what remained of Byzantine territory along the Asian shores of the Sea of Marmara. Beyond, they almost reached the Bosporus and did reach the Black Sea, waters they would have to conquer. In the first 15 years of the 14th century, Osman Bey extended Ottoman territory in two directions: southwestward to the slopes of Uludağ (the Bithynian Mount Olympus) and northeastward to take several small towns along the Sakarya river. Other Ottoman raiding parties ranged

Its glittering ceramic-tiled exterior gave the Green Mausoleum (**top left**) in Bursa its name. Built late in the 14th-century, the Ulu Mosque dominates Bursa (**top right and above**). The modern city is shrouded in the sub-tropical mist that often forms in the foothills of Mount Olympus (Uludağ).

Detail from a Koran stand, Konya, 1279 (**above**) and a manuscript bearing Orhan I's *tugra* (signature) at its top. At the Istanbul Gate of Iznik (Nicaea) knights of the First Crusade evicted the Seljuq garrison in 1097, but within 250 years the once-great late Roman and Byzantine fortress was back in Turkish hands again.

much further afield but did not permanently hold the lands they attacked.

Because the Ottoman state was still essentially a warlike frontier zone, Osman and his immediate successors continued to rule "from the saddle" rather than their newly conquered towns. Several towns and the southern coast of the Sea of Marmara (the Greek Propontis) remained under Byzantine control for some years after the Ottomans had taken the hills beyond. But even the lowland rural areas were increasingly dominated by Turcoman nomads who migrated to and from the hills according to season.

The Ottomans' first successes also became self-perpetuating. Victory over a small Byzantine field army at Koyunhisar (Bapheus) around 1301 spread the fame of Osman Bey, and settlers as well as gazi warriors reportedly flocked to Ottoman territory. The still modest realm seems to have been widely regarded as a true gazi state—"the instrument of God's religion, God's sure sword"—which existed primarily to defend and expand the realm of Islam. On a more prosaic level, the Ottoman leader had to pay or reward his followers and an increasing number of volunteers with booty; victory had to breed victory, or no booty would be won and the fighting men could not be paid. Ottoman successes were built on more than this, however. The other gazi beyliks and emirates of western Anatolia ran out of frontiers to press against or raid, so they either took to the sea to continue their traditions or focused on a more inward-looking and cultured form of Islam, expending their wealth and energy on art and architecture. Others withered away, losing both religious and military support, and as some beyliks turned their warlike enemies against each other, several were absorbed by stronger neighbors.

The culture of this Ottoman frontier march was as complex as its political situation. Its laws were as yet still those of Turkish tribal custom, the *yasa*, rather than the Şeriat (Sharia) Koranic law of more orthodox or established Islamic states. Its religion often seemed to have been a peculiar mixture of Sunni Islam, Shi'a Islam, ancient Turkish shamanistic belief and residual peasant Christianity. Almost heretical dervishes accompanied some—perhaps all—early Ottoman armies on their campaigns. A few of these mystics claimed that Islam and Christianity were essentially the same religion, and as a result attracted Christian followers, a fact that was to bear greatly on Ottoman successes during the conquest of the Balkans.

The progress of the first Ottoman military advances toward Constantinople is unclear, clouded by later pious or patriotic legend. The largest expansions of Ottoman territory were to the west, with the annexation of the Karasi beylik, and eastward with the absorption of small beyliks like that of Göynük, ruled by the Umur-Han family until conquered in 1331. Expansion northward was more limited and, without a powerful fleet, the Ottomans had to curve northeast and then west around the Sea of Marmara and Gulf of Izmit, to gradually take control of the peninsula which led to the eastern shores of the Bosporus. The claim that the Ottomans captured Kalolimne island in the Sea of Marmara in 1308 is probably a legend, though they may have raided it. This was imperial territory and the Byzantines did not relinquish it without a struggle.

A large-scale campaign of 1327/28 reached the outskirts of Üsküdar (Scutari) opposite Constantinople on the Bosporus and captured several towns. The Byzantines were defeated at Maltepe (Pelekanon) the following year and at Tavşancıl (Philokrene) in 1330. Meanwhile, Ottomans took the southern shore of the Gulf of Izmit, leaving the major Byzantine city of Nicomedia (now Izmit) virtually cut off, especially as Byzantine naval power was fading fast. These campaigns were on a relatively minor scale and focused on a much smaller area than later Ottoman activity in the Balkans, but their firm grasp of strategy was an indication of what was to come.

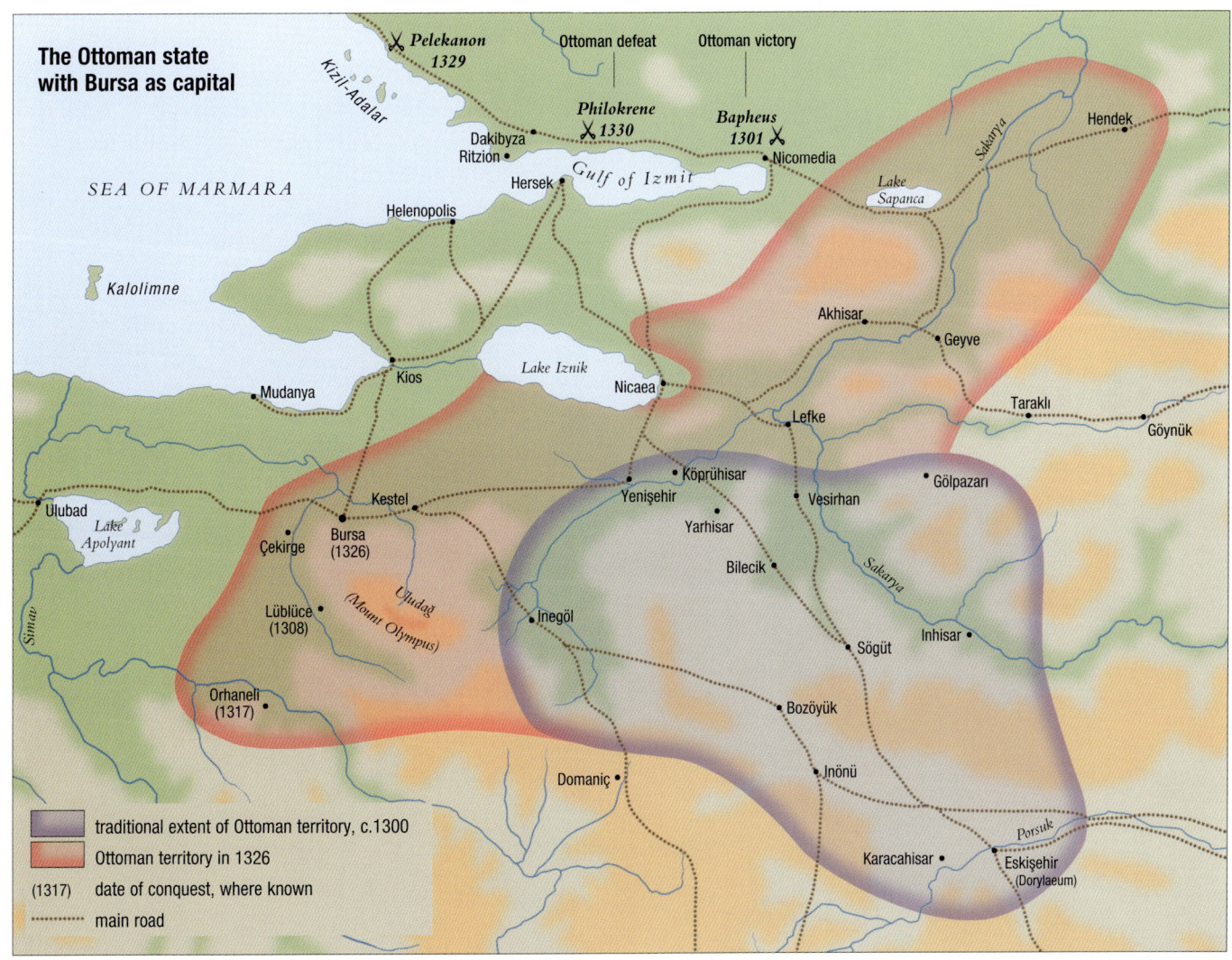

CHAPTER THREE

Across the Straits

Pushing beyond the Byzantine frontier

The Ottomans were still in competition with neighboring Turkish beyliks, their most significant rivals lying to the west and southwest, several of whom had engaged in similar expansion against what was left of Byzantine possessions in Anatolia. However, in most cases the beyliks had nowhere to go once they reached the Aegean coast, thus several took to raiding by sea, becoming what European chroniclers inaccurately but understandably called "pirate states." One such was the Karasi beylik in the northwestern corner of Anatolia. Though Karasi had only a small fleet, it seemed poised to cross the Dardanelles into Europe. But in 1346, before it could do so, the Ottomans conquered Karasi, which opened up huge strategic possibilities. By inheriting Karasi's small fleet, Ottoman gazis as well as those who had previously served under the banner of Karasi itself could raid Byzantine islands and coasts in the same way that Turkish beyliks further south had been doing for half a century. Even more significantly, perhaps, the annexation of Karasi placed Ottoman troops on the eastern shores of the Dardanelles, almost within shouting distance of the Gallipoli peninsula only a few hundred yards away in Europe.

Among those fighting men who entered Ottoman ranks as a result of the seizure of Karasi was Kara Timürtaş Gazi Evrenos. Whereas Köse Mihal may have been mythical, Gazi Evrenos Bey was a real historical figure; a man whose long career made him one of the most important, if still little-known, military leaders in

Built in 1280 by the Genoese, the castle at Anadolukavağı looks northward to the mouth of the Bosporus and the Black Sea.

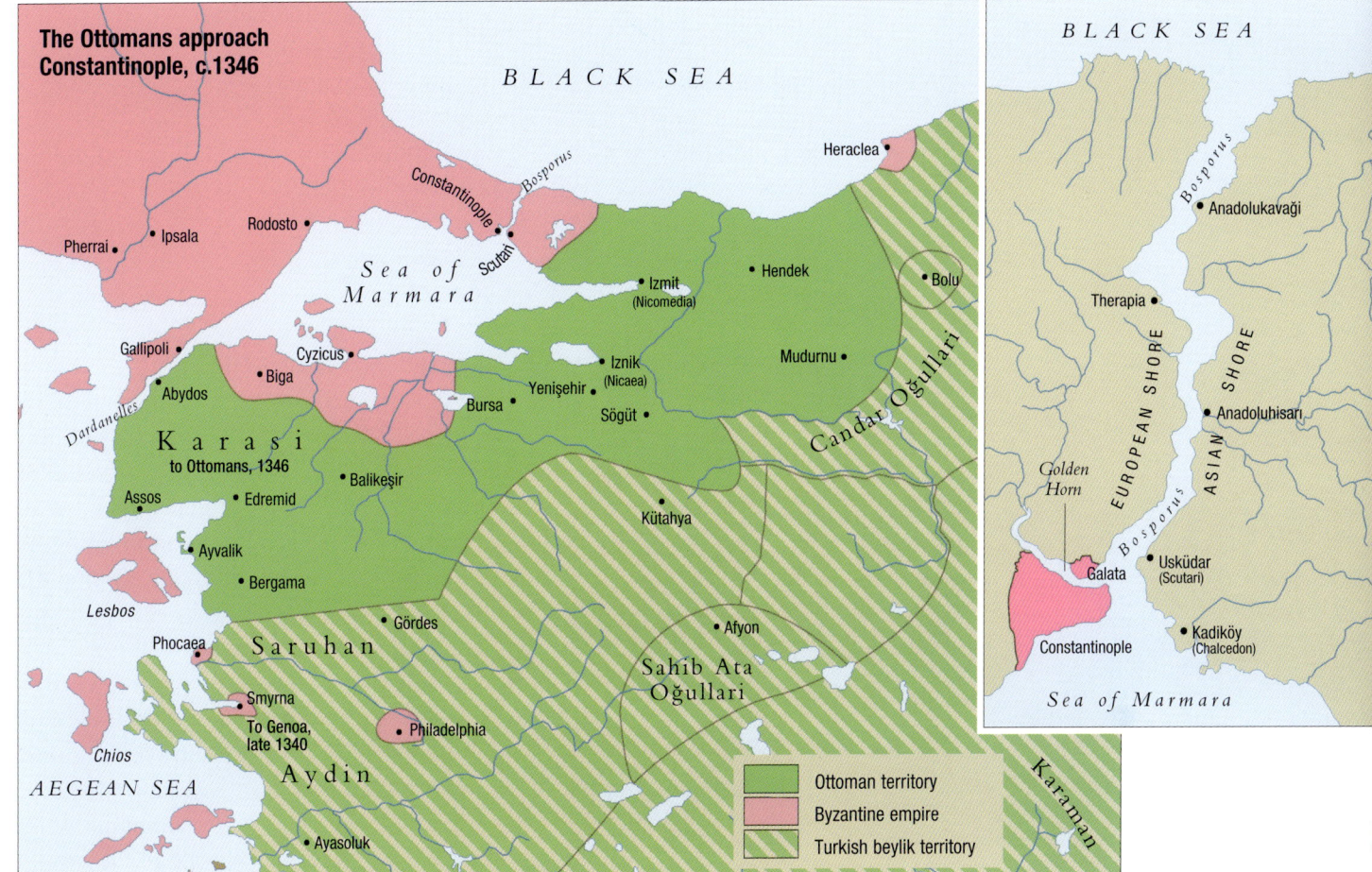

medieval European history. Gazi Evrenos's distinguished service under the Ottoman banner was also very dramatic. According to the most reliable sources, Evrenos was the son of Īsa (Jesus) Bey Prandi and came from a family of Byzantine origin that had transferred its allegiance to the rulers of the Turkish Karasi beylik early in the 14th century. They were among those who quickly converted to Islam and after the Ottomans annexed Karasi they served the new rulers loyally.

Gazi Evrenos was one of the soldiers sent by Orhan to help John VI Cantacuzenos during the Byzantine civil war against his rival John V. After the Ottomans won their initial foothold on the European side of the Dardanelles in 1352 (*see immediately below*), Evrenos became one of their most successful commanders in the Balkans. He campaigned on behalf of no less than five Ottoman rulers, becoming *uç-bey* or governor of the Left March, in which capacity he and his troops extended Ottoman control as far as Thessaloniki (Salonika, Greek Thessalonica), Macedonia, Albania, and down into the heartlands of Greece itself. Unlike many leading Ottoman commanders of that time, Gazi Evrenos was a relatively orthodox Muslim, perhaps reflecting his family's Orthodox Christian background. He made the hajj pilgrimage to Mecca and encouraged the building of mosques, religious schools, hostels for the poor, dervish convents, public baths, and caravanserais for travelling merchants. Under his governorship Komotini in what is now northeastern Greece became one of the first centers of Turkish-Islamic culture in Europe. Gazi Evrenos died at a great age on 17 November 1417. A dedicatory inscription on his tomb at Yenitsa, near Thessaloniki, still reads:

Transported from this Transient World to the Realm of Permanence,
The receiver of God's mercy and forgiveness,
The blessed, the martyr, the ruler of the Gazis
And the fighters of jihad, slayer of the infidels and the polytheists,
Hacı Evrenos, Son of Īsa,
May God illuminate his grave and may his dust be fragrant,
To the mercy of Almighty God and His approval.

View of the Gallipoli peninsula toward Kilitbahir from Çanakkale (near Abydos) on the Asian shore of the Dardanelles.

The first foothold in Europe

The first Ottoman outpost in Europe did not even have to be conquered. As a reward for mercenary services to Byzantium, John VI Cantacuzenos allowed the Ottoman ruler Orhan to garrison a fort on the Gallipoli peninsula. For many years the enfeebled Byzantine empire and its rulers, like some of their rivals in the Balkans and Greece, had been inviting Turkish troops—Muslim or otherwise—to support them in their mutually destructive struggles and self-defeating civil wars. By the 1340s Ottoman fighting men were among these troops. This helps to explain—given the huge significance for European history of the Ottoman Turks' first permanent toehold west of the Dardanelles (Hellespont strait) in Europe—that the event did not cause more of a stir at the time.

It is likely that the strength and persistence of Byzantine resistance along the Ottoman frontier, so close to the heart of the empire, had toughened both the Ottoman armies and the administrative system. Perhaps it also gave the Turkish settlers time to put down deeper and firmer roots and mix with the existing Greek population. The only other beyliks in a similar situation were those facing the equally tough and resilient Byzantine state on the Anatolian Black Sea coast known as the Empire of Trebizond, several hundred miles to the east. What differed was that these eastern Turkish frontiersmen found themselves up against much more challenging geographical and climatic obstacles.

On the death of Andronicus III in 1341, John VI Cantacuzenos enlisted Serbian and Turkish mercenaries in an effort to oust his coemperor John V Palaeologus. Most of the Turkish troops came from the Aydın beylik rather than the Ottoman state, but they were allowed to raid across much of Macedonia before returning to Anatolia with rich booty. Aydın went into steep decline after the death of its famous ruler, Umur Bey, so when next Cantacuzenos found he needed help he turned to Byzantium's immediate neighbors, the Ottomans. Orhan was supposedly encouraged to take 5500 troops over the Dardanelles into Thrace. With this small but effective army, he cleared John VI Cantacuzenos' enemies from the European Black Sea coast northwest of Constantinople to enable his paymaster-ally to regain the Byzantine imperial throne. As part of his reward Orhan was married to the

Early house of Osman (Ottomans)

Pre-imperial heads of the House
?–1227   Süleymanşah (bey)
1227–1281 Ertuğrul (bey)

Imperial heads of the House
1281–1324 Osman I (bey)
1324–60   Orhan I (bey)
1360–89   Murat I (sultan from 1383)
1389–1402 Bayezit I

(Interregnum, 1402–1413)

CHAPTER THREE: ACROSS THE STRAITS

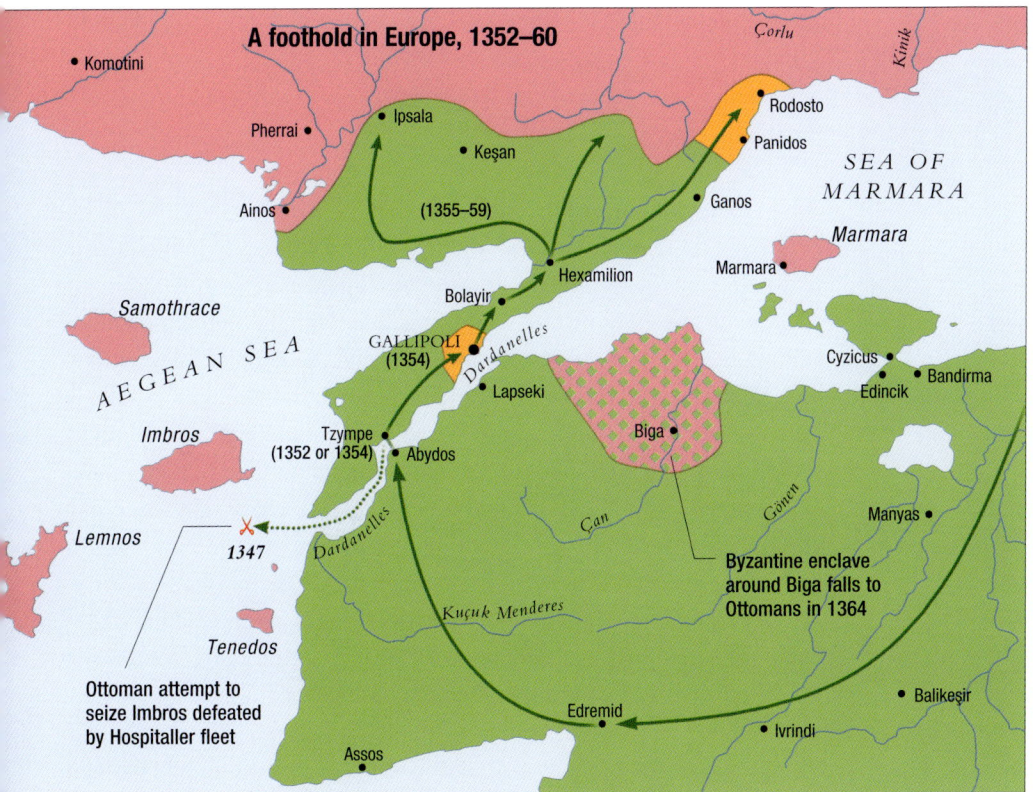

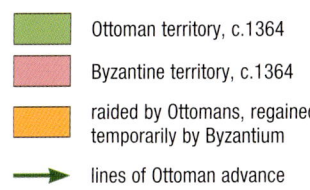

- Ottoman territory, c.1364
- Byzantine territory, c.1364
- raided by Ottomans, regained temporarily by Byzantium
- lines of Ottoman advance

The Byzantine civil war

In a confusing period, rivalry for the Byzantine throne allowed the Ottomans the freedom to seize whole tracts of the shrinking empire. In 1341 the nine-year-old son of Andronicus III came to the throne, but his 50-year reign was one of almost constant civil war, first against his grasping father-in-law John Cantacuzenos, who seized power as John VI in 1347. It was Cantacuzenos who invited Orhan and the the Ottomans into western Europe. When he turned to his old enemies, the Serbs and Bulgarians, for help against his now troublesome Turkish allies in 1354 the Byzantine ruling class—civil, military, and religious—lost patience and replaced him by his rival, John V. John's second reign was no more satisfactory than his short first. Regarded by his son as a weakling, Andronicus IV took the throne from his father for three years between 1376–79 before John's Venetian allies threw him out and restored the father. Having made a lengthy trip to Italy to appeal to the pope for aid and failed, John V was forced to recognize the legitimacy of Orhan's acquisitions in Europe, and died a broken man in 1391.

emperor's daughter, Theodora. Meanwhile, Ottoman troops under Orhan's son Süleyman were allowed to ravage those parts of Thrace and Gallipoli that did not acknowledge John as their ruler. They raided other places too, including some that recognized Cantacuzenos, who was in little position to complain. John continued to request Ottoman aid, having inadequate military resources of his own, and in 1349 Süleyman's men were ferried to Thessaloniki by the Byzantine fleet in order to regain the port from the Serbs who had recently captured it. Three years later, Orhan helped Cantacuzenos to defeat his rival John V and his Serb and Bulgarian allies outside Didimotikon. As a reward for this assistance and a means of ensuring that his Ottoman allies would be ready at hand on the European side of the straits, John VI Cantacuzenos allowed Orhan to garrison the little fort at Tzympe on the Gallipoli peninsula.

Orhan recognized that this outpost, though small and vulnerable, was a valuable strategic asset. His followers, and perhaps other enthusiasts not entirely under the Ottoman ruler's control, promptly began raiding the surrounding territory. Even in 1353, Süleyman reportedly rode north as far as Tekirdağ (Rodosto), apparently in alliance with Genoese ships. Genoa presumably hoped this new alliance might undermine the dominant position of its rival Venice in Byzantine trade. John VI complained, and stated that Tzympe was supposed to be a temporary base for his troublesome Ottoman allies. Orhan agreed that the over-enthusiastic Süleyman should come home, but also claimed that it was against Islamic law for him to abandon "infidel territory" that had been conquered by Islamic arms. He was particularly insistent that the more important town of Gallipoli and its strategic harbor must remain in Ottoman hands.

On 2 March 1354 a severe earthquake shook the Gallipoli peninsula and brought down many local fortifications, including those of Tzympe. Süleyman sent a reply to the Byzantine emperor, saying that the earthquake was a sign from God that the Turks must remain—which they did.

The Aegean: frontier and trading hub

During the early decades of the 14th century, while the Ottomans were establishing themselves in northwestern Anatolia, the Aegean Sea was both a war-ravaged frontier zone and a channel through which a great deal of trade flowed. In naval and to some extent military terms, the Aegean Sea was dominated by the Latins—people of western European origin and culture. Many Latins had, of course, been long resident in this region. It was they, rather than the Byzantines, whom the Turks had to face if they wished to extend their influence, power, culture, or trade across the Aegean. In 1204 the Fourth Crusade had conquered Constantinople to establish a short-lived Latin empire. This had little lasting impact on the Byzantine empire other than to weaken it still further in the face of its Turkish neighbors in Anatolia. The crusaders' presence in northern Greece was similarly ephemeral, but they and the Latin states they established in central and southern Greece were much more significant. Even after Latin settlers lost most of the interior to Byzantine counter-

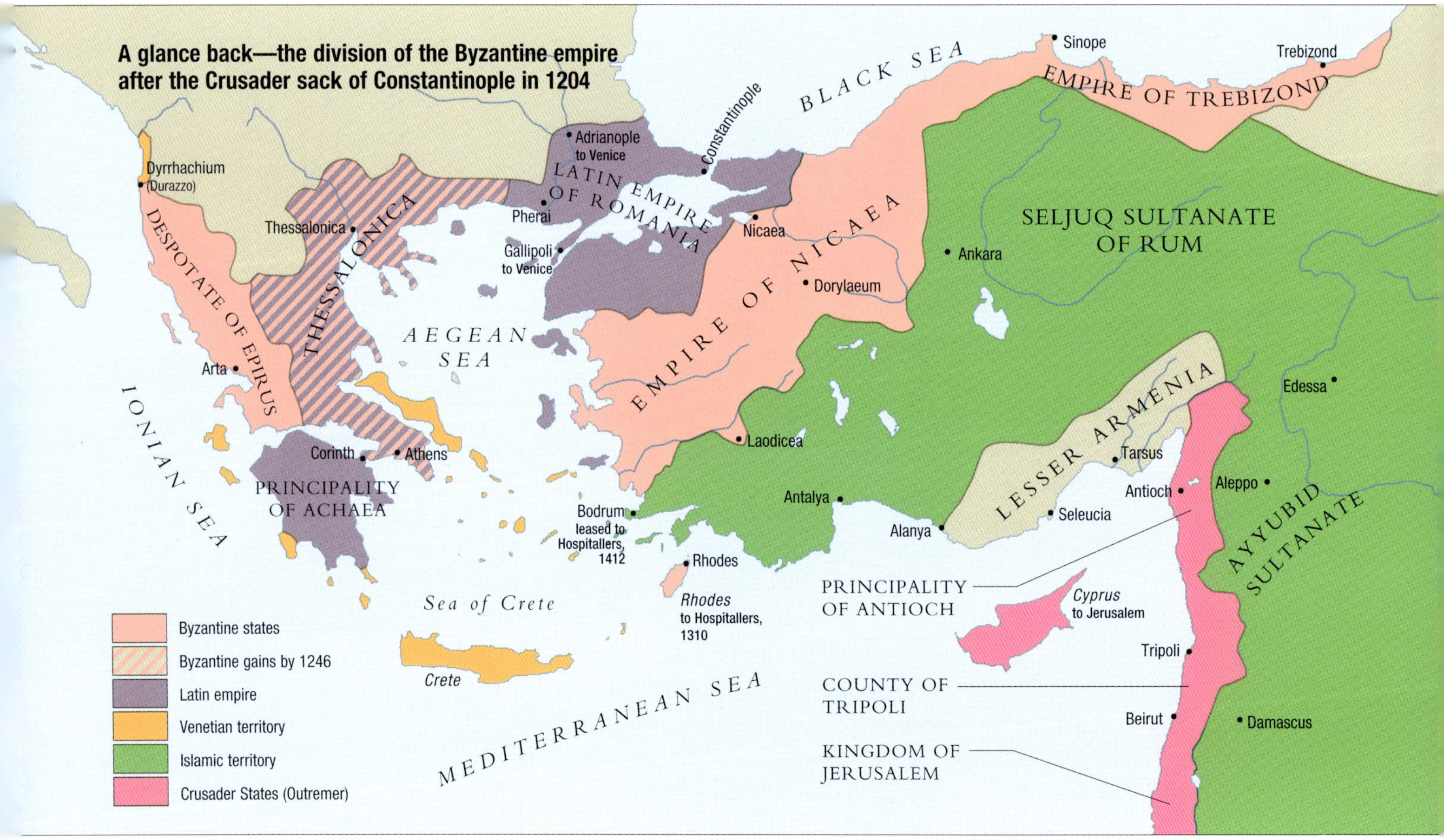

The Water Gate, Pherrai (now Féres in eastern Greece).

attacks, they remained and even flourished as an urban coastal aristocracy.

This process was reinforced by the arrival of Italian families who gradually came to dominate the previous French and Burgundian settlers. Many of the new Italian lords regarded their Greek fiefs as a form of financial investment, while the French-style chivalric society of 13th-century Latin Greece largely gave way to one based on trade and commercial priorities. The crusader states of Greece remained a recruiting ground for mercenaries of knightly and non-noble rank, who served many southern Balkan armies and even Turkish forces in Anatolia.

Carvings of combined Genoese and Byzantine heraldry from the 14th century in Mytilene castle on the island of Lesbos.

The crusader knights of the Aegean seem to have been more willing to assimilate existing Slav military elites and indeed to welcome Turkish settlers, provided they converted to Christianity, than to accept the larger and potentially more threatening Greek military lords. But as the years passed and the crusader states' shortage of military manpower became acute, some Greeks were knighted and given hereditary fiefs, despite remaining Orthodox rather than Latin-Catholic Christians. Motivations and processes may have differed, but there seem to have been remarkably similar absorption and cultural assimilation on both sides of the Aegean, in Turkish Anatolia and the Byzantine and Slav Balkans, and Greece.

As part of a new settler community, the Italian presence was not confined only to the mainland; the merchant republics of Genoa and Venice were much more prominent. Their valuable mercantile outposts around the Aegean and in the Black Sea were largely defended by troops of Italian origin, in some cases assisted by locals, most of whom were Greeks, and there is no real evidence that Muslim Turks were involved.

Following the Fourth Crusade in 1204, many of the numerous small islands in the Aegean became meeting places for pirates and freebooters of many nationalities, though again Muslim Turks rarely seem to have been involved. Many of these Christian freebooters were of noble origin, since piracy was not viewed in such a negative light as it would be in later centuries. Other "pirate knights" served Venice or Genoa; among the most successful, the Genoese Zaccaria brothers controlled several ports along with the vital alum mines of the Anatolian coast. In most cases such ports had been handed over by the Byzantine authorities because they could not defend the outposts against the advancing Turks. The Zaccaria brothers soon found themselves with occasionally aggressive but also commercially aware Muslim Turkish neighbors.

Genoese shields carved on the citadel wall of Amastris (Amasra). The Genoese trading enclave endured on the Black Sea coast until the Ottomans annexed the city in 1460.

The Zaccarias were wealthy enough to build a formidable fleet of their own and in 1304 they seized the large island of Chios in the name of their home city of Genoa. Chios was already an important staging post, harbor and source of provisions on several important maritime trade routes. In later decades the Zaccaria family, ruling on behalf of Genoa, Byzantium, or both, acquired several other islands and coastal enclaves, eventually holding these as vassals of the Ottoman sultan.

Sharing trade and power

Genoese outposts were governed in a very different way from those of Venice. Whereas the Venetians tried to impose strict governmental control in defense, trade, and relations with neighbors, the Genoese reflected the traditionally fragmented and almost anarchic nature of authority back in Genoa. Their outposts were usually governed by associations of wealthy ship-owners known as *mahonese*, some of knightly rank. They attempted, usually successfully, to win the support of local warlords and the acceptance of Turkish rulers by allowing them a share in the huge Genoese trading profits. Among the mahonese were men of extraordinary geographical knowledge. For example, Tedisio d'Oro was interested in the possibility of opening up a trade route to China, the most important source of the most expensive trading items, by sailing westward, across the Atlantic. It seems likely that

CHAPTER THREE: ACROSS THE STRAITS

Europeans like Tedisio d'Oro learned from, as well as traded with, their Turkish, Arab, Persian, and Mongol merchant partners.

The Muslims were described as *summa culpabilis*, the "most blameworthy" of people, by the Latin-Catholic Church, so religion had clearly motivated the crusaders. However, the knights of the Latin states in the Aegean soon showed themselves to be more down to earth and realistic, many simply abandoning the Latin emperor of Constantinople when he could no longer afford to pay them. Several generations later the Catalan Great Company of mercenaries (*see page 51*) similarly abandoned their poverty-stricken Byzantine paymasters and attacked the Latin states of Greece, finding no difficulty in making long-term alliances with the Muslim Turks of the Aegean region. By the 1330s the Italian rulers of some Aegean states or outposts also became *illik kafirleri* (non-Muslim frontier lords) under Turkish suzerainty.

Most historians highlight Italian naval dominance as a key consideration in the history of the Aegean region during this period. However, the Christians' naval superiority is too often overstated, just as it is in relation to the earlier history of the Crusader States of Outremer in the eastern Mediterranean. The idea that Christian navies dominated the Aegean and Black Seas well into the 15th century is simplistic and exaggerated. While it is true that Turkish Islamic fleets could rarely challenge Italian or crusader fleets face to face until the rise of Ottoman naval power in the late 15th century, instead, pre-Ottoman Turkish and early Ottoman naval expeditions used their numerous and almost invariably smaller ships to raid Christian-held islands and coasts. The fact that they launched these raids while the more powerful but less numerous Italian, crusader and indeed Byzantine warships were elsewhere, had a profound impact on the location, supplying and defense of Christian fortifications, as small forces put ashore by so-called Muslim pirates sometimes penetrated deep inland.

Naval warfare also became more important for the scattered Latin European possessions during the 13th and 14th centuries. Even so, raiding was usually on a small scale, with the military aristocracy engaging in little more than piracy. The heavily armored fighting men aboard most European or Latin galleys were much less agile than their lightly armored or even unarmored Turkish foes and their fellow Christian *almogavar* Catalan rivals. The crews of ships manned by Latin settlers in the 14th-century Aegean, especially those of the Venetian colonies, were summoned by a public crier a week before sailing, then again on the day of departure, with financial penalties imposed on men who arrived improperly equipped. Maritime expeditions involved considerable hardship, whichever side they originated from.

The Gothic architecture of the "Galata Tower" dominates the roofline of Istanbul's suburb, seen here at twilight. Built in 1348 by the Genoese who largely inhabited the district, it was named the Tower of Christ, and was the tallest, most powerful tower in the extensive fortifications of Galata.

The basic food was hard ship's biscuit, though figs and, for Christian crews, wine could be purchased along the way. In winter, the fragile galleys were taken out of the water, placed under cover and guarded by a garrison.

It is also important to note that galley slaves had not been used since the fall of the Roman empire. Byzantine and Islamic navies continued to be manned entirely by volunteers throughout the medieval period, except for the personal servants of senior officers. It was the crusading Military Order of the Hospitallers or Knights of St John who, from their base on Rhodes, reintroduced slaves to the Mediterranean. Even they should more accurately be described as galley serfs, since service as oarsmen was one of the obligations imposed on the Hospitallers' Greek Orthodox subjects. Muslims were rarely used as galley slaves for the simple reason that the Hospitallers did not usually take any prisoners when at war with their Muslim Turkish neighbors—captives were simply executed.

The dervishes of Turkey

Ever since the days of the Seljuq sultanate of Rum, Anatolia had been home to several mystical Islamic movements or dervish sects. Also referred to as *Sufis*, woolies or "wearers of rough woollen clothing," some of Anatolia's dervish groups reflected the Turks' pre-Islamic beliefs, including shamanist and Buddhist influences. Others owed more to early Persian-Islamic mysticism, and several clearly incorporated elements of the somewhat unorthodox "folk" Christianity seen in Byzantine Anatolia before the Seljuq conquest. Shi'a Islam had been strong in early Turkish Anatolia, especially among the gazi religiously motivated frontier communities and within nomadic Turcoman tribes. Even the early Ottoman rulers themselves, though proclaiming their Sunni Muslim orthodoxy, only became "mainstream" Muslims in the late 15th century. Orthodoxy became stronger after the Ottomans defeated the Mamluk sultans of Egypt in the early 16th century and took over the Middle Eastern heartland of Islamic civilization.

Three dervish or Sufi movements were to play a notable role in the conversion to Islam of many Anatolian and subsequently Balkan Christian communities: the Mevlevis, the Bektaşis and the Melami. The Mevlevis are today the most famous, popularly known as Whirling Dervishes. The sect was founded by the renowned Persian poet and mystic Jalal al-Din Rumi at Konya in Turkey in the 13th century. During the Ottoman period the Mevlevis were more prominent in Turkish Anatolia and some parts of the Arab world, while the latter two were widespread in both Anatolia and the Balkans—or Rumelia as the Ottomans called the region—though the Bektaşis had many adherents in Syria and Egypt.

It's difficult to separate truth from legend in the origins of the Bektaşi dervishes. They had a close association with the elite Janissary corps from its very earliest days and were even credited with responsibility for the Janissaries' distinctive tall, white felt caps. Headgear had been a form of religious identification for many years. The tall red hats worn by most early Ottoman troops, including the older and even more

Dervish cell in the Mevlana monstery, Konya, with seated display manikin and Mevlevi whirling dervish figurine, above.

Ladscape near Karaman, a Cilician Mevelevi meeting place.

CHAPTER THREE: ACROSS THE STRAITS

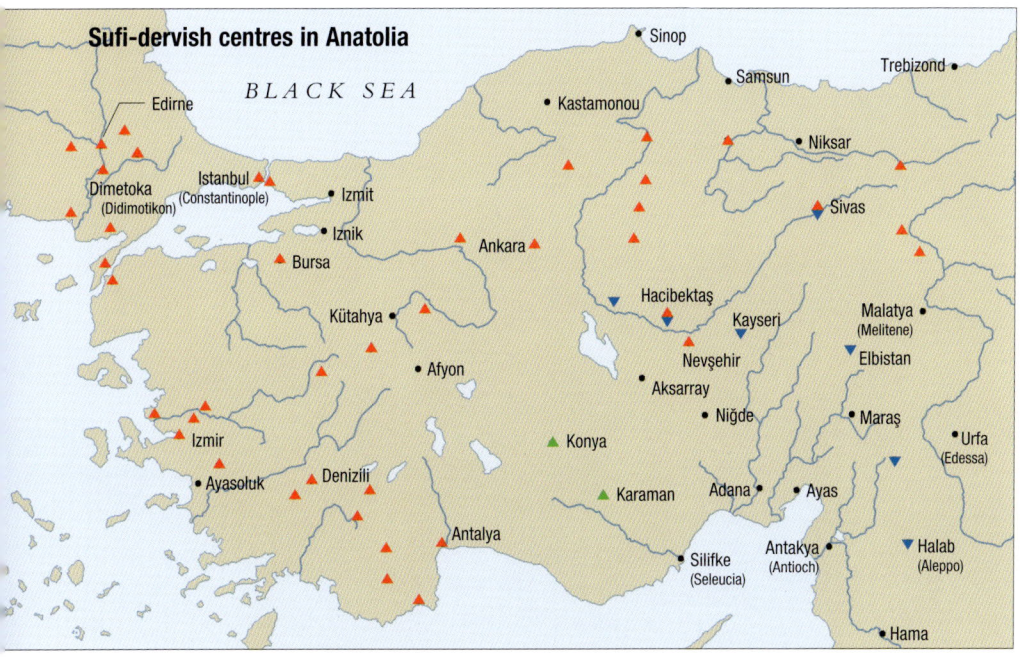

Haci (or Hajji) Bektaş was the possibly legendary founder, in the mid-13th century, of the Anatolian Baktaşi dervish movement. Originally from Nişapur, Iran, he was a follower of the Yasawi Sufi order that was active in Central Asia and working as a missionary among the region's Turkish tribes. Shaykh Ahmad Yasawi sent him to Anatolia to preach to the Turks there and where he remained in the town named after him—Hacibektaş—until his death. A Sufi order soon developed based on his teachings.

prestigious Silahtars, had been worn by revolutionary Shi'a sects in previous decades; a fact which may well reflect Shi'a influence in the earliest years of the Ottoman state. First recorded with certainty in 13th century Anatolia, the Bektaşis were widely regarded by orthodox Sunni Muslims as suspect, if not heretical—an attitude that survives to this day in several parts of the Islamic world. Nevertheless, they were very popular among recently converted, ex-Christian and often only superficially Islamic populations within the expanding Ottoman sultanate.

Christian influence can almost certainly be seen in a ceremonial distribution of bread, cheese and sometimes even wine when a new member was accepted into the order. The Bektaşi movement also developed a remarkable tradition of lyrical poetry and was characterized by what western European Christians would have described as a liberal attitude toward the role and status of women.

The original core of the Melami movement was, like that of the Bektaşis, in central Anatolia. They had *tekkes* or meeting places in Üsküdar on the eastern side of the Bosporus facing Istanbul, as well as in several other major cities. A refusal to be bound by the external forms of religion was a notable feature of Melami belief, and this often got them into trouble with the Ottoman authorities. Perhaps for such reasons most other Melami centers were near the European frontiers of the Ottoman state, in Albania, Bosnia, and in Budapest during the relatively brief period of Ottoman rule over Hungary. In later centuries the Melami suffered persecution because of their unorthodox views and, like the Bektaşis, they were eventually suppressed. The Bektaşis supposedly became an illegal organization in the 19th century but, like so many unorthodox religious communities, they, their beliefs, and their practices survive in semi-secret. Today there are substantial Bektaşi communities in Albania and America, among many other places.

The prayer hall of the 13th-century convent of Bektaşi, Haci (or Hajji) Bektaş.

Ahi Evren mosque of the dervishes, early 16th century, Kirşehir.

Non-Ottoman Anatolia

Many Turkish beyliks in Anatolia continued to flourish throughout the 14th century, while on the coast the Byzantine outpost of Trebizond prospered in relative peace. Trebizond's ally Georgia was a huge state which dominated most of the Caucasus mountains and the interior of northeastern Anatolia, while a series of other states rivaled the Ottoman sultanate. South and east of the Christian kingdom of Georgia lay the even larger realm of the deeply Islamic Jalayrids, one of the successor states of the Mongol Il-Khanate, ruled from the ancient caliphal capital of Baghdad. Two large beyliks, Eretna and Karaman, ruled the center of early 14th-century Anatolia. Other substantial states emerged to the southeast, Dulkadir and Ramazan, while the western half of Anatolia was far more fragmented.

Karaman, the realm of the Karaman Oğullari or Karamanids (c.1265–1475), occupied the old center of the Seljuq sultanate of Rum and was in many respects its most direct successor; it was certainly the longest surviving offshoot. The father of Karaman Ibn Nur al-Din, their first ruler, was a renowned Sufi mystical teacher, thus dervishes flourished under Karamanid rule. For many decades they were serious rivals to the Ottomans, making military and commercial alliances with powerful states to the east and west, before eventually being absorbed by the sultanate.

The Eretna Oğullari (1336–80) occupied much of the territory that had been the center of the Danishmandid state in the late 11th and 12th centuries. Some have suggested that the name of their founder, Eretna Ibn Ja'far, stems from the Sanskrit word *ratna*, meaning jewel, and that he was a military leader of Uighur, eastern Turkish, origin—perhaps even of Buddhist parentage. He may have served either the Mongol Il-Khanids or their local vassals, the Çobanids who ruled northern Anatolia before the rise of the Eretna Oğullari.

The Dulkadir Oğullari (1337–1521) was founded by the Oğuz Turkish chieftain Qaraj Ibn Dulkadir, whose name was later Arabized as Dhu'l-Qadr, "possessor of power," though its original Turkish meaning remains unclear. The Dulkadir survived so long partly because they held the same inaccessible mountainous territory that had served as a bastion for the Armenians of Cilicia, and partly because they made alliances with more powerful neighbors, the Mamluks and Ottomans. Their most persistent foes were the Karamanids and the Aq Qoyunlu (white sheep) Turcomans of western Persia.

The Ramazan Oğullari (c.1378–1608) were relative latecomers to this complex political and military situation, though Ramazan Bey, the father of their founder, was mentioned in the 1350s. He is said to have stemmed from the Oğuz of the west and thus claimed high status in the family or clan rankings of the Turks. The Ramazan built their state in what had been the prosperous economic heartland rather than the mountainous retreat of the earlier Cilician Armenian kingdom. At first enemies of the Mamluks, the Ramazan later adopted a generally pro-Mamluk policy and eventually formed a buffer state between Mamluks and Ottomans. They survived the Ottoman conquest and overthrow of the Mamluks in the early 16th century, after which the Ramazan were submissive vassals of the Ottomans for nearly a century before their lands were annexed as a directly ruled *eyâlet* or province of the sultanate.

The situation was far more fluid and complex in western Anatolia, where there were too many short-lived beyliks to describe in detail, but among the most important was the Candar Oğullari (1292–1462). Like several other tribal leaders, its founder seized power and then won recognition by becoming an Il-Khan vassal. The center of Candar power was Kastamonou, and after throwing off Il-Khan suzerainty they extended their territory eastward along the coast to take Sinop. Briefly dispossessed by Sultan Bayezit I in 1393, they were restored by Timur-i Lenk, the Mongol chieftain popularly known as Tamerlane, and adopted the new name of Isfandiyar Oğullari. Even after their final annexation by Sultan Mehmet II in 1462, the Candar or Isfandiyar family wielded considerable influence for many years.

The Germiyan Oğullari (1299–1428) first appear in the chronicles as a Turkish tribe in the service of the sultans of Rum at Malatya, at the eastern edge of the Seljuq state. During the late 13th century they migrated westward and eventually established a beylik around the powerful fortress city of Kütahya. Initially vassals of the Seljuqs and Mongol Il-Khans, the Germiyan Oğullari took advantage of the Seljuqs' decline and the Il-Khans' geographic distance to carve out what became for a while the most extensive Turkish *beylik* in western Anatolia, using wealth generated from their position astride several important trade routes to and from the Aegean coast. The ruler of the Germiyan state imposed his suzerainty of some of his smaller neighbors and for a while even the emperor of Byzantium was a tributary. However, the rise of small but rich and powerful beyliks on the coast as well as the Ottomans on the northern frontier led to the decline and fragmentation of the Germiyan Oğullari. Its last ruler, Ya'qub II, lost his throne to Sultan Bayezit I in 1390 and was restored by Timur-i Lenk, but then bequeathed Germiyan to the Ottoman sultan once again, Murat II taking over on the death of Ya'qub II in 1428.

The rulers of the Hamid Oğullari (c.1301–91) and Teke Oğullari (c.1301–1423) were descendants of a Seljuq frontier commander named Ilyas Ibn Hamid, who had carved out a beylik in southwestern Anatolia in the late 13th century. The Hamid and Teke remained small in territorial terms, but were sometimes wealthy because of their strategic location on the trade routes between the Aegean and Mediterranean

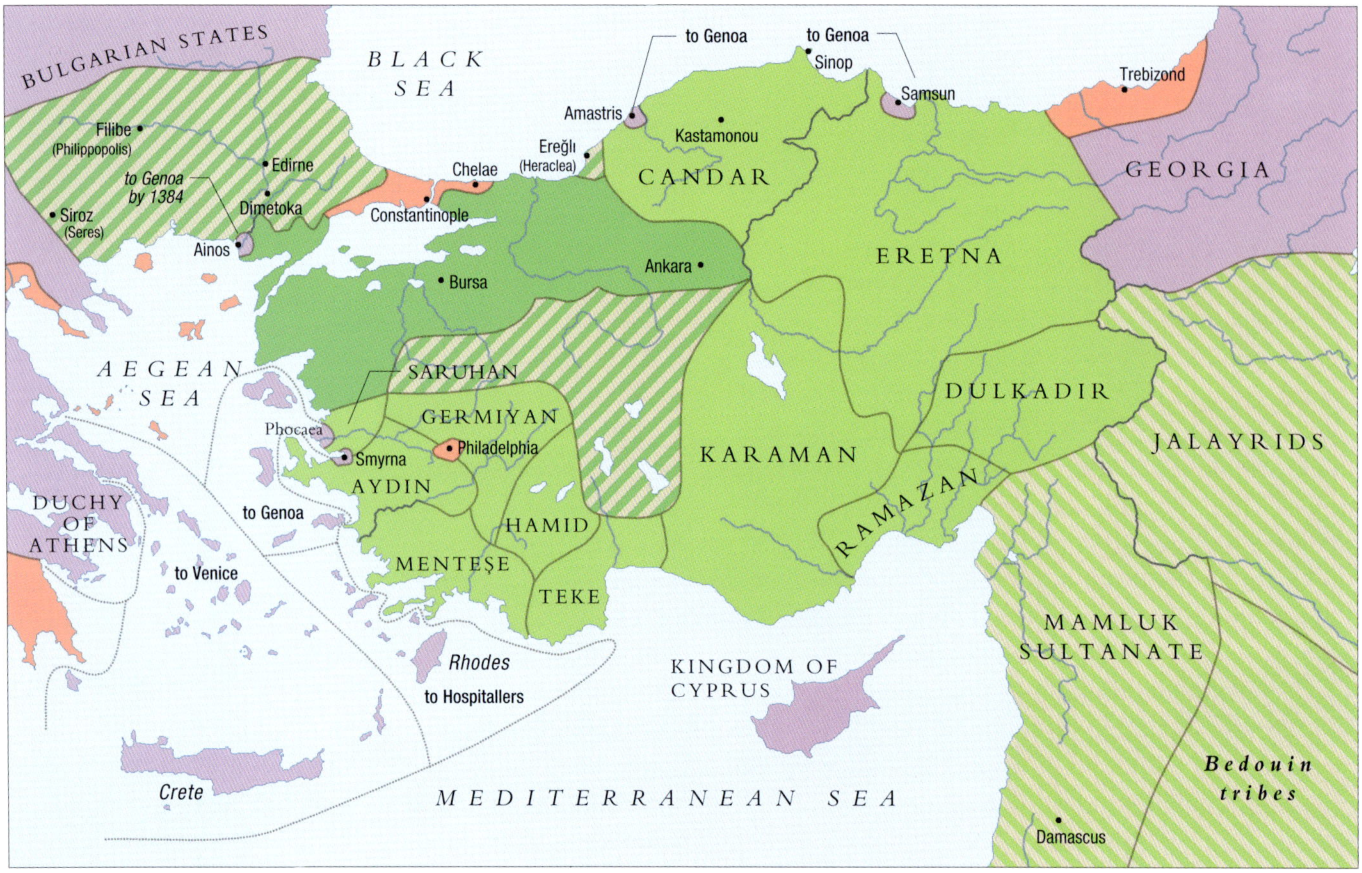

The Ottomans and the Turkish beyliks

- ▓ Ottoman territory, c.1362
- ▓ Ottoman conquests by 1382
- ▓ Turkish beyliks in Anatolia
- ▓ other Islamic territory
- ▓ Byzantine territory (empires of Constantinople and of Trebizond)
- ▓ other Christian territory

Alanya became an important Seljuq stronghold, ringed with powerful fortifications, including the famous '"Red Tower," guarding the harbor.

coasts. Their history was generally more peaceful than that of their larger neighbors but both were conquered by Bayezit I, after which the Hamid state disappeared permanently. Like so many other beyliks, Teke was restored by Timur-i Lenk, only to be finally reconquered by the Ottomans a generation later. On this occasion the last independent ruler was not absorbed into the Ottoman system but killed.

The Menteşe Oğullari (c.1280–1424) ruled, at least nominally, the rugged and indented coastal region immediately west of Hamid and Teke. The father of Menteşe Bey, the founder of this dynasty, may have been the Amir-i Sawahil or "governor of the coast" for the Seljuq sultans of Rum, but this might have been a family legend designed to justify Menteşe Oğullari rule. Given their geographical position it is hardly surprising that they soon took to the sea, raiding Venetian maritime trade routes and the island possessions of the crusader Hospitallers of Rhodes. Their troops struggled for control of the vital Aegean port of Smyrna, or Izmir to the Turks. Perhaps it was this naval orientation which enabled the Menteşe to survive for some years after the Ottomans had conquered their neighbors inland. However, they were among the beyliks seized by Bayezit, restored by Timur and then reconquered by the Ottomans within a generation.

The Aydın Oğullari (1308–1426) had an epic naval history. Aydın Oğlu Muhammad Bey had been an army commander in Germiyan service before creating a small state on the Aegean coast. His son, the famous Umur Bey, captured Izmir and built a small but remarkably effective fleet with which he seems to have challenged all the Christian navies of the Aegean, and some from further afield. He became the hero of an epic tale, the *Destan of Umur Paşa*, which remains one of the

CHAPTER THREE: ACROSS THE STRAITS

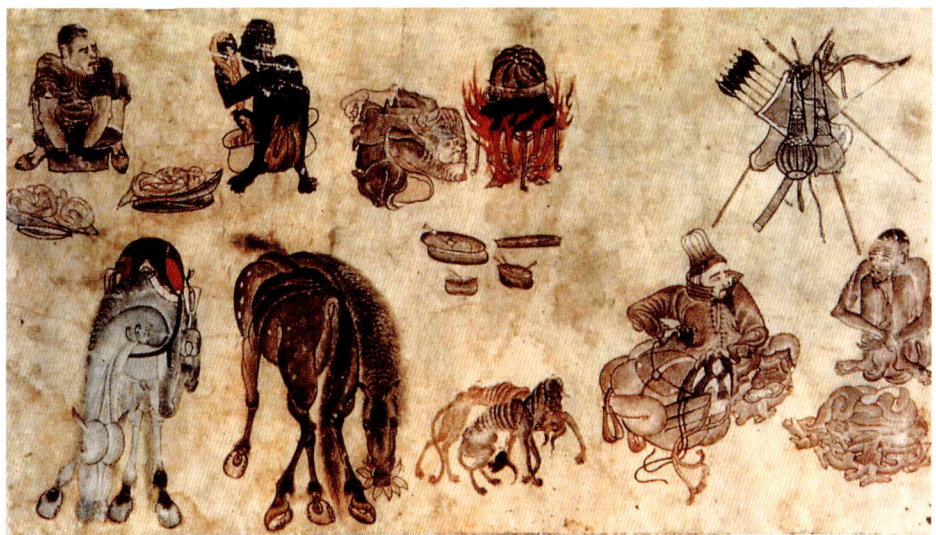

Drawings of Turkish momads in a manuscript of the late 14th or early 15th century.

> **The Grand Company of Catalans** was a nominally Spanish force of European mercenaries hired by Andronicus II in 1303. In the following year, the Catalans attacked the Turkish besiegers of Philadelphia, killing—it's said—18,000 Turks and driving off the remnant. Despite their speedy efficiency in defeating the Turks wherever they met them, it was soon clear that they were not within the emperor's control. The Catalans pillaged across a wide expanse of Anatolia, preying on Turks and Byzantines alike, until the emperor persuaded them to withdraw to Europe. When their captain, Roger de Flor, was murdered by members of the Alan cavalry (he had previously insulted them), the Catalans suspected their paymaster and turned against the emperor. Soon, reinforced by malcontents including Turkish freebooters eager for a share of the spoils, the Catalans went on to ravage large parts of Thrace before seizing one of the Latin states in Greece, the Duchy of Athens, which survived for only 70 years before falling to the Ottoman sultanate.

finest examples of medieval Turkish literature. Eventually Umur and his fleet were defeated and Izmir was retaken, for a while, by a crusader and Hospitaller army. Aydın shared its fate with most of its Turkish neighbors, annexed by Murat II in 1426, after its last ruler backed the wrong side in an Ottoman civil war.

The history of the Saruhan Oğullari (1313–1410), whose beylik lay immediately north of Aydın, was similar. As a minor naval power in the Aegean, the Saruhan sometimes fought against and sometimes traded peacefully with the Genoese and the Byzantines. The Gattilusi-Genoese coastal enclave of Phocaea (Turkish Foça) was surrounded by Saruhan territory.

Squeezed between Germiyan and Aydın was another remarkable outpost of Christian rule. The city of Philadelphia (Turkish Alaşehir) and its immediate surroundings remained an outpost of Byzantine territory until 1390 or 1391, long after the rest of western Anatolia had been lost to the Turks. This survival was largely achieved by diplomatic means, playing one neighboring beylik off against another. However the Byzantines, or rather the Catalan Grand Company of mercenaries in their pay, marched all the way from the Sea of Marmara to Philadelphia in the spring of 1304, decisively defeating a Turkish army that was besieging the city. As a result, Philadelphia was left in relative peace until Bayezit I decided to mop up all non-Ottoman territory in western Anatolia.

Karaman has many fine monuments, including the Hatuniye Madrasa. This theological college in Karaman—which is also known as either the Nefise Hatun or Nefise Sultan Madrasa—was built in 1382. At the time, it was regarded as one of the most distinguished universities in the Muslim world.

CHAPTER FOUR

The Invasion of Europe

United against the fragmenting Balkans

The Balkans have too often been seen merely as a region crossed by crusaders on their way to the Holy Land, periodically invaded by Asiatic hordes, and then suddenly collapsing before the Ottoman Turks. The enduring kingdom of Hungary dominated the northern regions of this corner of Europe, while the Byzantines recovered to form a Greek state at its southern extremity. The Serbs won a brief but extensive empire in the 14th century and the Bulgarians—though never repeating the glories of their first empire from the 7th–10th centuries—established an effective and highly cultured state. Other players on the confusing Balkan scene included the Albanians, Croatians, Bosnians, Macedonians, Wallachians, Moldavians, and Transylvanians, plus various nomadic or semi-nomadic peoples from the steppes, most of whom were of Turkish origin.

A 14th-century Turkish fort sits on an island in the harbor of Kusadasi, to the south of Selçuk (Ephesus) on the Turkish coast. Kusadasi's well protected position between the island projections of Chios and Samos made it an ideal sea-raiding base for the Turkish fleet after the Ottoman annexation.

The role of Hungary was significant. Unlike the other major Balkan states, which were largely Orthodox Christian, Hungary was Latin Catholic and became an enthusiastic participant in what are generally known as the Later Crusades. Part of the Russian principality of Galich was temporarily conquered by a Hungarian feudal aristocracy, which was itself under increasing French cultural and military influence. With the death of King Andrew III in 1301, the Arpad dynasty that had ruled Hungary since its creation was supplanted by the Italo-French Angevins who already ruled southern Italy and parts of Greece.

Charles Robert I curbed the barons' power and spread French and Italian Gothic culture across Hungary, along with more up-to-date military ideas. Louis the Great, who became king in 1342, used German and Italian mercenaries against Venice in Dalmatia, pagan Lithuanians and Catholic Poles in the north, and Orthodox Serbs in the south. Louis presented himself as a champion of the Church but his dreams of leading a great crusade against the Ottoman Turks were frustrated by chronic religious divisions. Instead, Louis' successors had to face the full might of the Ottomans in a struggle which brutally highlighted the failings of the Hungarian army. As the Ottomans advanced deep into the Balkans, Sigismund of Hungary (1387–1437) called a crusade, but the ill-disciplined multi-national force met total disaster at the battle of Nicopolis in 1396 (*see pages 64–66*).

Following a brief period of independence in the 11th century, Croatia formally united with Hungary in 1091. It retained a considerable degree of autonomy, but its *bán* or viceroy had difficulty controlling the turbulent feudal nobility who tended to pursue their own ambitions in neighboring Dalmatia and Bosnia. By the 14th century a local form of light cavalry had evolved that would stand the Croats in good stead in the 15th century.

Bosnia was culturally, religiously, and militarily more mixed. Emerging from tribal confusion in the late 12th century, it was dominated by local chieftains or *zupe* who accepted the leadership of the regional bán, when it suited them. While Lower (northern) Bosnia consisted of two Hungarian duchies, established as outposts against Serbian expansion, Upper (southern) Bosnia retained anarchic independence. Militarily and culturally, most Bosnians had more in common with the neighboring Serbs than with the Croats or Hungarians. Bosnian light cavalry was characterized by distinctive shields, which developed into the specialized *scutum bosniensem*. A peculiar feature of this region was the Bogomil heresy, which had features in common with the early medieval Paulicians of Anatolia and the more recent Cathars of southern France. Bogomilism survived persecution and crusader assaults but would disappear with the arrival of the Ottomans, when most Bogomils converted to

Serbia's brief supremacy in the Balkans came to a sudden end with the defeat of her army at the 'Field of Blackbirds' (Kosovo Polje) in 1389. However, despite the Turkish victory Sultan Murat I fell to an assassin's sword only days later, as shown on the left of this 18th-century illustration of the battle. This setback slowed the pace of Serbia's subjection to Ottoman rule.

Islam, a faith that shared their deeply egalitarian outlook. Bosnian cavalry would, however, continue to serve under an Ottoman banner.

Bosnia had its own golden age in the 14th century, although it only achieved real independence under Stephan Tvrtko (1353–91). During his reign Bosnia conquered part of Croatia and won an outlet onto the Adriatic Sea. When the sprawling Serbian empire fragmented, the Bosnian bán adopted Byzantine court ceremonial and titles, defeated an Ottoman army at the battle of Plocnit in 1386 and briefly became the most powerful among the admittedly weak southern or Balkan Slav states. Serbia was to fall to the Ottomans in 1459, and four years later Bosnia would be conquered.

The Albanians claimed descent from the ancient Illyrians—who had produced some of the toughest late third-century Roman emperors—and throughout the Middle Ages were divided into numerous mountain tribes. The development of a national identity was also hindered by the division between Catholic (Arbanite) and Orthodox (Epirot) Albanians. After the collapse of Byzantine authority and period of independence under numerous localized leaders, the area was briefly united under a single *archon*, then absorbed into the Byzantine Despotate of Epirus in 1216. A degree of autonomy followed an Angevin invasion from southern Italy, when a small Angevin kingdom was briefly installed on the coast before collapsing in the face of a local revolt. The Angevins returned in strength in 1304 and this time allowed greater freedom to Albanian leaders. Most of the mountain peoples of the interior were still semi-nomadic, which enabled them to migrate to Greece in large numbers when a series of famines struck the country in the 14th century. Most of their homeland was incorporated into the huge but fragile Serbian empire of Stephan Dusan (*see pages 58–59*). The Albanians, perhaps with Ottoman Turkish

CHAPTER FOUR: THE INVASION OF EUROPE

support, were even able to defeat invading Knights Hospitaller crusaders in 1378. Relations with the Turks were not usually so friendly and it was the Albanian leader Skanderbeg's defiance of the Ottomans in the mid-15th century which caught the imagination of Christian Europe.

After the fall of its first empire in 1018, Bulgaria remained part of Byzantium for almost two centuries. The Bogomil heresy also flourished in some parts of the country. The second Bulgarian empire won independence under a mixed Bulgarian Slav, Vlach Romanian, and Kipchaq Turkish warrior aristocracy. After trying unsuccessfully to forge an anti-Byzantine alliance with those crusaders who conquered Constantinople in 1204, the second Bulgarian empire became their implacable foe. However, deep social divisions appeared between the common people, many of whom had been strongly influenced by Bogomil egalitarian ideas, and an elite increasingly dependent on forced labour and military conscription. Territory was lost to Hungarians and Byzantines and the authority of the Bulgarian king weakened. A ferocious peasant uprising led by the swineherd Ivailo tore the country apart and Bulgaria was also forced to accept the overlordship of the Mongol Golden Horde.

The Murder of Murat I, illumination of the late 15th century, in a history by Ahmedi.

Although Bulgaria enjoyed peace and an economic revival as part of the Mongol "world empire," the process of political decline continued, just as the power of neighboring Serbia grew. Eventually Bulgaria broke into three principalities: Dobrudja in the northeast, Vidin in the northwest, and Tarnovo in the south. A few places flourished through international trade, but heresies persisted and much of the lowlands were depopulated as a result of wars, nomad raids, and plague. Bulgaria was then hardly in a state to resist the Ottomans.

In the mid-14th century, from their toehold on the Gallipoli peninsula given them in 1352 by John VI Cantacuzenos, Ottoman troops raided further afield, advancing into Thrace to seize Çorlu, Tekirdağ (formerly Rhaedestum), Lüleburgaz, and Malkara, each of which became a forward base for further raids. Meanwhile, Ottoman Turkish rule was imposed on the surrounding villages and a more solid bridgehead was established in and around the Gallipoli peninsula. This would be the starting point for the Ottomans' eventual conquest of the entire Balkans and much of central and eastern Europe. Plovdiv (formerly Philippopolis) fell in 1364 and the rest of Bulgaria soon accepted Ottoman suzerainty. The remaining peasant communities of the eastern lowlands and Black Sea coast entered an era of unexpected prosperity under their new Turkish lords. A few of the old Bulgarian aristocratic class fled to the western mountains, where they maintained a precarious autonomy for a few decades, but eventually persistent revolts led to the imposition of direct Ottoman rule on the last of the Bulgarian principalities by 1396.

It became almost impossible for the Orthodox Christian Balkans states to join forces with their Catholic Christian neighburs from central and western Europe; and certainly the once mighty Byzantine empire was in no position to lead any resistance against the Ottomans. The crushing of peasant uprisings, urban revolts, and the ravages of the Catalans had left large parts of Thrace and Macedonia sparsely inhabited. Everywhere in what remained of Byzantine territory there seemed to

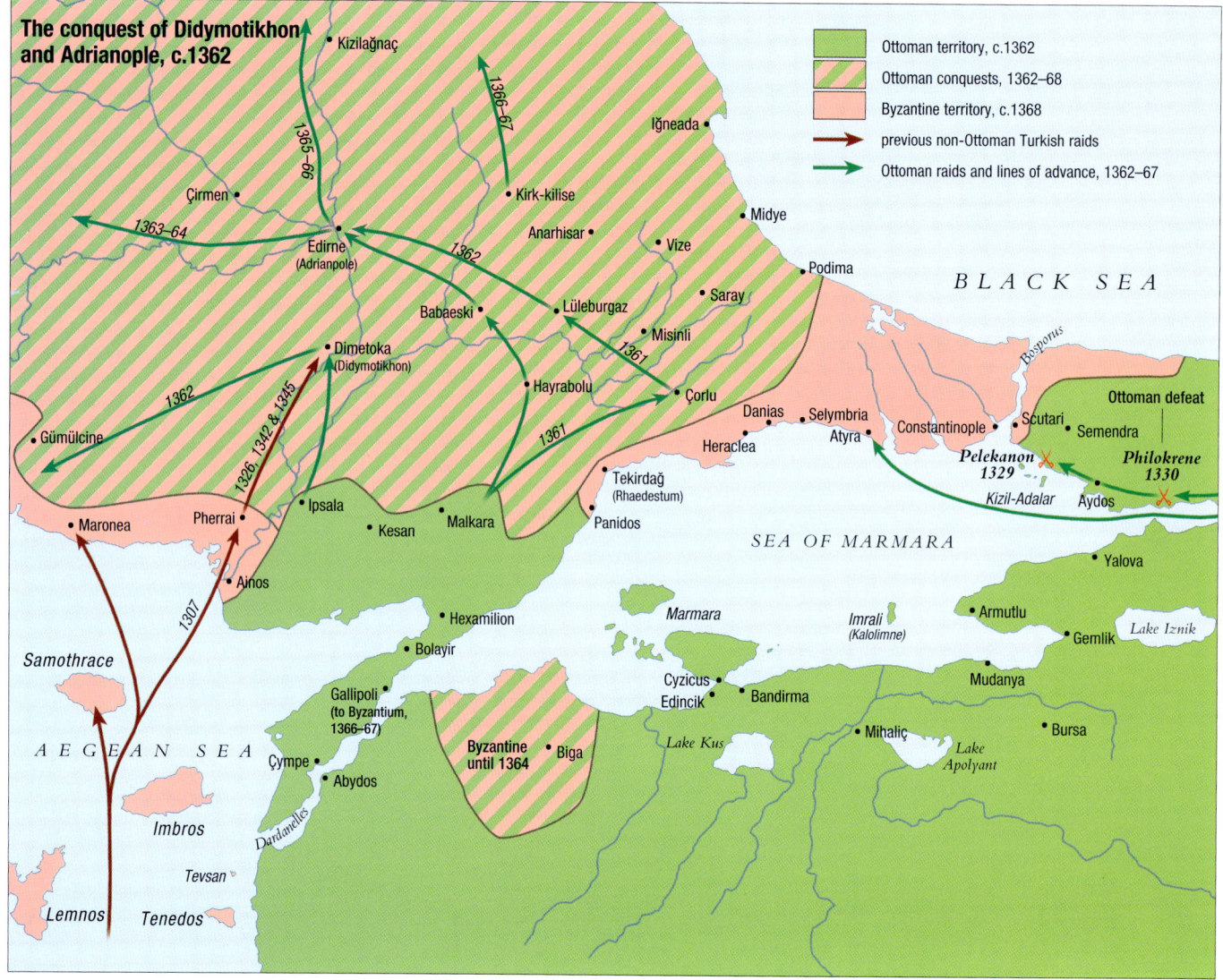

be hostility between the military and civilians, between ruling classes and common people. While many of the ruling classes looked northward for help, ordinary people often preferred Ottoman-Islamic rule to that of the Catholic Hungarians, who seemed to be the only viable alternative to a crumbling and humbled Byzantium.

Under the restored John V Palaeologus in the final decades of the 14th century the Byzantine empire of Constantinople consisted of little more than the city and its adjoining coasts, plus southern Greece (the Morea) and some Aegean islands. Other rival Byzantine or quasi-Byzantine states included the Empire of Trebizond on the northeastern coast of Anatolia and the Despotate of Epirus in what is now northwestern Greece and southern Albania. Similarly, little was left of the crusader states in Greece, while Bulgaria was already under Ottoman domination. The extensive but fragile Serbian empire had fallen apart before the Ottomans had reached the heart of the Balkans.

The seriousness of the Ottomans' intentions at last began to be appreciated in Europe and some rulers as well as senior churchmen started talking about another crusade. Nothing happened for several years, and in the meantime Orhan's eldest son and designated heir, Süleyman, was killed in an accident. Orhan himself died

After decades of war and famine, the plains of Thrace were devoid of people and ready to be repopulated by the Turkish newcomers. This shepherds' camp between Dedéagach (Alexandroupoli) and Komotini, now in eastern Greece, has probably changed little in appearance from those early nomadic Ottoman settlements.

CHAPTER FOUR: THE INVASION OF EUROPE

only two years later in 1360. This might have proved a vulnerable moment for the young Ottoman state and its fragile hold on parts of eastern Thrace, but Orhan's successor, his second son Murat, proved to be an even more effective and ambitious leader than his father. Murat already had command of the European front or *uç*, but on becoming ruler he focused on consolidating the Ottoman position in central Anatolia. One of the most significant developments in this region came when the virtually independent *ahi* religiously based militia and urban authorities in Ankara recognized the Ottoman emir rather than the Germiyan bey as their ruler. Other extensions of rule strengthened what would, in effect, become the Ottomans' base for their forthcoming conquest of the Balkans.

Murat next extended Ottoman authority deeper into Thrace, Macedonia, Bulgaria, and Serbia to become one of the most remarkable conquerors in medieval European history. At the start of this process, Gallipoli's harbor was essential to maintain communications and transport troops across the strait. The small Ottoman fleet could not have retained control of the narrow Dardanelles waterway if the far more powerful Christian fleets had been determined to break this vital link between the Turks' old and new territories. This weakness was fully understood in Europe and the Byzantine capital, but the competing Christian powers never allied long enough to control the Dardanelles or permanently retake Gallipoli. Instead the Ottomans copied the Byzantine emperors and forged valuable though temporary alliances with one or other of the Christian naval powers, taking advantage of their rivalries to strengthen the weak maritime link between Anatolia and Rumelia, Asia and Europe.

In the wake of Murat's conquering armies, the almost empty plains of Thrace and the valleys of eastern Macedonia were recolonized by people from the Anatolian provinces of the Ottoman state. They included Turkish nomadic groups who merged with, and to a large extent became the *yürük*, warrior-herdsmen who were to dominate several Balkan upland regions for centuries. Others included Muslim and Christian peasants from Anatolia. The role of the Bektaşi dervishes who accompanied many Ottoman armies was more important than is generally realized,

The 13th–14th-century towers of Baba Vida castle at Vidin, on the Danube, one of the last Bulgarian outposts to fall to the Ottomans.

not only as Muslim missionaries but also by encouraging the settlement and recultivation of abandoned lands. Much of the latter had been devastated by wars and plague long before the Ottomans arrived.

Serbia: A rival Balkan empire

At the time of the first Ottoman expansionist campaigns into the Balkans, the empire of Serbia was actually a larger state than the Byzantine empire. Serbia had evolved from two principalities among the partly tribal, partly feudal and only partially Christian Serbs back in the 11th century, Zeta in the west and Raska in the east. They were united as a single kingdom in 1172, but for a century and a half after its unification Serbia struggled to survive in the face of Byzantine, Bulgarian, and Hungarian ambitions, while the Bogomil heresy was suppressed and the kingdom became thoroughly Orthodox Christian. The Serbs did, however, win a small outlet on the Adriatic coast in the 1190s.

Wall painting in the Patriarchate of Péc, 1350–75; Serbs looked to the Byzantine empire and Orthodoxy for their faith.

Since its foundation as a kingdom, Serbia had looked south toward Byzantium as the source of civilization and an area for Serbian expansion. The first significant advances came in the reign of Stephan Uros II (1282–1321), but it was his son Stephan Uros III who made a breakthrough by defeating Bulgaria at the battle of Kyustendil in 1330, making Serbia the leading Balkan power. The victory also highlighted some interesting differences between a Bulgaria under strong eastern military and political influence and a Serbia already being influenced by western Europe. At Kyustendil the Bulgarians had been supported by numerous Mongol and Wallachian horse-archers, whereas the Serbian army included about a thousand Spanish mercenaries, many of them perhaps Catalan veterans who had previously fought for—and then almost destroyed—the Byzantines.

Despite his success, Stephan Uros III was overthrown by the Serbian aristocracy, which seemingly considered him too cautious and too peaceful. In his place they installed his son, Stephan Dusan (1331–55), who became the greatest conqueror in Serbian history and the most famous ruler of its Nemanja dynasty. Trade and mining had made Serbia rich, and Dusan used this wealth to recruit a large, mainly German, mercenary army. While striving for peace along Serbia's northern frontiers, Dusan overran huge areas of Byzantine territory in the south as well as taking substantial provinces from his neighbors to the west. Eventually Stephan proclaimed himself emperor of the Serbs and the Greeks, to which he added Bulgarians and Albanians in 1346. Apparently he intended to replace the ailing Byzantine empire with a new and vigorous Orthodox Christian comonwealth of his own. He was preparing to attack Constantinople when he suddenly died in 1355, barely three years after the Ottomans had taken control of Tzympe on the Gallipoli peninsula.

Under Stephan Dusan, the turbulent Serbian aristocracy had been forced, or were at least willing, to accept royal authority. A self-governing Serbian Orthodox Church fully emerged, with its own patriarchate based at Péc in what is now Kosovo. The king's lands were expanded, as were those of the Serbian kingdom as a whole. By the time of his death, Dusan's empire included not

CHAPTER FOUR: THE INVASION OF EUROPE

only Serbia, southern Bosnia and parts of Herzegovina, but also Macedonia, Epirus, and Thessaly in northern Greece, and, at least nominally, most of Albania. He even transferred the capital southward to Üskup (modern Skopje), in what is now the Republic of Macedonia.

Stephan Dusan's successors to the hugely expanded Serbian state were unable to continue his ambitions, though several of them are remembered as heroes of the epic Serbian resistance to Ottoman Turkish conquest. Some wielded only nominal authority and Dusan's empire rapidly disintegrated into a series of local, occasionally competing, principalities, some of which had to accept Hungarian suzerainty. Meanwhile, neighboring Bulgaria was fragmenting into three principalities, as described on page 55. By the time the Ottoman threat became serious, the Balkans comprised more than 20 separate states, all relatively small, some tiny. Many were deadly rivals of one another; none was in a position to offer effective resistance to the approaching Ottoman armies. Byzantium was in terminal decline, wracked by its Cantacuzenos-Palaeologus civil war which opened up tempting possibilities for Ottoman interference. The Genoese had been allowed to take over the strategic trading island of Chios, while mainland Thessaly and Epirus had been lost to the Serbs, leaving the Byzantines with part of Thrace, some northern Aegean islands, and the Morea in the Peloponnese in southern Greece. This lack of unity gave the Ottomans a golden opportunity.

As the Ottomans advanced through the Balkans, they introduced the civilized comforts Turks in Anatolia took for granted. Public baths, like this late 14th-century Hamam of Bayezit I at Bolu, sprang up in Thrace, Bulgaria, and Serbia (*see also the photograph on page 67*).

A new power in Europe

The first real Ottoman capital had been Bursa in the foothills of the northwestern Anatolian mountains. Now, after perhaps using Didimotikon (Turkish Dimetoka) as their first or temporary European regional capital, the Ottomans settled on Adrianople, which was renamed Edirne, as the base from which the greatest wave of conquests would be launched. The expansion was carefully planned and carried out with utter conviction. However, retaining full control of an army powerful enough to conquer the Balkans was not easy. Most of the fighting was done by armies operating on three frontier uç or marches. The first thrust northeast through Thrace was normally commanded by the Ottoman ruler. The second aimed northwestward through Bulgaria; its most famous commander was Kara Timürtaş. Gazi Evrenos—whom we have already mentioned (*pages 38-39*)—was the most renowned leader of the third uç, directed westward into Macedonia and Greece.

Official Ottoman attitudes toward their Christian and Jewish subjects were almost as sympathetic and accommodating as that of the unorthodox Bektaşi dervishes who accompanied their armies. Previously persecuted minorities like the Bogomils of Bosnia would soon convert to Islam in large numbers, while elsewhere in the Balkans Orthodox Christians often welcomed the Ottomans as liberators from Catholic domination and the peasantry appreciated the generally less oppressive Turkish administration. The Ottomans demanded fewer taxes than previous Byzantine, Bulgarian, Serbian, and other ruling classes. Their insistence on dividing the population into military and civilian classes enabled existing Christian warrior elites to remain without conversion to Islam. The higher aristocracy were almost all slain, or they fled, or accepted a lower status than they had enjoyed before the Ottoman conquest. The Church hierarchy also bemoaned their change of masters, not only because Islam had seemingly triumphed over Christianity but also because they had much to lose.

Most of the existing Byzantine Greek, Bulgarian, Serbian, and other Balkan military aristocracies who came to terms with the Ottoman sultanate converted to Islam after a few generations. In the newly conquered Balkan provinces, known to

CHAPTER FOUR: THE INVASION OF EUROPE

the Ottomans as Rumeli or Rumelia (Rum Ili or the Roman lands), many of the old feudal *pronoai* fiefs simply became Ottoman *timar* fiefs. Some went to Turkish warriors, others to Christian soldiers who now fought for a new ruler.

Even in the second half of the 14th century, most Ottoman armies seem to have consisted of a large proportion of Turcoman cavalry supported by a smaller number of foot soldiers, but the emphasis was gradually changing. By the time the Ottomans first established a bridgehead on the Gallipoli peninsula they had some sort of standing army capable of defending fixed positions and conducting offensive raids. This led to the incorporation of Byzantine and classical Islamic elements into the battle array. Byzantine influence appeared particularly strong in siege warfare. Although its enemies constantly exaggerated the size of the Ottoman army, in the mid-14th century it was large in comparison to the Ottoman state. Many vassals and volunteers followed the horse-tail *tuğ* ensigns of the Ottoman emir. Only later, when Bayezit I claimed the title of sultan, did any leader have more than one horse-tail. Thereafter the sultan would have four, his senior vizirs three, provincial beylerbeyis two, and ordinary beys one.

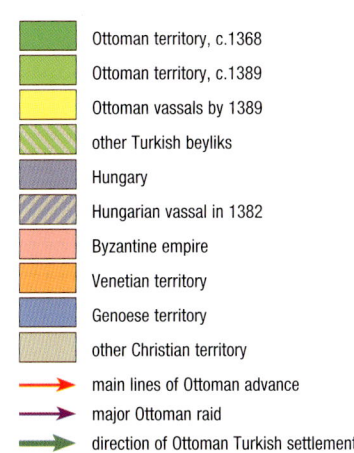

- Ottoman territory, c.1368
- Ottoman territory, c.1389
- Ottoman vassals by 1389
- other Turkish beyliks
- Hungary
- Hungarian vassal in 1382
- Byzantine empire
- Venetian territory
- Genoese territory
- other Christian territory
- main lines of Ottoman advance
- major Ottoman raid
- direction of Ottoman Turkish settlement

The Uç "fronts" in the Balkans and Ottoman expansion, c.1389

Turcoman nomads were known as *akincis* if they served for one campaign, receiving booty instead of pay, and *yürüks* if they formed a tribal contingent. These horse-archers rarely owned more than leather *lamellar* armor and still used the central Asian lasso as a weapon. Such Turcomans could rarely even hold occupied territory and were almost impossible to govern, thus Emir Orhan had long ago relegated them to the frontiers as raiders. Most of the gazi volunteers fought in traditional Middle Eastern or Iranian Islamic styles as mixed cavalry and infantry, and were much more amenable to discipline than Turcomans, though their essentially religious motivation may sometimes have made them difficult. Their code of *futuwa* provided a model for a virtuous life and formed a bond between a ruler, his gazis, and the caliph or other senior Islamic spiritual leader. It included comparable ceremonies to the western European code of chivalry and inspired a similar sense of comradeship based on shared ideals. From the late 13th century, Anatolian gazis are said to have worn tall felt caps, red or white, similar to those later adopted by some Ottoman elite units. Ex-Byzantine troops probably included both cavalry and infantry. Though they often used a bow, their military traditions no longer normally included horse-archery.

A professional force

Despite the existence of highly motivated soldiers, Ottoman tradition maintains that Emir Orhan (1326–62) felt the need for a disciplined and more easily controlled professional army. Legend and fact are so intertwined that the truth is almost impossible to identify, but it seems a regularly paid force of both Muslim and Christian horsemen and foot soldiers was established, supposedly by Orhan's vizir, Alla'al-Din. The horsemen were known as *müsellems* (tax-free) and organized under the overall command of *sancak beys*. They were theoretically divided into units of one hundred led by *subaşis* and thousands led by *binbaşis*. The foot soldiers, known as *yaya*, were similarly divided into tens, hundreds, and thousands. They fought as infantry archers and were occasionally recorded in Byzantine service, where they were called *mourtatoi*. Müsellems and yaya were at first paid regular wages, but by the time of Murat I they were normally allocated fiefs in return for military service, the yaya also having responsibility for the protection of roads and bridges. Being free Turkish landholders or farmers, the yaya again proved difficult to control and their loyalty tended to be to their immediate commanders. As a result müsellems and yaya were gradually relegated to second-line duties by the late 14th century. By the end of the 16th century they had been abolished altogether, or had been reduced to non-military status.

In a further attempt to create a reliable and loyal army, the Ottoman rulers adopted the centuries-old Islamic tradition of recruiting soldiers of slave origin, but added distinctive variations. The result was the famous Kapıkulu, whose name meant "slaves of the gate [of the palace]." Once again historical fact is buried beneath heroic and pious legend. According to a mythical version of events, the Kapıkulu corps was created by Kara Halil Çandarli, the brother-in-law of the

Hrvoje Vukčić, a bán of Croatia and—through Stephan Tvrtko's patronage—Grand Duke of Bosnia, was the strongest of the three main lords of medieval Bosnia. In a long career of bitter opposition to Hungarian ambition, Vukčić both sought Ottoman aid and fought against the Turks until a weakened Bosnia finally fell to Turkish rule soon after his death.

CHAPTER FOUR: THE INVASION OF EUROPE

A Turcoman warrior out hunting, from a Turco-Iranian manuscript illumination of c.1380.

saintly Shaykh Edebali whose daughter Malkhatun was supposedly married to Osman, founder of the Ottoman dynasty. Another story, which may contain an element of reality, maintained that the Yeniçeri (or Janissary, "new troops") infantry of this Kapıkulu corps were founded in 1326 when the first recruits were supposedly blessed by Haci Bektaş whose name meant "Bektaş who has been on Hac"(Arabic hajj) or pilgrimage to Mecca. By this date he would, in reality, have been long dead, if he had ever existed at all. The broad upraised sleeve of the *haci* (pilgrim) is said to have draped down a recruit's back as he gave the blessing, thus leading to the Janissaries' distinctive folded version of the tall white felt cap.

In reality, it seems more likely that the first Yeniçeri were prisoners of war, perhaps from the captured garrisons of one or more Thracian towns at least a generation later than 1326. The Kapıkulu included a smaller number of cavalry units. Established at an earlier date than the Yeniçeri infantry, they enjoyed higher status and wore upright or unfolded versions of the Janissary cap. These elite Kapıkulu horsemen are sometimes confused with Ottoman feudal, provincial fief-holding cavalry, as both were called *sipahis*. Known more specifically as the *süvarileri* or *bölük halki* (regiment men), they eventually consisted of six units. The oldest were the left and right *ulufeciyan* (salaried men), founded in the 14th century by Kara Timürtaş Paşa and Murat I who selected them from their finest troopers. The left and right *gureba* (poor foreigners) had almost as long a history, having been recruited from gazi volunteers, while the *silahtars* (weapons carriers) were a very early bodyguard formation identified by their tall red felt caps. The silahtars were replaced as the Ottoman ruler's mounted bodyguard by a new unit, the *sipahi oğlan* (sipahi children) early in the 15th century. Each unit of Kapıkulu cavalry was commanded by a *kethüda yeri* and eventually recruited from the sons of süvarileri horsemen, Arab, Persian, and Kurdish Muslims, and Janissaries who had distinguished themselves in battle. In later years the Kapıkulu corps also included artillery and engineer units.

Ottoman tactics had at first been those of tribal Turcomans, harassing their foes with horse-archery and only closing when the enemy was sufficiently disorganized to make victory almost certain. To take a fortified town the Ottomans continued the traditional tactic of ravaging the surrounding countryside to intimidate the defenders and deny their food supply. Where necessary they built their small forts to strengthen a blockade. Once in possession, however, the Ottomans put great effort and perhaps expense into reviving a town's trade and bringing in settlers to increase its population. Their earliest successes, even in the Balkans, had been against small and isolated garrisons, rarely against a large enemy field army. Land had been gained either by defeating local Byzantine noblemen, by buying Muslim and Christian castles from those unable to defend them, by absorbing existing landowners into Ottoman society, or occasionally by marriage alliances.

The moustaches may be fake but the spirit isn't. Turkish soldiers reenacting the historical Janissary corps march past the ancient walls of Constantinople during Istanbul's 2004 aniversary ceremony of the conquest of the Byzantine capital.

Defeating the Crusade of Nicopolis

By the end of the 14th century, despite early success the new Ottoman emir, Bayezit I, who was besieging Constantinople, decided that his position in the Balkans was not yet sufficiently secure. He summoned his Christian vassals to a conference in 1393/4, at which they swore oaths of allegiance in the European feudal manner. When Bayezit I selected Prince Stephan Lazarevic of Serbia as his most trustworthy subordinate ruler to help secure the Balkans, the emperor, by this time Manuel II Palaeologus, knew that Byzantium was doomed unless he summoned massive military help from Catholic western Europe. Sigismund of Hungary had also responded to events by trying to get his fellow European rulers to support a crusade to "go against the Turks to their loss and destruction." The pope, as usual, offered sympathy but little else.

Charles VI of France was suffering one of his renowned bouts of madness when Sigismund's emissary arrived in Paris, but his energetic uncle, the Duke of Burgundy, immediately set about raising the finance for a crusade. He assembled a massive army of French, English, Scottish, German, and Italian troops, supported by a fleet supplied and manned by Venetians, Genoese, and the Knights Hospitaller of Rhodes. This was probably the most international force ever to take the Cross against

Right: Bayezit I as portrayed in the *Book of Sultans*, created for Murat III in the late 16th century. While Beyezit was a substantial patron of public building (and undoubtedly a lover of scented flowers), he was also a powerful and ruthless military leader. His siege of Constantinople brought the emperor Manuel II Palaeologus to his knees—seen here in supplication to the Archangel Michael—who begged the West to raise a crusade to save his realm.

CHAPTER FOUR: THE INVASION OF EUROPE

Muslims, and it was joined by Sigismund's army at Buda in July 1396. To the east, Bayezit was obliged to raise his months-long siege of Constantinople to march and meet the threat.

Sigismund, who was already expecting an Ottoman invasion, favored a defensive strategy but the western European nobility scorned such an unchivalrous attitude. They persuaded the reluctant Hungarian king to join a great offensive along the

CHAPTER FOUR: THE INVASION OF EUROPE

Danube which, they claimed, would eventually take them through the Balkans and Anatolia to Syria and Jerusalem itself. Accompanied by a supply fleet, the army followed the river into Bulgarian territory, which already accepted Ottoman suzerainty. They slaughtered the Ottoman garrison at Vidin and massacred virtually the entire population of Rahova, Orthodox Christians included. Only a few miles further down the Danube at Nicopolis, the crusaders suffered their first setback. The Ottoman garrison held a strongly fortified town but neither Burgundy nor Sigismund had brought siege engines. These large, cumbersome weapons were aboard the crusader fleet which had sailed from the Aegean, so the crusaders had to wait before beginning a siege of Nicopolis, while discipline and health in the Christian lines declined as "camp fever" took hold.

Title page of *Schildtberger's Travels*. Captured by Turks during the defeat of the Christian crusade at Nicopolis in 1396, Schildtberger traveled around Asia for 22 years. On his return home in 1421 he was an acknowledged expert on the Ottoman military and techniques of warfare.

Bayezit had not been idle. After breaking off his siege of Constantinople he assembled his palace troops at Edirne, while summoning vassals from Anatolia and Rumelia, including the Serbs. Bayezit marched toward Nicopolis, collecting contingents on the way. After some initial skirmishing, the main battle was fought outside Nicopolis on September 25, 1396. It resulted in an overwhelming Ottoman victory, though Bayezit also suffered severe losses. As a result of reduced manpower, many of the Turks' prisoners were slaughtered. Senior men were taken for ransom while other captives were sold as slaves or to the "ransom brokers" who were a feature of warfare during this period.

The defeat outside Nicopolis had a profound impact on Hungary, undermining Sigismund's already weak authority but leading to a prolonged period of military reform. It also sparked the beginnings of a mixture of fear and respect for the Ottomans within Hungarian society, and chroniclers eventually became less vitriolic about the Turks. The greatest terror would be reserved for the Ottomans' "false

An Ottoman hamam of the late 14th–early 15th centuries stands next to the mosque of Sinan Paşa in Prizren, Kosovo.

kindness," which "worked against the soul" and encouraged Christians to convert to Islam. In the aftermath of the battle, a series of Ottoman raids reached as far as Styria in southern Austria, sending waves of fear as far as Germany and northern Italy. It was a sign of things to come, though in the meantime the Ottomans would have to surmount problems of their own before they could launch a major offensive toward central Europe.

Ottoman Edirne—the jeweled city

In 1367 Emir Murat I made Adrianople the administrative capital of his expanding Rumelian or Balkan provinces. The Byzantine city—which had been in Turkish hands since the year before, following the small but historically significant victory over a combined Byzantine Greek and Bulgarian force somewhere between Babaeski and Pinarhisar—was known as Edirne to the Turks, who tended to simplify the sometimes convoluted Greek city names. As demonstrated earlier in this chapter, Edirne became the point from which Ottoman campaigns thrust in four directions: along the coast of the Aegean Sea through Thrace to Macedonia, northwestward into the heart of Bulgaria, northward toward the eastern end of the Balkan range and the lower course of the Danube, and eastward across eastern Thrace toward Constantinople.

Ottoman successes attracted scholars as well as soldiers and Bayezit I had several famous people in his new court at Edirne, even before his victory over the crusaders. They included the historian Ibn al-Jazari, who finished his epic poetic verse *History of the Prophet and Caliphs* three days after the battle of Nicopolis, while living in the Ottoman army camp. Prior to that remarkable victory, Ottoman rulers had been addressed as emirs, but after it Bayezit persuaded the titular 'Abbasid caliph in Cairo to grant him and his successors the more senior title of sultan. The fact that this was permitted by the Mamluk sultan of Cairo, who ruled the biggest and most prestigious Islamic state in the Middle East, suggests that the shortsighted Mamluks did not yet see the Ottomans as dangerous rivals. Bayezit's new status encouraged yet more scholars to the increasingly wealthy and cultured Ottoman court. Not surprisingly, Edirne was soon graced with fine new Islamic buildings. The Eski Cami or Old Mosque dates from the start of the 15th century, but remained traditional in design. This was also true of the Mosque of Murat II, which was not completed until 1435/6.

The beautiful Üç Serefli Cami or Three Balconies Mosque was also built for Murat II and although it was finished only a few years later, architectural historians regard it as the first significant building in a new and truly Ottoman architectural style. The great dome is almost 82 feet across and would not be surpassed until Sultan Mehmet the Conqueror built his victory mosque in Istanbul a generation

Ottoman capital after its capture at some point before 1366 until the taking of Constantinople in 1453, Adrianople—renamed Edirne—benefited from a lavish building program, typified by the minarets of the Üç Serefli Cami

CHAPTER FOUR: THE INVASION OF EUROPE

later. Each of the four minarets of the Üç Serefli mosque is decorated in a different manner, one having a remarkable multiple spiral pattern in red and white, while the tallest has the three balconies which give the mosque its name.

Senior military leaders paid for the construction of secular buildings. These included the bridge of Gazi Mihail, a convert from Christianity, which dates from 1420, and the Orta *ımaret* or soup kitchen. Sadly nothing remains of the great 15th century palaces built in Edirne but a huge *bedestan* or covered bazaar constructed at the start of the 15th century survives largely intact.

The transfer of the Ottoman capital to Istanbul after its capture as Constantinople in 1453 had little impact on the importance of Edirne, which remained the administrative center of the Rumelian or European provinces, as well as being the site of the sultans' favorite country retreat until the 19th century. The city was to continue to serve as the main strategic military base for the conquest of southeastern Europe and, in much later years, for the defense of what remained of these possessions. Its magnificent monuments suffered severe damage during the Russian invasions of 1829 and 1878, and more was inflicted during the long siege and brief occupation by the Bulgarians in 1913. Today most guidebooks describe Edirne as a quiet, old-fashioned city wedged into a curve of the river Tunca, hiding masterpieces of Ottoman architecture. It could be described as the only true Ottoman city remaining in Europe.

Above: Edirne's Bayezit II medical complex and mosque from 1484 and, **below**, interior of the Eski Cami, built 1413–14.

CHAPTER FIVE

Survival and Expansion

Tamerlane, civil war, and European crusades

Nicopolis had been an overwhelming victory for Bayezit and the Ottoman army, but it would soon be overshadowed by greater and far more dangerous events. Immediately after his victory next to the Danube, Bayezit decided against the invasion of further territory in Europe, though he sent raiders remarkably deep into Hungarian territory. Instead the sultan chose to consolidate authority within those parts of the Balkans the Ottomans had already taken. The little Bulgarian Principality of Vidin, previously a vassal, was placed under direct Ottoman rule and the entire southern bank of the lower Danube river became an uç frontier zone. Colonization by those considered entirely loyal to the sultan was encouraged, and as a result the bulk of the population of the uç soon became Muslim. Elsewhere troops raided central Greece while Bayezit returned to his previous desultory siege of Constantinople.

As mentioned in the last chapter, some scholars had already been attracted to Bayezit I's exciting court, but after Nicopolis this became a flood of highly educated administrators, religiously motivated soldiers, talented craftsmen, and renowned scholars. However, many were seeking protection from the savage Mongol campaigns of conquest led by Timur-i Lenk, which had thrown the eastern Islamic lands into near anarchy.

Timur-i Lenk—Timur the Lame, or Tamerlane as he is better known—was actually a Turk, though he claimed to be a Mongol. Partially lame as the result of a battlefield wound early in his career, Timur was now elderly and many thought he was at last settling down to enjoy the spoils of conquest. From 1396, the year of Bayezit's great victory over the crusaders at Nicopolis, to 1398, Timur-i Lenk spent much time in his favorite city of Samarkand, far away in Central Asia, where he indulged in feasting and supervized the building of those architectural monuments whose beauty stood in stark contrast to their patron's bloodthirsty life. These quiet years would pass, however—Timur had by no means retired from the battlefield. During 1398–99 Timur-i Lenk led his superbly equipped and disciplined army into northern India, leaving a trail of massacre, destruction and looting in its wake.

Timur-i Lenk in mounted procession, protected from the sun by a parasol; from a Persian manuscript, Shiraz c.1434.

The following winter he struck at Christian Georgia for the third time, and in August 1400 he marched against Sivas in the heart of Anatolia, a town which had only recently been incorporated into the Ottoman sultanate. Prisoners were forced to work as sappers, undermining the walls and erecting earth platforms from which Timur's siege machines could hurl rocks and fire-pots into the town. The garrison, largely consisting of Christian Armenian sipahi feudal cavalry, put up a stout resistance but eventually had to capitulate. They were buried alive in the city's moat, though the Muslim inhabitants were spared. Timur-i Lenk's treatment of Christians in eastern Anatolia was particularly savage, and probably contributed to the loyalty these communities developed for the mild rule of the Ottomans.

Captured Turks, including those from the warlike Qara Qoyunlu, were sent east to be held ready for Timur's proposed invasion of China. The second main Turcoman tribe in this area, the Aq Qoyunlu, came to terms with Timur and even sent troops to help him fight the Ottomans. First, however, Timur had to deal with the Mamluks of Syria and Egypt who had declined an offer of alliance from the Ottoman sultan but also refused to become Timur's vassals. Timur's assault on Mamluk territory was fiercely resisted, but in vain. Aleppo was taken by assault and the usual massacre followed. A palace coup in Cairo led to a sudden withdrawal of the main Mamluk army, leaving Damascus defenseless. Its inhabitants then suffered some of the cruelest tortures in even Timur's sadistic career.

An illustration from a late 14th- or early 15th-century manuscript depicts two cavalrymen and two foot soldiers in combat—either Mongol or more probably Aq Qoyunlu—in Azerbaijan or western Iran.

Taken at Ankara—the end of the first Ottoman sultan

Timur-i Lenk next turned to face his most powerful foe. Both Bayezit and Timur were successful conquerors and the Ottoman army enjoyed the same record of success as did Timur's. Not surprisingly, the leaders were wary of each other and at first did no more than exchange threats written in peculiarly flowery language. In the winter of 1401-02 Timur tried to draw local Christian rulers into an anti-Ottoman alliance but they demurred. The war was to be land-based: though the emperor of Trebizond was already Timur's vassal, he did not have the 20 galleys that Timur demanded and while the Byzantines of Constantinople and the Genoese of Galata may have promised Bayezit naval support, nothing came of it.

Timur's first action against Bayezit was to seize Erzinjan, where he demolished the Armenian cathedral of St. Sergius. From there his army returned to Sivas where he held a full-scale, highly public and well recorded review which showed just how modern and sophisticated its organization and equipment had become. Timur then completely outmaneuvered Bayezit, despite the latter's formidable military reputation. Whereas Timur's army was still a highly mobile Turco-Mongol force based on cavalry, the Ottoman army already included large numbers of infantry. These no longer served merely as siege troops or skirmishers but had a central military role. Yet it was Bayezit's men who were obliged to do most of the marching while Timur besieged Ankara.

On July 20, 1402, tired and thirsty, the Ottomans were thrown into what has been described as one of the first modern battles in Middle Eastern history. It was hard fought and long, with the Ottomans' Serbian vassals distinguishing themselves by their skill and determination. But by the end of the day Timur had won and Bayezit was his prisoner. Later sources claim that Bayezit was held captive in an iron-barred cage, but this is probably a legend that grew out of Ahmad Arabshah's poetic

Bayezit's conquests and Timur-i Lenk's invasion

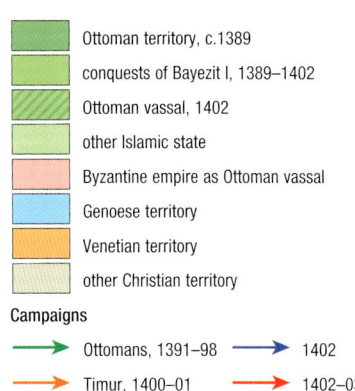

- Ottoman territory, c.1389
- conquests of Bayezit I, 1389–1402
- Ottoman vassal, 1402
- other Islamic state
- Byzantine empire as Ottoman vassal
- Genoese territory
- Venetian territory
- other Christian territory

Campaigns
- Ottomans, 1391–98
- 1402
- Timur, 1400–01
- 1402–03

description of the Ottoman sultan having "fallen into the hunter's snare and been confined like a bird in a cage." Yet Bayezit seems to have attempted an escape and thereafter was chained at night, traveling by day in a wagon or litter surrounded by a stout grille. The Elizabethan English playwright and rival of Shakespeare, Christopher Marlowe, took the story a stage further in his play *Tamburlaine the Great* by having Bayezit use these same bars to end the misery of his defeat:

Now Bajazeth, abridge thy baneful days,
And beat thy brains out of thy conquered head,
Since other means are forbidden me,
That may be ministers of my decay.

The shattered and largely leaderless Ottoman army fled westward, where many of the survivors were ferried across the Dardanelles to Europe in Genoese and Venetian ships. While Genoa thought the time ripe for an alliance with Timur,

CHAPTER FIVE: SURVIVAL AND EXPANSION

Venice kept the conqueror at arm's length. Timur ravaged right up to the Aegean Sea, using the great citadel of Kütahya as his base. Down on the coast, the city of Smyrna had been in crusader hands since 1344, though the occupiers never took control of the surrounding territory. Many different people had contributed to this extraordinary Christian outpost, including Venetians, Genoese, the remaining crusader principalities in Greece, the Kingdom of Cyprus, a French army under the Dauphin of Vienne and, above all, the Knights Hospitallers. The garrison now consisted of 200 knights and their followers under the Spaniard Inigo d'Alfaro. Timur demanded that they surrender but d'Alfaro refused and on December 2, 1402 a siege began. Smyrna's harbor was partially blocked by causeways built out into the bay, while Timur's engineers also constructed huge mobile wooden towers manned by up to 200 soldiers. The towers were rolled against the walls, which Timur's sappers also undermined. After less than 15 days the city fell. As the massacre of the population began, the survivors fled to the neighboring island of Chios. From then on Smyrna became Turkish Izmir.

Though the evidence is not entirely clear, it seems that Bayezit I's sons Musa and Mustafa had also been taken prisoner by Timur-i Lenk after the battle of Ankara but were later released. Bayezit died at Akşehir in March 1403, after which Timur returned to Central Asia to prepare for the invasion of China. Timur left Anatolia in a situation similar to that which had existed before Bayezit had conquered so many beyliks in the late 14th century. The greatest of these independent states was again Karaman, which Timur had hoped would serve as a strong buffer and vassal state between himself and what remained of the Ottoman sultanate. In the event the Chinese were spared—the bloodstained conqueror died in 1404 while leading his army toward the Chinese frontier.

The defeat and subsequent death of Bayezit threw the Ottomans into turmoil, but their empire was already as much a Balkan-European state as an Anatolian-Asiatic one. They not only survived but also recovered to reconquer what is now modern Turkey, half the Middle East, North Africa, and Europe almost to the gates of Vienna. In the short term, Timur's invasion strengthened the nomadic Turcoman element in Anatolia in relation to the settled peasantry and townsfolk, a factor which in fact actually helped the revival of Ottoman fortunes. But before that happy future, the Ottomans were divided by a bloody civil war between Bayezit's four sons.

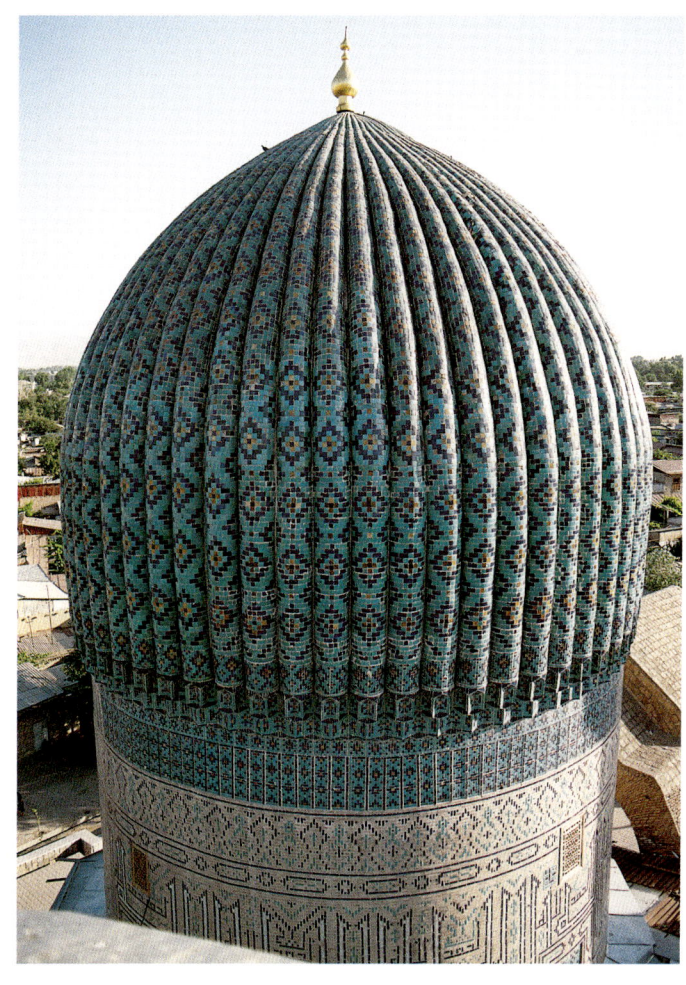

Architectural monuments whose beauty stood in stark contrast to their patron's bloodthirsty life— the dome of Timur's mausoleum in Samarkand.

The towers Kütahya's citadel jut up like stumps of teeth from the hillside.

Civil war and revival

Loyalty to the descendants of Osman remained strong and there were hardly any attempts to break away from Ottoman rule. The gazis continued to raid deep into central Europe even as rival forces fought on behalf of the four brothers. At one time Bayezit's eldest son Süleyman seemed likely to emerge victorious— he was the most effective battlefield commander. At first he controlled the capital Edirne, most of the European provinces, and was supported by powerful Christian vassals. İsa controlled Bursa but not all of the other Anatolian provinces. Instead, another brother, Çelebi Mehmet, governed Amasya while the fourth brother Musa was virtually a prisoner of the beylik of Germiyan at Kütahya. As early as 1403 Mehmet marched west to defeat İsa and overrun most of northwestern Anatolia. The following year İsa returned from the European side of the straits, where Mehmet again defeated him. Meanwhile there was a revolt in and around the devastated city of Izmir, from where an adventurer named Cüneyt Bey had taken control of the beylik of Aydın.

After seizing Aydın, Cüneyt was removed by Süleyman, who put him in command of Ottoman forces at Ohrid in Macedon. By 1412 he was back at Ayasoluk (Selçuk) on the Aegean coast of Anatolia, where he declared himself independent. This time Mehmet brought Cüneyt to heel but unwisely left him in charge of the town and its citadel. In return for fighting an ally of Mehmet, Cüneyt was given command of the strategic frontier sancak of Niğbolu (Greek Nicopolis), but a few years later gave his support to "the False Mustafa," an unsuccessful pretender to the Ottoman throne. After deserting the False Mustafa, Cüneyt rebuilt an autonomous province around Izmir and took control of the neighboring islands, only to be defeated and executed by the new sultan's Genoese allies in 1426.

After his defeat at Mehmet's hands in 1404, İsa made a final attempt in the following year by forming an alliance with the beyliks of Aydın, Saruhan, Menteşe, and Teke, but was nevertheless defeated and disappeared from the scene. In 1406 Süleyman invaded his brothers' territories and their beylik allies in Anatolia. Although this campaign was successful, Mehmet formed an alliance with Karaman and sent his brother Musa to Wallachia, from where he in turn invaded Rumelia. Süleyman had to withdraw across the straits to defeat Musa in Thrace.

Mehmet controlled Anatolia and Süleyman ruled Rumelia until 1410, when Musa again invaded the European provinces, defeating and killing Süleyman near Edirne. Now Mehmet invaded Rumelia, but was defeated by Musa and had to withdraw to the Asian shore. The climax came in 1413 when Mehmet forged an alliance with Constantinople and Serbia in the west and the beylik of Dulkadir in the east. Assembling a formidable army he defeated Musa near Samokov and later had him put to death. Ottoman power in Anatolia and the Balkans was not fully restored by the time of Mehmet I's death in 1420. He was succeeded by his son Murat II, who improved the civil administration and military structures and handed the sultanate to his own child, Mehmet II, the Conqueror.

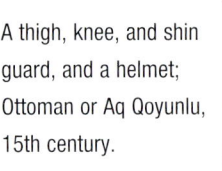

A thigh, knee, and shin guard, and a helmet; Ottoman or Aq Qoyunlu, 15th century.

CHAPTER FIVE: SURVIVAL AND EXPANSION

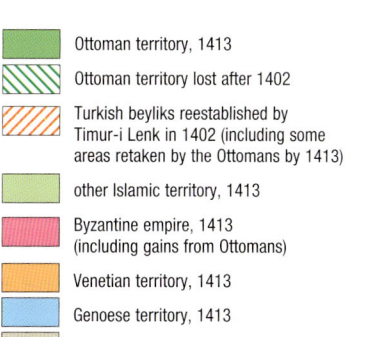

The reconquest of Anatolia

After Timur-i Lenk had defeated the Ottomans outside Ankara in 1402, he permitted if not actively encouraged the reemergence of the independent Turkish beyliks. However, they never regained their old strength and only survived as long as the Ottomans were diverted by civil war, but with victory in Europe Mehmet I quickly set about using his European provinces as a springboard from which to regain lost territory in the east. In some ways this was a European conquest of Anatolia, mirroring the previous Anatolian conquest of the Balkans in the 14th century. Even so, it took Bayezit I's successors many years to reach his earlier eastern frontiers.

At first it had seemed possible that the Ottomans would be driven from Asia altogether. The most immediate threat was probably posed by Isfandiyar Mubariz al-Din, who had regained control of the beylik of Candar and after whom the Candar Oğullari family subsequently took its name. He had already extended power from his family's original powerbase at Sinop (ancient Sinope) to control Kastamonou, Safranbolu, and Samsun. Isfandiyar Mubariz al-Din now formed an

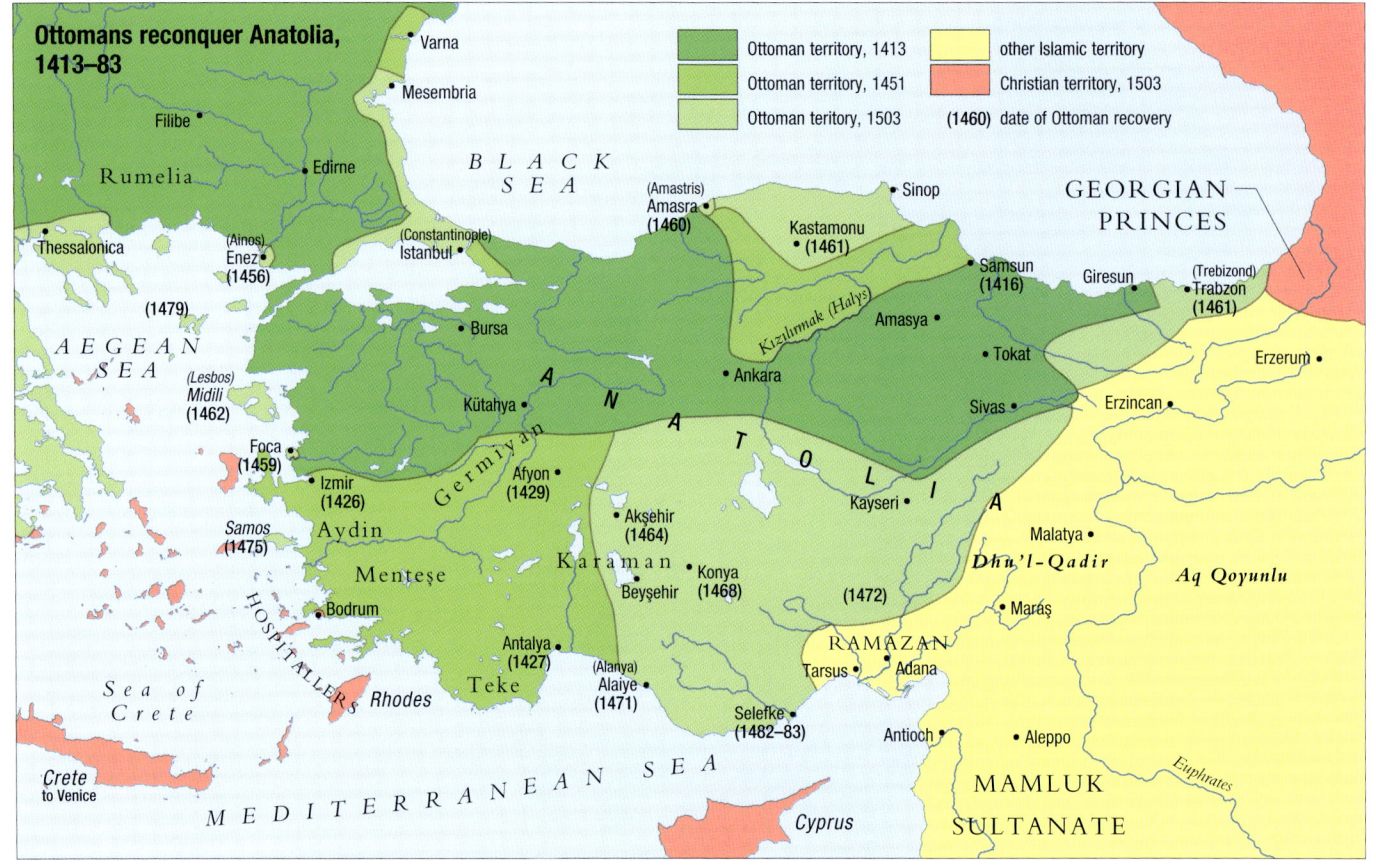

alliance with the revived Karaman Oğullari beys of south-central Anatolia. Further east Ottoman rule was threatened by the growing power of the Qara Qoyunlu or Black Sheep Turcomans. Mehmet I rose to both these challenges, defeating Isfandiyar and forcibly transferring most of his Turcoman fighting men to Ottoman-ruled Bulgaria, where they were settled near Filibe (Bulgarian Plovdiv, ancient Philippopolis). The town which developed as the center of this new warrior community came to be known as Tatar Pazarcik, "the Market of the Tatars" (now Pazardzhik). As this proved to be a success, such transfers developed into common Ottoman policy, thus removing troublesome peoples from Anatolia and turning them into generally reliable garrisons within Rumelia. The Candar or Isfandiyar Oğullari would lose the last of their territory to Mehmet II in 1462 but remained a locally dominant family for many generations.

Anatolia was still a source of trouble for Mehmet I's son and heir, Murat II. His first problem in the early 1420s was the ambitious adventurer Cüneyt Bey at Aydın, but once he was removed with Genoese help, the Ottomans moved south to reoccupy Menteşe and Teke. This brought the whole of the Aegean coast of Anatolia back under the sultan's control, which would soon enable the Ottomans to build a proper navy (see pages 89–92). Meanwhile, in return for Genoese naval assistance, Murat allowed Italian merchant enclaves to be reestablished along the Black Sea coast. He also tried to weaken the powerful beylik of Karaman by sowing dissention within the ruling family of the Karaman Oğullari. This was partially successful, and the new ruler of Karaman, Ibrahim Bey, became an ally of the Ottomans rather than the Mamluks. The latter had also been extending their influence, particularly in the

CHAPTER FIVE: SURVIVAL AND EXPANSION

strategic and fertile region of Cilicia. Germiyan was the next beylik to be taken over, whose last ruler, Ya'qub II, bequeathed his lands to the sultan on his death in 1428. This left the whole of western and central Anatolia either under Ottoman rule or its vassals; the only exceptions were the restored Genoese coastal enclaves on the Black Sea coast. Eastern Anatolia largely remained beyond Ottoman reach, with the independent Byzantine Empire of Trebizond in the northeast and Mamluk-dominated minor rulers in the southeast.

Despite their promises of friendship and support, the Karaman Oğulları were the least reliable of the Ottomans' allies against their Christian European foes, but the dynasty was finally overthrown by the Ottomans in 1475. The neighboring Ramazan Oğulları of Cilicia became vassals in 1516, having previously been more linked to the Mamluk sultans of Egypt and Syria. Five years later the Dulkadir Oğulları who ruled Maraş and Malatya followed them into the Ottoman sphere of influence.

Defeating the Hungarian crusades

The civil wars of 1403–13 had allowed Serbia, Bosnia, and Wallachia to throw off suzerainty, but during the first of his two reigns, 1421–44, Murat II subdued these three states once again, while extending direct Ottoman rule westward into the Epirus region of Greece. Murat's younger son Mehmet had shown himself to be a skilled and enthusiastic soldier, which made him popular with the frontier beys and a significant number of the Kapıkulu household troops. They urged the elderly sultan to nominate Mehmet as his heir, but Murat had more immediate problems. The dramatic revival in Ottoman fortunes had come as a shock in the courts of western Europe and by 1443 another crusade marched against the Turks. It was led by King Wladislaw V (Ladislaus V, 1443–57), who ruled both Hungary and Poland.

Janos Hunyadi's massive castle at Hunedoara—now in Romania—once stood in Hungary and was known as Vajdahunyad. It later inspired a copy which was built in Budapest at the end of the 19th century.

The Ottomans had also suffered a number of painful setbacks in Wallachia, where they faced Janos Hunyadi, one of the greatest heroes in Hungarian and indeed Romanian history. His origins are unclear, for though he was born in largely Romanian-speaking Transylvania, where his huge castle still stands at Hunedoara, Janos Hunyadi was a member of the Hungarian aristocracy. He had been appointed *voyvoda* or governor of Transylvania by the new Hungarian king and promptly defeated several Ottoman raids. His reputation earned him the role of military leader, though not titular commander, of the Hungarian crusade.

The first phases of the campaign were a great success, penetrating deep into Ottoman-dominated Serbia, where Niş was seized. The crusaders advanced over the mountains into Ottoman-ruled Bulgaria, where Sofia fell. Murat was campaigning in Anatolia and the local Ottoman forces of Rumelia could do little but harass the invaders. Mehmet hurried back to Europe with a relatively small army of Kapıculu

household regiments, regrouped his now scattered Rumelian forces and tried to stop Hunyadi's larger army in a mountain pass known as the Trayan Gate (Trajan's Gate). Though defeated, the Ottomans soon had the weather on their side as the brutal Balkan winter arrived. Hunyadi had to abandon the invasion and, after slaughtering thousands of Muslim prisoners, returned to Hungary. Nevertheless, the Ottoman position remained highly vulnerable, so the sultan negotiated a truce in July 1444. The following month the aged Murat abdicated in favour of Mehmet II and retired to Bursa, where he planned to spend the rest of his days in prayer and study.

The youthful Mehmet II enjoyed widespread support and it seemed likely that he could prepare the Ottoman defenses for any future crusader assault. Unfortunately Mehmet's accession led to increasing friction between the Kapıkulu and the older established Turkish aristocracy led by the Çandarlı family, whose most senior member Çandarlı Halil was also the ruler's vizir or senior minister. To make matters worse, a series of rebellions flared up in the Ottomans' Balkan provinces while resistance stiffened in Albania. Then the pope declared that oaths sworn by Christian princes to maintain a truce with the "infidels" were not binding; a new Hungarian crusade was proclaimed and soldiers flocked to join it from all over Europe. Again

CHAPTER FIVE: SURVIVAL AND EXPANSION

Carving of local militia troops on a house in the Dalmatian city of Šibenik. Venice annexed the Adriatic port in 1412 and defended it against the Ottomans, to whom it never fell despite repeated threats.

led by Wladislaw V, it marched out of Segedin in Hungary on September 1, 1444 and was joined at Orsova by Janos Hunyadi with his own highly experienced troops. Hunyadi had been unwilling to break the promise of peace he had made to Murat, but he also felt honor-bound to follow his king.

George Brankovic, the Serbian prince, refused to join this renewed attack and warned Mehmet of the approaching storm. The local Rumelian commanders decided that Mehmet was too young to cope with such a crisis and so Çandarlı Halil asked Murat to return and take command of the Ottoman resistance. The old man abandoned his retirement and persuaded the Genoese to ship his Anatolian forces across the straits to Europe. Meanwhile the crusaders reached Varna on the Black Sea coast. There, on November 10, 1444, the Ottoman army at first appeared to be losing the day, but Murat II rallied his men, the elite Janissaries stood firm against the Hungarian cavalry and by the time the fighting ended, the invaders had been routed and Wladislaw killed.

Turk in Byzantine service by Pisanello (**above**) and a Janissary by Gentile Bellini.

Once again, a victory against the biggest and best army that Christendom could send against them brought huge prestige to the Ottomans. It was also the signal for a renewal of Ottoman advances in the Balkans, campaigns partly proclaimed as punishment for the Christians' breaking of truce agreements. In most regions, resistance was crushed or brushed aside, but in Albania the Turks came up against an extraordinary guerrilla leader, George Castriota, better known by his Ottoman name of Skanderbeg (Iskander [Alexander] Bey). He and his followers used their exceptionally rugged and mountainous homeland to defy the sultan from 1443 to 1468, and even then the Ottomans found it expedient to allow the Albanian tribes to retain a considerable degree of autonomy. Eventually the majority of Albanian people converted to Islam and became some of the sultanate's fiercest defenders.

Another crusade was launched four years later, again led by Janos Hunyadi. Again the Serbian ruler, George Brankovic, refused to turn against his Ottoman neighbors but Skanderbeg of Albania sent soldiers, as did the ruler of Wallachia. Murat met the invaders in Kosovo, routing them at the second battle of Kosovo, October 18–20, 1448, on much the same battlefield as the Serbs had been defeated by Bayezit almost a century before. One of the first places to feel the Ottomans' renewed wrath was Wallachia, where one of the strangest figures in European history appeared on the scene. Vlad Tepes, nicknamed Vlad the Impaler, was born in about 1430 at Sighişoara, where his father, Vlad II Dracul, held a border command post under the Hungarian crown. Dracul became the Hungarian king's voyvoda in 1432 but had to regain the title by force four year later at the head of a dissident faction of Wallachian boyars or noblemen. He switched allegiance and supported the Ottoman cause, taking part in two raids into Hungarian-ruled Transylvania.

Situated about 15.5 miles southwest of Brasov in the Transylvanian Alps, Bran is Romania's most spectacular castle. In the mid-15th century Vlad Tepes held Bran in his fight against the Turks, thus branding it with his bloody cruelty. In the 19th century, Bram Stoker used the castle and parts of its history when writing his famous vampire story about Dracula.

Changing sides once again, Vlad II Dracul joined the Hungarian crusade against Murat in 1443 but argued against the new campaign which came to grief at Varna the following year. For a while he even held the famous Janos Hunyadi captive, who had Dracul dethroned in 1446. However, the Hungarian-supported voyvoda who replaced him reputedly betrayed them at the second battle of Kosovo.

The younger Vlad, the future Tepes or "Impaler," had been brought up in his father's palace at Tirgoviste with several brothers, but at the age of around 13 his family's varying fortunes forced him to lead a nomadic and sometimes terrifying life. This must surely have had some influence on his later cruel and bizarre conduct. In 1444 Vlad Tepes and his brother Radu the Handsome were sent to the Ottoman court as hostages to maintain their father's good behavior. Given Dracul's unpredictable action, the boys suffered a precarious existence in the Turkish fortress of Eğrigöz. In 1447 Vlad II Dracul and his eldest son Mircea were killed by dissident Wallachian boyars and Vladislav II, a man more pliable to Hungarian wishes, was made voyvoda. The sultan freed Vlad Tepes and gave him an Ottoman officer's rank and some Turkish troops before sending him across the Danube into Wallachia. Vlad briefly captured Tirgoviste in 1448 but was soon driven into exile again.

For the next eight years Vlad Tepes lived by his wits in Ottoman territory, Moldavia and Transylvania, sometimes as a tolerated pawn in the power game, sometimes as a fugitive. Finally winning the support of Janos Hunyadi, he fought his way to the bloodstained throne of Wallachia in September 1456. He swore formal oaths to both the king of Hungary and the Ottoman sultan, and began the first of his two reigns. The fact that Vlad Tepes became the relentless and quite successful leader of Wallachian resistance to Ottoman domination has been obscured by the horrendous savagery with which he slaughtered huge numbers of enemies and those he believed unreliable. The most famous epitaph to Vlad Tepes is his Impaler nickname and his identification with Bram Stoker's vampire Dracula.

The sultan's vassal

The final half-century of the Byzantine empire of Constantinople was a period of raised and dashed hopes, of imperial humiliation, desperate attempts to get help, and final, almost epic, collapse. Deals were made with the Ottomans to keep the empire alive, especially after the crusader army's defeat at Nicopolis in 1396, which had been a severe blow for Manuel II. As he later wrote to the scholar and departing prime minister of Constantinople, Cydones, "To prudent men, life is not worth living after that calamity, that deluge of the whole world [the Biblical Flood], but one worse than that in so much as it carried off men better than those of old." The Ottoman siege of Constantinople was pressed harder and Bayezit demanded that Manuel II hand the city over to his pro-Ottoman nephew, John VII. Many of the inhabitants agreed, while the sultan and his aides were so confident that they stood on a hill overlooking Constantinople and discussed who should get which palace after it fell. However, the massive fortified walls defied their assaults and Bayezit scaled down the siege.

Reconciliation between the rival emperors Manuel and John calmed the situation, but Manuel's lengthy visit to western Europe from 1399 to 1403 failed to gain substantial help. By the time Manuel delivered the funeral oration for his late brother, the despot Theodore of the Morea in 1407, the names of the defeated western crusaders stuck in the throat of such a cultured Byzantine gentleman: "The great army which was struck down at Nicopolis— I mean that collected from the Panonians, the Celts, and the Western Galtians, at all of those names I shudder at, as an entirely barbaric thing."

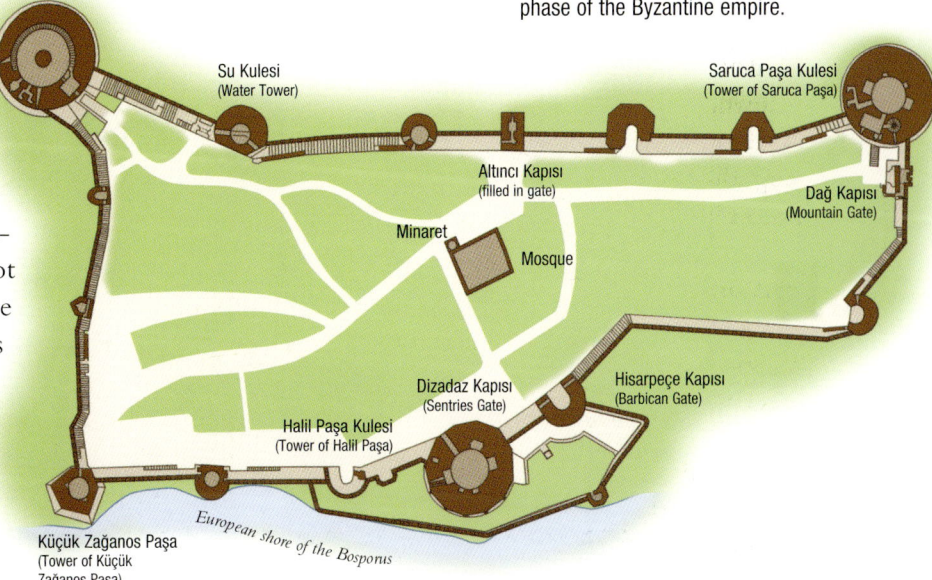

Standing on the European shore of the Bosporus, construction began on the fortress of Rumeli Hisarı in April 1451, the year Mehmet succeeded his father Murat. Designed to cut off Constantinople from its northern territories along the Black Sea coast, Rumeli Hisarı (its ground plan below) marked the beginning of the last phase of the Byzantine empire.

The remnants of the Byzantine empire withdrew into their cultural shell, but the Ottoman catastrophe at Ankara in 1402 allowed Constantinople to survive for another half-century. While some Christian states in the Balkans tried to take advantage of the resulting Ottoman civil wars, and were later punished as a result, the Byzantines were more cautious or more clever. The empire, having been virtually reduced to the city and its immediate environs, regained a significant amount of territory. Manuel II at first supported Bayezit's son Süleyman in return for the Ottoman ruler handing over the southwestern coast of the Black Sea, perhaps including the important port of Varna, as well as the Chalcidice peninsula, Thessalonica and perhaps a small area southwest of that city. Inland, the fortified town of Vize (Greek Bizya) was also given back to the Byzantines. Much if not all of this was lost after Süleyman was defeated. However, Manuel then supported Mehmet against Musa, ferrying him across the Bosporus in imperial galleys and allowing him to use Constantinople as a base. Once Mehmet had defeated Musa, he rewarded Manuel by handing back much of the territory previously ceded to Süleyman, this time certainly including Varna. Nevertheless, the writing remained on the wall and in 1437 John VIII (1425–48) traveled to Italy with a desperate plea for help.

The only Byzantine territory with real, if limited, military potential was the Despotate of the Morea in southern Greece. Here the military elite included Greeks, Albanians, and Slavs, as well as descendants of Venetians and other Italian or French knights from the virtually defunct Latin crusader principalities. Greek scholars Plethon and Bessarion, who would later play a key role in the Italian Renaissance, took a keen interest in military affairs as armchair generals. Plethon advocated a trained full-time citizen army supported by the labor of demilitarized peasants; an idea based on his interpretation of the armies of ancient Sparta. Plethon's student, Bessarion, went further by demanding that prisoners no longer be used as slave labor, but be offered full citizen rights, with the associated military obligations. A new fortified capital should be built on the Isthmus of Corinth to defend the Peloponnese from attack from the north—Ottoman territory.

Whether these academic ideas had much practical influence is unknown, but a wall *was* erected across the isthmus more than once. Unfortunately this Hexamilion Wall, with its 153 towers plus castles at each end, was not very strong. Built in only 25 days, it failed totally when the Ottoman Turks decided to make a serious assault.

Constantinople—the final days

Shortly after Sultan Mehmet II came to the throne for the second time in 1451, Byzantine Emperor Constantine XI tried to extract concessions by threatening to release another claimant to the Ottoman throne, Prince Orhan. This convinced Mehmet that the time had come to crush Constantinople once and for all. Even the cautious old Ottoman chief vizir, Çandarlı Halil, lost patience and, turning to the Byzantine envoys, blurted out, "You stupid Greeks! I have known your cunning ways long enough. The late sultan [Murat] was a tolerant and conscientious friend of yours. The present Sultan Mehmet is not of the same mind. If Constantinople eludes his bold and impetuous grasp it is only because God continues to overlook your devious and wicked schemes."

On his way back to Edirne from Anatolia, Christian warships blocked Mehmet's passage across the Dardanelles, so he crossed via the Bosporus instead. It was apparently during this journey that he decided to build a massive fortress on the European shore, the Rumeli Hisarı. The older and much smaller Anadolu Hisarı had been built on the Asian shore by Bayezit I back in late 14th century. Together the fortresses could close the straits to enemies, or at least make unfriendly ships run a gauntlet of gunfire from both banks. The newly made cannon of the Rumeli Hisarı

John VIII Palaeologus (school of Gentile Bellini) and (**top**) as a Magi, painted by Gozzoli while the emperor was on his fruitless visit to Italy seeking aid.

CHAPTER FIVE: SURVIVAL AND EXPANSION

An illustration by Jean Mielot dated 1455 shows the Turkish army camped before Constantinople. While almost contemporary, Mielot—a Dutch illuminator—never actually witnessed the events depicted.

opened fire on November 10, 1452, on a pair of Venetian ships returning from the Black Sea that had refused to stop. The Italian crews reached Constantinople safely but the artillerymen adjusted their ranges and, on November 25, sunk a Venetian ship commanded by Antonio Erizzo. When Mehmet heard the news he ordered Urban, his Hungarian chief gun-founder, to make a cannon capable of shooting a ball weighing 1000 lb. This was tested near the sultan's new palace outside Edirne and duly shot a massive cannonball over a mile.

In the face of these obvious military preparations, Constantine brought food supplies, wine and even winnowing fans into Constantinople, along with people from outlying villages. During the winter of 1452/3 he sent ships to the Aegean to purchase food and military equipment. The city's defenses were strengthened and silver was taken from churches and monasteries to pay the troops. But many maintained that only God and the Virgin Mary could now save Constantinople, and that it was folly for the emperor to flirt with the schismatic Catholic western Europeans. In truth, little more than warm words had come from the West so far. The Byzantine Empire of Trebizond was preoccupied with its own problems, while on the Morea peninsula of Greece, the Byzantine codespots Demetrios and Thomas faced a substantial raid by Ottoman troops in October 1452. Byzantine forces under Matthew Asanes had captured a senior Ottoman leader, Ahmet Bey, but little help for Constantinople could come from this region.

It was the same in the Balkans where George Brankovic of Serbia supported his Ottoman overlord. According to Byzantine chronicler George Sphrantzes, the great Hungarian military leader Janos Hunyadi had demanded Mesembria or Selymbria in return for helping Constantinople. Sphrantzes also claimed that the Aegean island of Lemnos was given to King Alfonso V of Aragon to use as a naval base from which to help the Byzantine capital. Nothing came from either of these proposals, while the independent Turkish beys in Anatolia were either friendly toward the Ottomans or too frightened to oppose them.

In January 1453 large numbers of volunteers mustered in and around Edirne, in addition to Ottoman Kapıkulu palace contingents and those from Rumelia or the European provinces. Furthermore, thousands of supporters arrived, including merchants who would supply the Ottoman army with food and other necessities. Over the next couple of months a Serbian vassal contingent of 1500 Christian cavalry plus auxiliaries arrived, while the highly regarded and vital Serbian miners followed later. Meanwhile Beylerbeyi Karaca Bey, the senior governor in Rumelia, sent 50 carpenters and 200 assistants to repair and strengthen the land routes from Edirne to Constantinople—their archaic bridges had not been designed to carry the Ottomans' massive cannon. In February Karaca Bey's troops took control of the remaining Byzantine towns along the Marmara and Black Sea coasts, so the Turkish artillery train could bring its heavy guns up to the walls of Constantinople. The biggest required 60 oxen to pull its flatbed transportation wagons. The final siege of the Byzantine imperial capital could begin.

Mehmet and the main Ottoman army left Edirne on March 23, 1453 and assembled a few miles from Constantinople. Mehmet's heavy artillery was already in position, in 14 or 15 batteries with additional groups of smaller cannon alongside or between the big guns. The first Ottoman infantry assault was probably launched on April 7 when irregulars and volunteers advanced, supported by archers and handgunners. However, they were met on the outer rampart and driven back with relative ease. Byzantine artillery was notably effective until their largest cannon blew up, after which the remaining smaller guns were largely restricted to an anti-personnel role. As the siege progressed, Mehmet had most of the cannon taken off the Ottoman ships which were attempting to blockade the Golden Horn and the sea-walls of Constantinople. Instead these weapons were brought ashore, where they bombarded enemy ships defending a boom which blocked the entrance to the Golden Horn. This was when Mehmet was credited with devising a new or improved form of high-trajectory, long-range gun or mortar.

Work was accelerating on the construction of a wooden slipway from the Bosporus to the Golden Horn, around the outside of the northern wall of the fortified suburb of Galata. By April 22 it was complete and, under the cover of an intense artillery bombardment, 72 of the Ottomans' smaller fighting ships were hauled across the hills on rollers before being slid into the waters of the Golden Horn, thus taking control of it. The northern walls of Constantinople could now be threatened from the Golden Horn itself so Byzantine and allied Italian defenders had to be withdrawn

The conquest of Constantinople, 1453

1. Byzantine galleys raid Ottoman coastal villages as far as Cyzicus (winter 1452–53).

2. Some Ottoman contingents from Anatolia cross the Bosporus to watch Constantinople and begin construction of siege-lines (winter 1452–53).

3. Mehmet II leaves Dimetoka to winter in Edirne; plans siege of Constantinople.

4. Genoese fleet arrives with reinforcements for defense of Constantinople (January 1453).

5. Ottoman advance guard takes siege cannon from Edirne to siege-lines outside Constantinople (February); other Ottoman contingents capture most remaining Byzantine outposts along the Marmara coast (February–March).

6. Another Ottoman contingent captures remaining Byzantine outposts along Black Sea coast (February–March)

7. Ottoman fleet sails from Gallipoli to help transport remaining Anatolian contingents across the Bosporus, then imposes a naval blockade on Constantinople (March).

8. Remaining Ottoman contingents cross the Bosporus (March).

9. The formal siege of Constaninople begins on April 2 and continues until the city falls, May 29, 1453.

CHAPTER FIVE: SURVIVAL AND EXPANSION

from other parts of the wall to man this newly exposed area.

On May 26 Mehmet summoned a council of war. The following day he toured the army while heralds announced that a final assault would take place on the 29th. Celebratory bonfires were lit and from then on there was continuous feasting within the Ottoman camp. The defenders of Constantinople saw so many torches that some thought the Turks were burning their tents and abandoning the siege. But about three hours before dawn on the appointed day there was a ripple of gunfire from the Ottoman artillery and the Turkish irregulars surged forward. Their attack focused on the battered fortifications near the Gate of St. Romanus. Despite suffering terrible casualties, few retreated until, after two hours fighting, Mehmet ordered them to pull back. Ottoman ships similarly attempted to get close enough to the sea walls of Constantinople to erect ladders.

After another artillery bombardment it was the turn of provincial troops from Anatolia and Rumelia to attack, but they were hampered by the narrowness of the breaches in Constantinople's walls. More disciplined than the irregulars, they occasionally pulled back to allow their artillery to open fire, and during one such bombardment a section of temporary defensive stockade was brought down. Nevertheless this second assault failed.

A portrait attibuted to the Venetian artist Gentile Bellini (c.1429–1507) of Sultan Mehmet II the Conqueror.

The only fresh troops still available were Mehmet's own Kapıkulu regiments, the elite Janissary infantry among them. All sources agree that these soldiers advanced with terrifying discipline, slowly and with neither noise nor military music. This third phase of the assault lasted an hour before some Janissaries discovered that a small postern door had not been properly closed following a previous Byzantine counterattack. About 50 soldiers burst in and climbed to the top of the wall where they raised their banner over the battlements. Despite the huge boost to Ottoman morale, the intruders were soon in danger of being wiped out. Now the Ottomans had another stroke of luck. Giovanni Giustiniani Longo, a renowned Genoese soldier who was commanding the most threatened sector of Constantinople's fortifications, was mortally wounded. Panic spread among the defenders and the Janissaries took control of the inner wall. Word also spread that the Ottomans had broken in via the Golden Horn harbor and that Constantine XI Palaeologus had been killed. The defense of Constantinople collapsed.

Around noon that same day of May 29, 1453 Sultan Mehmet II Fatih—Mehmet the Conqueror, as he was henceforth known—rode through the defeated city to the great church of Santa Sophia. There he prayed; a sign that it would be converted into a mosque, the Aya Sofia. This it remained until it was made into a museum in 1935. To Western minds Constantinople's fall to the Turks had enormous significance; for the Ottomans it was merely the tidying up of a particularly irritating loose end.

CHAPTER SIX

Ottomans in the East

From Istanbul to Egypt, Persia, and Arabia

Immediately after conquering Constantinople, or Istanbul as the Turks and most Muslims already knew it, Mehmet II set about reconstructing his new capital. He had the fortifications damaged during the siege repaired and renewed the much-reduced population (*see the side panel opposite*)—those wealthy enough, had fled in the immediate aftermath—with Christian Greeks, Muslim Turks and others. Some were encouraged by tax privileges but many were forced to settle in the city. This rapid growth led to food shortages because the surrounding countryside had similarly suffered decline and depopulation during the final century of Byzantine rule—a problem whose solution would lie in a drive northward, to the grain-producing regions beyond the Black Sea (*see page 92*).

Detail from a 16th-century Ottoman manuscript depicting mathematicians and astronomers in discussion.

One of Mehmet the Conqueror's greatest ambitions was to make Istanbul a multi-faith centre for all Peoples of the Book—Muslims, Christians, and Jews alike. This grand imperial statement was intended to create an intellectual crossroads where the cultures of east and west, Europe and Asia, could meet and mingle. Furthermore, Mehmet declared himself the new *qaysar* or caesar, the legitimate heir and successor to the Roman and Byzantine emperors with a claim to territories far beyond the Ottomans' existing frontiers. This was widely accepted, not only by the sultan's Muslim subjects but by Greek scholars like George of Trebizond, who wrote to Mehmet in 1466: "No one doubts that you are the emperor of the Romans. Whoever is legally master of the capital of the empire is the emperor, and Constantinople is the capital of the Roman empire."

Few places show the relaxed religious Ottoman attitude toward the non-Islamic populations more dramatically than Mount Athos in northern Greece. Since early Christian times, an extraordinary concentration of monasteries had been built on the easternmost of the three slender peninsulas that thrust into the Aegean Sea from the larger Chalcidice peninsula. Already under the Byzantine empire, Mount Athos had become a major center of Orthodox Christian culture and power within the Greek, Serbian, and other Orthodox church hierarchies.

Precisely when Mount Athos and the rest of Chalcidice fell under Ottoman control remains unclear, though it probably accepted the sultan's authority at the same time as the nearby city of Thessalonica in 1430. The "Holy Mountain" of Mount Athos, however, seems to have kept both Turks and women at bay, with the blessing of a sultan who wanted as good relations with the Orthodox Church as possible. Mehmet II clearly renewed and perhaps clarified the privileges of Mount Athos

and its numerous monasteries in the early years of his reign, before his final attack on Constantinople. This was to remain the basis of the relationship between the monasteries and the Ottoman authorities, confirmed by various later *firmans* or government documents. These described Mount Athos, or the Island of Aynaroz as it was known in Turkish, as "the country in which day and night the Name of God is revered" and as "a refuge for the needy and for travelers." Under the fully formed eyâlet provincial government system of the 17th century, the special status was again made clear, as was that of the Orthodox Monastery of St. Catherine in Egypt's Sinai peninsula and, for different reasons, various troublesome or warlike communities in Greece, Macedonia, Albania, and Serbia.

After suffering centuries of war and raiding, Mount Athos prospered under Ottoman rule and was to continue to do so through the 16th century, when a new monastery was founded. The Stavronikita was built on a headland overlooking the sea between the much older monasteries of Iveron and Pantokrator, perhaps on the site of an abandoned earlier monastery. In 1533 the ruins were sold by the Monastery of Philotheou to Gregorios Giromereiatis, abbot of Giromerios monastery in western Greece. Three years later this sale was confirmed by a decree from the Greek Orthodox Patriarch in Istanbul, which also reinstated the Stavronikita as a separate monastery in its own right.

Within a short time Gregorios Giromereiatis settled at Stavronikita. Under his rule the revived monastery was rebuilt, enlarged and given impressive defenses which eventually included a tall, fortified tower and an aqueduct bringing fresh water to the site. It became one of the wealthiest monasteries on Mount Athos, not least because it had rich and powerful supporters in the Ottoman capital. Nevertheless, monasteries were heavily taxed, including those on Mount Athos and

Byzantine Constantinople—a shell of its former glory:
In the years of decline, the once populous city had bled people. With economic failure came famine through the intermittent food supply system. Malnourished citizens were vulnerable to disease, which further lowered numbers. Housing, too, was poor, since whole tracts had been torn down after war damage to provide fields to grow food. The churches were largely shells, even the imperial palaces were in disrepair. By 1453 Constantinople housed fewer than 50,000 inhabitants —a fraction of its heyday population, hardly sufficient to mount a defense.

many of their estates beyond the mountain were lost. Economic hardship was overcome and the monasteries became more self-sufficient, especially from the 18th century onward. They also received considerable financial and political support from outsiders, ranging from the czars of Russia to governors of autonomous provinces such as Wallachia and Moldavia. It allowed widespread and sometimes quite magnificent restoration and decoration; in return the monasteries gave leading donors holy relics, including many supposed fragments of the True Cross.

The conquest of Greece

As pointed out above, after the Ottoman conquest of Constantinople much of the old Byzantine upper classes fled, some to the tiny quasi-Byzantine principality of Theodore Mangoup in the mountains of southern Crimea. Others migrated to the Byzantine Empire of Trebizond or the Despotate of the Morea in southern Greece. The latter had formed part of Constantinople's empire, but now the Morea peninsula was being torn apart by internal dissentions and rebellions between and against the codespots Demetrios and Thomas. There was also bitter rivalry between Greeks and Albanians within the despotate, and especially within its army. In October 1454 Mehmet II sent Turahan Bey to help Demetrios and Thomas, already his vassals, regain control of southern Greece. But as soon as Turahan left, civil war flared up once more. In 1460 the sultan lost patience and the Byzantine Despotate of the Morea was incorporated directly into the Ottoman sultanate. Its capital, Mistra, fell to Ottoman forces on May 29, exactly seven years after the fall of Constantinople. This coincidence of date cannot have been accidental.

The remaining Latin possessions also fell, relics from the aftermath of the Fourth Crusade in 1204. It is fascinating to learn that Mehmet allowed special privileges to the newly conquered city of Athens because of his interest in the Classical civilization of ancient Greece. Some of the Genoese outposts in the Aegean lasted a little longer. The port of Ainos (Turkish Enez) at the mouth of the river Maritsa on the coast of Thrace remained under the rule of the Genoese Gattilusi, though under Ottoman suzerainty. Palamedes Gattilusi was also entrusted with the island of Imroz, which had been under the direct rule of the Byzantine emperor. The similarly ex-Byzantine island of Lemnos was allocated to Dorino I Gattilusi, the lord of Mytilini on Lesbos island. They again ruled as vassals of the Ottoman sultan and paid him an annual tribute. In 1460 Ainos was transferred to Demetrios, the deposed codespot of the Morea. Elsewhere the Gattilusi family retained Lesbos under Ottoman suzerainty until 1462, while a Genoese *mahona* or merchant commune held the island of Chios until as late as

Wall painting of monks at Lavra Monastery, 16th-century. During the 17th and 18th centuries Mount Athos became a major intellectual center of Greek Christian culture. Many Greek nationalists even claim that the Holy Mountain "enlightened the enslaved Greek people" under Turkish rule. Many emerged from their monastic retreat to serve the Orthodox Church as patriarchs, bishops, teachers, and preachers, culminating in the foundation of the Athonite Academy near the Vatopedi monastery. A monk named Kosmas Lavriotis established a Greek printing press at the Lavra monastery which operated until shortly before the Greek War of Independence. During this war of 1821 monasteries offered practical advice to the rebels and many monks left Athos to join the struggle. Not surprisingly, such actions severely undermined the centuries-old tradition of trust that had been nurtured between Mount Athos and the Ottoman sultans.

CHAPTER SIX: OTTOMANS IN THE EAST

1566. The Ottomans then transferred it to the Jewish Duke Joseph Nasi of Naxos.

All that was now left were the Venetian enclaves, which were well fortified, well garrisoned, well provisioned and could be supplied from the sea by the Venetian fleet. The Venetians were still the strongest naval power in the region, which made these possessions too strong for the Ottomans to attack until they could challenge the Venetians at sea, a lack of power which was to be soon remedied (*see below*). The Ottoman conquest of Constantinople and Greece had come as a terrible shock to a western cultural elite, which was increasingly influenced by the Renaissance and its admiration of ancient Greek civilization. Nowhere was this more apparent than in Italy, the birthplace of the Renaissance. Here the Humanists, who spread the idea that the Classical civilizations of Greece and Rome should be the source of European ideals in art and culture, were appalled at the idea that Greece should lie under Turkish domination. As the renowned scholar Aeneas Sylvius Piccolomini, the future Pope Pius II, wrote, "Here is a second death for Homer and for Plato too… Now Muhammad reigns amongst us. Now the Turk hangs over our very heads."

Even though other writers pointed out that the Ottomans were good and honest people, horrendous propaganda soon led to the popular and widespread image of the "Terrible Turk." Ottoman victories over Europeans were seen as somehow unnatural, along with the Turks' supposed blind obedience to their officers. Nevertheless, most Europeans felt secure behind the powerful Catholic Kingdom of Hungary, and the fate of the Orthodox Christians was regarded as God's punishment for their weakness and sins.

The ruins of Mistra, southern Peleponnese, Byzantium's penultimate enclave, which was taken into Ottoman hands seven years after the fall of Constantinople. In the following year, the Byzantine Empire of Trebizond also lost its dubious independence to its Turkish overlords.

Ottomans as a naval power

The Venetians—clinging like limpets to many Aegean possessions—pointed up the great weakness in the Turks' armed forces, and without a competent Ottoman navy Constantinople might have remained in Byzantine hands for much longer than it did. Despite great successes on land, it was not until the mid-15th century that the Ottomans created a substantial fleet. The first decades of Ottoman history had been landlocked. The supposed capture of the island of Kalolimne in 1308 (*see page 37*) seems impossible, because this was before they held any coastline at all. The small but steadily expanding state reached the southern coast of the Sea of Marmara in about 1333, with the seizure of Gemlik (formerly Greek Kios), but there is virtually no evidence that they used any of the ports and fishing villages of this shore to range further afield. The Sea of Marmara lay next to Constantinople and was also a major maritime trade route dominated by the powerful Italian fleets of Genoa and Venice.

The gradual conquest of the neighboring Turkish beylik of Karasi, completed in 1346, gave the Ottomans a much extended coastline, some useful and defensible harbors, and a small raiding fleet. It was a turning point in Ottoman history, not only because it was from ex-Karasi territory that they first invaded and held some European soil, but because the Ottoman emirate started to develop as a naval power. Initially its maritime ambitions were extremely modest. European influence on the development of the fleet was also important and apparent from the very start. Ottoman ship-builders, mariners, navigators, and tacticians also drew on the naval traditions of the Islamic Middle East and the Byzantine empire. Nevertheless, where the eastern Mediterranean, Aegean, and Black seas were concerned, the Islamic and Byzantine maritime heritages had for centuries been almost identical to those of medieval Italy and the western Mediterranean. It would only be with the arrival of northern European and Atlantic naval traditions and technologies from the late 14th century onward that all Mediterranean fleets underwent major changes. The small Karasi navy had been built by Greeks and was largely manned by ex-Byzantine sailors and gazi warriors. The sailors remained largely Christian and would do so for many years, and not all of the so-called gazi were Muslims, recently converted or otherwise. Many are likely to have been adventurers; men whom their foes would have described as pirates.

An illumination from a French Book of Hours depicts a naval skirmish between Hospitallers and Turks, late 15th century.

The Ottomans' lack of a formidable fleet left their expanding Balkan conquests vulnerable throughout the 14th century. Not until the first half of the 15th century did Turkish ships confront the Venetians whose coastal possessions still dotted the eastern Mediterranean. During those early years, most Ottoman naval campaigns were hit-and-run affairs. The earliest version of the *Düsturname Destan* was written by a Turkish poet named Enveri in 1465. The text is a verse history of several earlier dynasties, and one of the most interesting sections deals with the epic adventures of Umur Bey, ruler of the Aydın beylik (1334–48). However, the maritime warfare it describes is that of the mid-15th century.

In these verses Umur has a large *qadirğa* war-galley built, which he named the *Gazi*; otherwise his fleet largely consists of smaller *qayiqs*, the name still used for the traditional coastal craft of Turkey and Greece. Medieval qayiqs, however, were fighting ships carrying 30–40 men and armed with a boarding "beak" (sometimes mistranslated as "ram"). Although their weapons included some firearms, the mid-15th century Ottoman fleet—like those of their Turkish beylik predecessors—largely relied on bows, crossbows and close-combat weapons for boarding. Trumpets and horns were used for communication and to maintain morale in combat. During one naval expedition in

CHAPTER SIX: OTTOMANS IN THE EAST

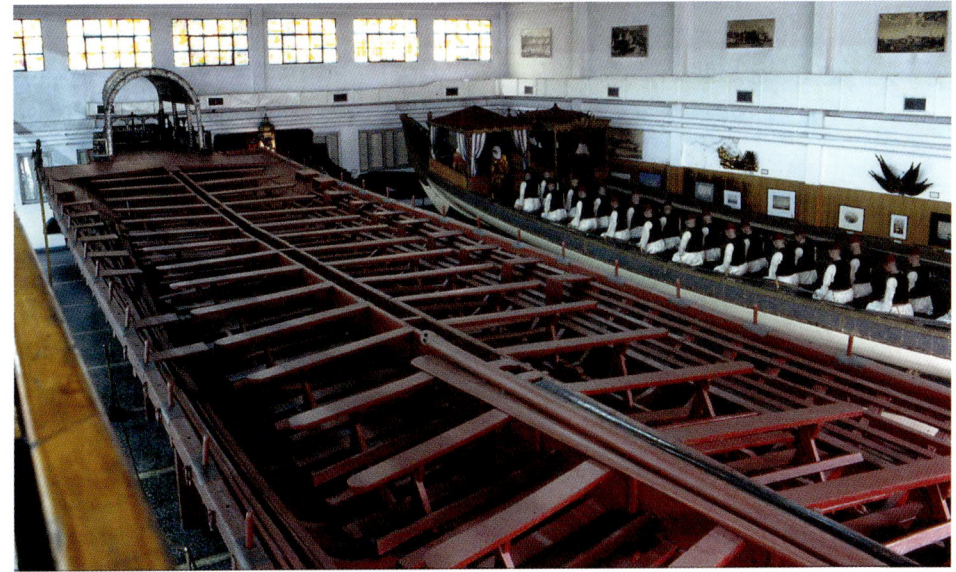

A *qadirğa* or galley which once served as the Ottoman sultan's personal barge, on display in the Naval Museum, Istanbul; **above:** detail of the stern covering.

the *Düsturname*, Umur's little fleet found five enemy *köke* or cogs at the island of Bozcaada (Tenedos). The cog was a northern European type of ship which reached the Mediterranean during the second half of the 14th century, where it was soon adopted by Spaniards, French, Italians, and others. First Umur studied the enemy:

Their topsails towered like fortresses,
The cogs carried enemies without number.
Their topsails, solid like fortresses, were full of rocks,
Large and small crossbows were numberless.

Umur then attacks, and Enveri's description of the ensuing struggle must surely be based on what the poet heard from Ottoman sailors of his own day:

They shot at the oarsmen and cried "Oh Muhammad!"...
Some carried spears in their hands, others had swords,
Striking without pause the enemies' armour of blue iron.
Others brandished cutlasses, crash! crash!...
The Turks defended themselves from the rocks behind wooden planks,
The cogs were broken apart...
The cogs were chopped into pieces with picks.

On another occasion Umur's ships and their armament are described in greater detail, again reflecting the reality of the mid-15th Ottoman fleet rather than that of mid-14th century Aydın he's supposedly representing:

He had built twenty-eight ships,
All were greased and coated with pitch.
He had there seven qadirğa, seven iğribar [smaller galliots]
And fourteen qayiqs, the construction was rapid.
They armed the ships with crossbows, arrows and tüfeks

The Ottoman fleet, as depicted in an Ottoman manuscript of c.1540, showing a mix of sailing ships and oared galleys with lateen sails.

> *They deployed the sails, they pulled up the boarding ramps…*
> *On each ship they planted banners,*
> *The drums made a sombre and piercing sound,*
> *The horns, the zurnas [bass clarinets] and the flutes played.*

The mention of the *tüfek*, an early form of handgun, arquebus or musket, in the hands of Turkish naval personnel is particularly interesting at this early date, as they were still a new form of weapon even aboard western European warships.

A generation before Enveri wrote his epic *Düsturname*, Murat II had built a substantial fleet which, in 1430, helped Ottoman land forces recapture Venetian-held Thessalonica. By 1456 the Ottoman fleet had around 60 ships manned by *azap* "marines" and Christian oarsmen and crossbowmen. That year it took control of Genoese-ruled Ainos, as well as other islands in the northern Aegean Sea. By 1470 the Ottoman war fleet had increased to 92 galleys, which enabled the sultanate to dominate the Black Sea and compete with Italians in the Aegean. Over the next decades the expansion of the Ottoman navy was quite astonishing—western observers soon claimed that the entire fleet, including fighting galleys and transports, numbered around 500 vessels. During the 1499–1502 war against the Venetians Ottoman shipyards launched two great ships of 1800 *tonilato* (roughly equivalent to modern tons)—the largest yet seen.

During its first centuries the primary role of the Ottoman fleet was to transport land forces and, after the adoption of gunpowder artillery, to support them where possible by coastal bombardment. As the sultanate expanded still further, the fleet tried to control or at least to police its exceptionally long, rugged and indented coastlines. Control of the numerous offshore islands may have been easier, though they often remained havens for Christian pirates.

Black Sea becomes Ottoman Lake

A greater confidence in their sea power enabled the Ottomans to extend the sultanate's sphere of influence around the Black Sea, and after the seizure of Constantinople and the subsequent mopping up of the remaining relics of the Byzantine empire the political, strategic and economic situation around the Black Sea was changed dramatically.

The fast-expanding population of Istanbul following the conquest led to food shortages, and so the Ottomans began to look to the fertile grain-producing plains north of the Black Sea as a possible source of wheat for bread. Constantinople's fall had also cut Italian trade through the Dardanelles and Bosporus to the Crimea. The changed political and military situation soon led to steady emigration away from the Genoese merchant colonies all around the Black Sea, not merely in the Crimea. Many Armenian families who had lived in these colonies for centuries under Italian and Byzantine rule moved to the Ukraine or Poland. The same was true of Italian colonists and more temporary residents, some Italian craftsmen from the Crimea soon being recorded as far away as Moscow. After little more than 20 years, Genoa's possessions beyond the Bosporus had all been lost to the Ottomans.

Ottoman campaigns elsewhere had confirmed domination throughout most of the Balkans, though they also suffered significant reverses. Wallachia moved firmly into their sphere, accepting a suzerainty that would remain in place for another four

---

Manning the Ottoman fleet:
By the end of the 15th century, the Ottoman navy had grown massive, but the sultanate's administrative and financial system was up to the task of maintaining this huge but still young navy. The money came from the maritime sancaks (provinces) of Al-Cezayir (*see also pages 116–17*), consisting of the Aegean islands and Gallipoli, Galata, Izmit and, at a later date, Algiers in North Africa. Galley sailors and marines, called *levents*, were recruited from Turkish coastal communities, Greeks, Albanians and, again at a later date, Dalmatians and North Africans. The oarsmen included criminals, prisoners-of-war and some volunteers. Sailors specializing in all-sail ships were at first called *aylakçiler*, though with the adoption of new styles of western European warships they came to be known as *kürekçiler* or galleon men. Several Janissary *orta* battalions either specialized in naval service as marines or had historically close associations with the fleet. The 88th Orta had an anchor for its insignia, often tattooed on the men's hands or arms, as did the 8th and 31st Bölük regiments. The 25th and 37th Bölük had a fish while the 56th had a galleon. This was probably the unit shown in several Ottoman and European illustrations where a large model galley is thrust into the plume holder of their distinctive white *börk* caps while on parade.

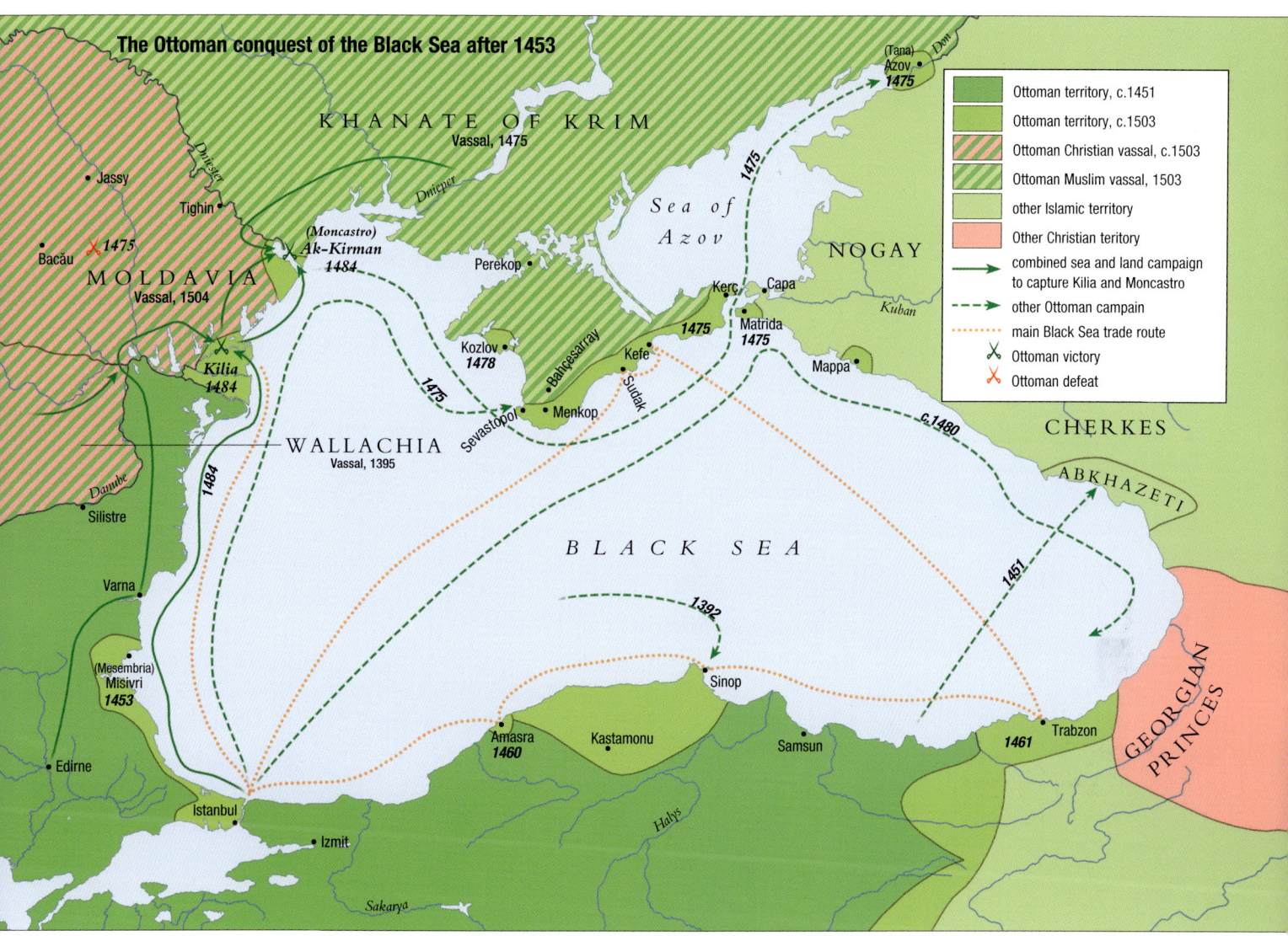

centuries. Even Moldavia was theoretically tributary to the sultan from 1456, but Stefan III Cel Mare, Steven the Great, came to the throne of Moldavia a year later, threw off Ottoman domination and spent much of his 47-year reign competing with the sultan for domination over neighboring and similarly Romanian-speaking Wallachia. Stefan III was a near-contemporary of Vlad Tepes of Wallachia but a man of very different character, a deeply religious patron of the arts as well as an effective military leader and tireless diplomat. The fall of Constantinople, followed by Byzantine Trebizond (Trabzon) in 1461, was disastrous for Moldavian trade. Now virtually surrounded by foes, the principality had to fight Ottomans, Mongols, Poles, Lithuanians, and Hungarians, and was eventually obliged to pay tribute to the sultanate. When Stefan became *hospodar* or prince he promptly refused further payment. Yet, after a series of fierce campaigns, even he had to kneel.

Meanwhile Stefan had married his daughter to the son of Grand Prince Ivan of Muscovy, cementing an alliance against the vast and rambling Polish-Lithuanian realm on Moldavia's northern frontier. What his daughter thought of this is unrecorded, though a combined Moldavian-Muscovite army routed a Polish-Lithuanian force in the Kozmin forest in 1497. These bloody struggles availed the

The last of the Byzantine states, Trebizond survived the fall of its metropolis and remained a wealthy Christian entrepôt until 1461; detail from a Florentine painting shows the inevitable Turkish assault overwhelming the Greek-Armenian defenders outside Trebizond.

peoples of Romania little, and Moldavia, like Wallachia, eventually fell under Ottoman domination as a vassal state. Thereafter they retained their autonomy until both won independence during the 19th century. In the meantime The Principalities, as they came to be known, had to pay the sultanate a substantial tribute in foodstuffs, money and armed men.

The consolidation of Ottoman power in the Black Sea had a profound impact far away in the Middle East, by cutting the largely Genoese maritime link between the Mamluk sultanate of Egypt and Syria and the Mongol khanate of the Golden Horde north of the Caspian and Black seas. This strategic partnership had existed for several centuries, not only bringing wealth to the three partners, but also serving as the channel through which slave recruits reached the Mamluk army. Without it the entire Mamluk system gradually withered, as this supply of slaves not only filled the ranks of their military but also formed the pool from which the ruling class was drawn. For Genoa the impact was largely financial and, though expensive, not fatal. The Golden Horde had been in decline throughout the 15th century. Its defeat and partial absorption by the rival Khanate of Krim (Crimea) in 1502 was only fractionally attributable to events in the Black Sea.

The Tartar khanate of Crimea

For over 300 years the Giray dynasty—Mongols descended from Genghis Khan's son Jochi—ruled the supposedly Tatar khanate of Krim. They were useful allies of the Ottomans but domination remained beyond the sultanate's power. At first vassals of the much larger Golden Horde, they achieved independence early in the 15th century and soon dominated vast territories in what are now eastern Ukraine and southern parts of European Russia. The khanate and the sultanate found themselves to be natural allies, initially against the Golden Horde to the northeast and the similarly gargantuan Polish-Lithuanian confederation to the northwest. Later they continued as a natural alliance against the rising power of Muscovite Russia in the north. The Crimean "Tatars" also supported the Ottomans against the Habsburg dynasty of central Europe.

It was, however, an uneven relationship. The far stronger and wealthier Ottoman sultans treated the khans of Krim as their vassals and had imposed direct rule over the Krim coastal enclaves that in earlier centuries had been Greek, Roman, Byzantine, Venetian, and finally Genoese. The same was true of the little-known sub-Byzantine principality of Theodore Mangoup (Turkish Menkup), ruled by an offshoot of the Comnenid imperial dynasty from the late 11th- and 12th-century Byzantine empire.

The 14th-century lower castle of Lutsk, a town whose position made it the axis of struggles between Poland, Lithuania, Muscovy, and the khanate of Krim. Here, English Morris Dancers attend an international folk festival.

CHAPTER SIX: OTTOMANS IN THE EAST

The Giray khans regarded themselves as the legitimate heirs of the Golden Horde that had once been overlord of most of Russia. Krim certainly seems to have incorporated most of the military manpower of the Golden Horde in 1502. For part of the 16th century they even extended their rule as far as Kazan on the upper Volga river and into the foothills of the Ural mountains. These developments were a major challenge to the Russian principality of Muscovy, itself in the process of imposing domination over other Russian states. The most important pastures used by the khans of Krim and their subordinate tribes were closer to Moscow than those of the Golden Horde had been. It was largely from these grasslands immediately north of the Crimean peninsula that

the Krims launched raids deep into Russian and Polish-Lithuanian territory. Only in the 18th century did the balance of military power shift sufficiently in Russia's favor for the raids to end. Meanwhile the Giray khans built a small but beautiful and remarkably sophisticated capital at Bahçesaray on the northern slopes of the Crimean coastal mountains. Its architecture and decoration reflect strong Ottoman influence, as might be expected.

For the Ottomans, an alliance with, and theoretical suzerainty over, Krim opened up huge strategic possibilities. However, some of these remained pipe dreams far beyond the economic and military capabilities of even the powerful Ottomans. One such was a proposal in 1569 to excavate a canal linking the Don and Volga rivers at a point where they were only 37 miles apart. Only a few years earlier Muscovite forces had raided down the length of both the rivers, threatening what had for centuries been the Turkish, Mongol, and now Islamic domination of the western steppes. If practical it would have enabled Ottoman warships and merchant craft to sail between the Black Sea, which was already virtually an Ottoman lake, and the Caspian Sea, where none of the littoral states or tribal peoples had so far attempted naval domination.

A maritime European threat through the "back door"

There was a widespread belief in the medieval Islamic world that the Turks had been sent by God to save Islam from destruction at the hands of Mongols, crusaders, and others. Nor was this admiration for Turkish warriors and rulers confined to Turkish countries or even those governed by Turks. The main beneficiaries of such prestige were, however, the Mamluks of Egypt, Syria, and some neighboring territories. It was they who had finally evicted the crusaders from the Middle East and, more importantly, had stopped the pagan Mongol hordes in their tracks. This enabled the sultans in Cairo to proclaim themselves to be not only the Defenders of Islam, but also Protectors of the Holy Places because, as rulers of Egypt, they had suzerainty over the Hijaz with its sacred cities of Mecca and Medina. During the 15th century, however, the Ottoman sultanate rose in both power and prestige, taking the battle deep into Christian lands, reversing the tide of aggression against Islam that had characterized the 10th–13th centuries. It was the Ottomans who had taken the great Christian-Roman-Byzantine citadel of Constantinople and it was their ruler who now claimed greater right to the title of Defender of Islam.

It was inevitable that Anatolian rulers who feared the Ottomans should seek alliances with the Mamluks. These included the Karamanid beys, when they were not forced to be vassals of the Ottoman sultan, and the Dulkadir Oğulları. The Mamluks were particularly keen to maintain the Dulkadir as a buffer state between the Ottomans and their own territory in Syria. On the other hand, the international situation had changed by the start of the 16th century so there were good reasons for Ottomans and Mamluks to co-operate. Both had Sunni Muslim rulers, whereas the rising and expansionist Safavid shah of Persia was Shi'a. Furthermore, the entirely new threat of the Portuguese Christians had appeared in the Indian Ocean.

At first the Mamluks tried to contain the Portuguese on their own or in alliance

The great Portuguese navigator Vasco da Gama became the first European commander to sail in the Indian Ocean when his small fleet of ships rounded the Cape of Good Hope over the Christmas of 1497. Aided by the sultan of Malindi, a port north of Mombasa on the East African coast, da Gama was also the first European to reach India by sea in his own ships. His voyage of exploration opened up the Indian Ocean to aggressive Portuguese mercantile dominination and war with the Muslim states of Africa and the Middle East.

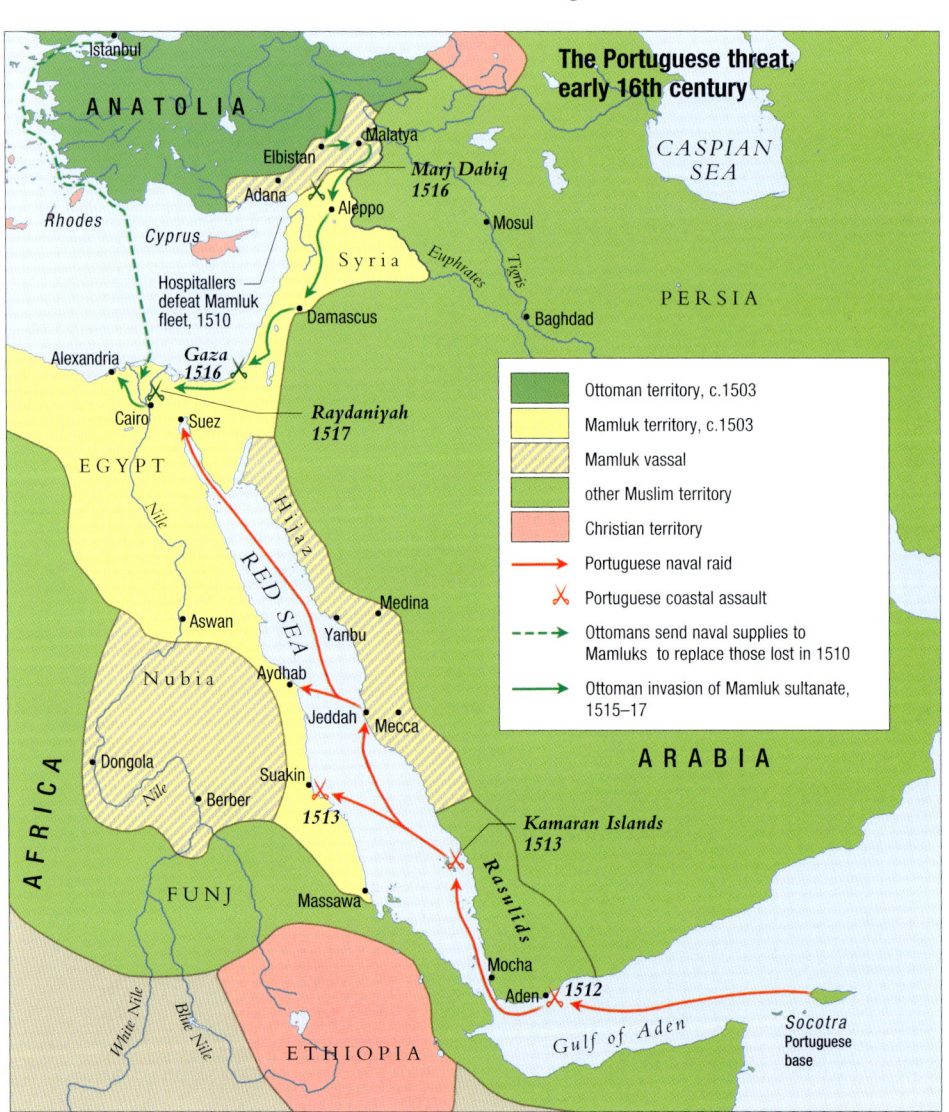

with the Muslim rulers of India, at the cost of a great deal in interrupted trade, military and naval effort but with little result. The Portuguese and other western European fleets who would follow in their wake virtually destroyed Arab domination of maritime trade between Egypt and India, and in the Indian Ocean as a whole. The Mamluks' failures in the Red Sea and Indian Ocean exposed the Hijaz and its Islamic holy sites to danger from Christian raiders, undermining their claim to the role of protector. Initially, the Ottoman sultan agreed to help, not only out of solidarity in defense of Mecca and Medina, but because he feared an alliance between the rising power of the Safavids in Persia and the Christians, not only in the Indian Ocean but also Europe. Such a strategic nightmare would hang over Ottoman policy for hundreds of years, and was a tempting possibility to the courts of Europe.

The European threat to Muslim control of the wealthy Indian Ocean trade was utterly unexpected. In 1498 a flotilla of Portuguese ships commanded by Vasco da Gama (1460–1524) had rounded the southern tip of Africa. Not far up the East African coast they found Arab merchants and mariners who showed them the way to India. Two years later Pedro Álvarez Cabral (1467–1520) took command of the Portuguese presence in the Indian Ocean. He established a base on the Indian coast and seized the island of Socotra (now part of Yemen) off the Horn of Africa. Cabral and his fleet attempted an astonishingly ambitious blockade of the entrances to the Persian Gulf and the Red Sea. If successful, this would have compelled all Indian Ocean trade with Europe to go southward, around southern Africa in Portuguese or Portuguese-controlled ships—a mortal threat to the prosperity of Mesopotamia, Syria, and Egypt.

Pedro Álvarez Cabral, who was sent to India to found Portugal's first permanent settlement (at Cochin), used it as a base to blockade Muslim trade in the Indian Ocean and Arabian Sea.

Beginning of the end for the Mamluks

The Mamluks reacted as strongly as they could. Despite their supposed but very much exaggerated dislike of naval warfare, on November 5, 1505 they sent a substantial fleet under Amir Husayn to fight the Portuguese. Although there were some elite Mamluk soldiers onboard, most of the crews and marines were North Africans, Sudanese, and Turcomans. Even so, Husayn's fleet could not stop 20 or more Portuguese ships penetrating the Red Sea, where they captured many Islamic merchant vessels and severely disrupted traffic. The results were soon felt in the markets of Cairo, where Indian goods became virtually unobtainable. Worse still, the customs revenue from Indian exports to Europe dried up. The Mamluk government verged on bankruptcy.

Threatened by the Portuguese at sea, Safavids to the northeast, and Ottomans to the northwest, the Mamluk rulers seemed uncertain what to do. Younger Mamluk soldiers mutinied and demanded payment. Embassies from various Indian Muslim rulers arrived in Cairo, begging for help against the Portuguese. Needing timber to build warships, in 1510 an Egyptian squadron sailed to Cilicia, where they also loaded canvas for sails, rope, and other naval equipment. But they had hardly set out on the homeward journey before they were attacked by warships of the Knights Hospitallers and slaughtered. Whether from a sense of Islamic solidarity or because Shah Isma'il Ibn

Mamluk cannon of the late 15th–early 16th centuries captured by the Ottomans during the campaigns in Syria and Egypt.

Haydar of Iran (1501–24) was trying to forge an alliance with several European Christian powers, Bayezit II (1481–1512) promptly sent the Mamluks a substantial consignment of naval stores, including timber, plus iron, 300 arquebuses, gunpowder, and more traditional military equipment, which arrived in Cairo in January 1511.

Meanwhile, Amir Husayn and his fleet had been campaigning in the Indian Ocean, forming an alliance with the ruler of Gujarat and destroying a Portuguese squadron. He and his allies were routed off Diu island in February 1508. Husayn continued the struggle as best he could, but in December 1512 he returned to Cairo. The following year the Portuguese were back in the Red Sea, occupying several islands and attacking Islamic ports. It was not all. The Mamluk government was growing increasingly alarmed by the power and ambition of the new Ottoman sultan, Selim, nicknamed Yavuz (the Grim, 1512–20). In contrast, Mamluk Sultan Qansawh al-Ghawri (1500–16) was old, infirm and almost blind. Having defeated Shah Isma'il at the battle of Çaldiran in 1514 and while preparing for a further campaign against the Safavids, Selim changed his focus. The Mamluks had been trying to bolster the buffer-state of Dulkadir and were reported to be building up their forces in northern Syria. Finding an excuse in the supposed mistreatment of a Dulkadir prince by the current ruler, 'Ala al-Dawlah, Selim led his army from their winter quarters in eastern Anatolia, virtually wiped out the Dulkadir army, killed 'Ala al-Dawlah and annexed his territory. The last ruler of the Dulkadir Oğullari dynasty, he had been a Mamluk vassal and war between Mamluks and Ottomans now seemed inevitable. Nevertheless, the army and fleet which the Mamluks had raised to fight the Portuguese in the Red Sea still set sail from Suez on August 21, 1515.

Ottoman cannon from the time of Selim I —the Turks' superior firepower helped to defeat the Mamluks.

The final crisis came early in 1516. Two hundred extra guns were sent to Alexandria to face an expected Ottoman naval assault and on May 14, Sultan Qansawh led the Mamluk army out of Cairo toward Syria. Selim had seized Malatya on the Mamluk frontier and now he led the Ottoman army south. They met at Marj Dabiq, north of Aleppo, and in the resulting battle on August 24, 1516 the Mamluks were routed. The aged and infirm Qansawh al-Ghawri died of a stroke at the height of the battle and this army collapsed, its survivors fleeing back to Egypt. Selim proceeded to occupy what are now Syria, Lebanon, Jordan, Palestine, and Israel.

The Mamluk army belatedly tried to copy some features of Ottoman organization, recruitment, and armament. By 1517, on the orders of the last Mamluk sultan, Al-Malik al-Ashraf Tuman Bey II (1516–17), one hundred or so ox-drawn wagons had been built to carry infantry armed with handheld guns, probably of the arquebus type, and light bronze cannon. The army now included camel-riding sharp-shooters, a form of mounted infantry for whom the Arab world would later become famous as far afield as Moghul India. Virtually every available artillery piece had been assembled from various Egyptian citadels for use in the field, although they remained static, not mobile field artillery in the modern sense. All the Mamluks could then do was wait.

CHAPTER SIX: OTTOMANS IN THE EAST

Overthrow of the Mamluk sultanate; the battle of Raydaniyah, 1517

Legend:
- irrigation and transportation canal
- Mamluk fortified line
- Ottoman advance
- Ottoman turning movement
- major fighting
- retreat of Tuman Bey to Upper Egypt

The battle of Raydaniyah

Once Selim had completed his occupation of Syria in 1516, he led his army on a well organized and rapid march across the northern Sinai desert to seize the Egyptian Nile Delta town of Bilbays. As the Ottomans approached, the Mamluks—perhaps still demoralized by their previous defeats—abandoned their traditional offensive strategy in the belief that their best hope lay in a defensive battle against an enemy who would be tired after their long march and possibly ill-supplied as a consequence of extended lines of communication. Given the existing balance of forces and recent Mamluk acceptance of new military ideas, not to mention new weapons, this was a prudent decision.

On January 22, 1517, Selim's army reached Birkat al-Haj, a small lake northwest of Cairo, between the desert to the east and a fertile area irrigated by the Nile to the west. Its name, meaning Pool of the Pilgrims, reflected the fact that it also lay close to the main route taken by Muslim pilgrims from the Egyptian capital to the Islamic holy cities of Mecca and Medina; it was one of the main assembly areas for the great annual pilgrim caravans. A little further south lay the village of al-Marj, whose name meant the Meadow, again reflecting the fact that this was no parched desert. The closest substantial settlement to the west was clustered around the Coptic monastery of Siryaqus, which in turn stood close to one of the most important medieval irrigation canals in Lower Egypt. During the Middle Ages this canal had at various times been extended to link the Nile with the Gulf of Suez, forming a version of the Suez Canal by allowing ships to sail up the Nile to Cairo, then via this canal to the Red Sea. The stretch leading from the irrigated Nile Delta to the Gulf of Suez had, however, been silted up and disused for centuries.

Beyond al-Marj were several other villages, that of Ayn Shams clustered around a spring of the same name. Just west of Ayn Shams lay the hamlet of Raydaniyah in an area where Egyptian armies often mustered before campaigning in Palestine and Syria. The city of Cairo, though large by medieval standards, was much smaller than it is today and lay further to the southwest, between the Nile and the steep and rugged though not particularly high Muqattam Hills. One of the northern spurs was known as Jabal Ahmar, the Red Mountain, which would be a significant feature in the forthcoming battle.

99

At dawn on January 22 the Mamluk army, which had been encamped around Raydaniyah, moved forward to occupy their prearranged and almost certainly pre-constructed defensive positions. But Selim had either been informed of the Mamluks' plan or could work it out from reports sent by his scouts. Tuman Bey II had decided to construct a strong Mamluk defensive line anchored on the canal on its left flank and embedded in the Jabal Ahmar on the right. Instead of advancing against this formidable position, Selim kept his own artillery out of range and led some of his troops over, or perhaps around the back of, the mountain. Outflanked, with their baggage train and camp attacked from the flank or rear, the Mamluks had little choice but to resort to their traditional tactics. Charging on horseback armed with spears, swords, and javelins, rather than the horse-archery of earlier Mamluk armies, they suffered appalling losses from the Janissary infantry's firearms. The opposing sultans are said to have fought in person, Tuman Bey killing one of Selim's closest advisors in the mistaken belief that he was the Ottoman leader.

Inevitably, perhaps, firepower triumphed and the broken Mamluks were forced to flee. They tried to rally in Cairo, and there was some bitter street-fighting in the Nile-side dock area of Bulaq on January 28–31. Perhaps the Mamluk leaders and their closest followers were attempting to take ships up the Nile to fight another day. Although there was another smaller battle at al-Giza on the western side of the Nile in April, the Mamluk regime had been smashed. Tuman Bey fled but was found and executed. Egypt was to remain an Ottoman province, more or less under the sultans' authority, for another 400 years.

Before the loss of their state, the Mamluk sultans had enjoyed the prestigious role of Servants or Protectors of the Holy Places, which included the two main Islamic holy cities of Mecca and Medina. Jerusalem, the third holiest city in Sunni Islam, also fell within their domain. This important role now fell to the Ottomans. With it went the duty to keep the *hajj* (Turkish *hac*) pilgrimage routes open, and to provide protection for the *hajjis* or pilgrims themselves. At this time the Arabian peninsula was in much the same fragmented state as it had been since the collapse of the 'Abbasid Caliphate in the tenth century. It was virtually ringed by a series of small coastal states, some independent, some vassals of greater Islamic powers. Meanwhile, the desert interior was dominated by Bedouin tribes whose histories remain obscure.

South of the Hijaz lay Yemen, a relatively fertile and prosperous though backward land with flourishing cities and wide trading links. Yemen also dominated the entrance to the Red Sea; a fact which became increasingly important after Portuguese and other European fleets appeared in the Indian Ocean beyond. The Ottomans conquered Yemen in the early 1540s and this distant region remained a province until they were expelled in 1636. On the other side of the Red Sea the Turks held Suakin in Eritrea and Zayla on the Somali coast which, with the Arabian port of Jidda, were under the overall authority of Egypt's governor. Zayla was lost by 1540, but the Ottomans continued to dominate the Red Sea and its coasts, despite efforts by the Portuguese to defeat them on both land and at sea. Meanwhile, in those areas of the Hijaz under their immediate control, the Ottomans built forts and improved roads along the main pilgrimage routes, while *sharifs* made similar improvements within the Hijaz and the holy cities themselves.

Intricate decoration of colored tiles adorns the minaret of the Shaykh Omar Mosque, Baghdad.

CHAPTER SIX: OTTOMANS IN THE EAST

Ottomans, Safavids, and the Kizilbaş

A far less satisfactory situation existed in connection with the rising power of another major Islamic state: Persia. Isma'il Ibn Haydar, the first of the Safavid dynasty, had seized power in 1501. His origins are clouded by legend, though he was probably of Turcoman rather than Persian ancestry. What was most important was that the Safavids were Shi'a Muslims; their dynastic name reflected their status as hereditary leaders of an unorthodox, though not yet specifically Shi'a, sufi mystical, or dervish order based at Ardabil in the Azerbaijan region of northwestern Persia, adjacent to the Caspian Sea. Their rise to power had begun back in the mid-15th century when Shaykh Junayd, head of the Safaviyya order, started to take political as well as spiritual power. By the time Isma'il became shah or ruler of Iran, the Safavids were enthusiastically Shi'a and had established an essentially theocratic state.

Between the Ottomans and the first Safavids lay a number of local powers dominated by tribal leaderships. The strongest were the White Sheep Turcomans, the Aq Qoyunlu. In 1501 Ismai'l defeated the Aq Qoyunlu and conquered Azerbaijan, a

Voluntary migrations and deportations

1. 7000 Üstaclü families to Iran, 1500
2. Sultan Bayezit II deports Shi'as to southern Greece, 1502
3. 5000 Dhu'l-Qadar tribesmen to Iran, 1507
4. Deportation of Shi'as to southern Greece, 1512 onward
5. Sultan Selim I deports Shi'as to the European provinces, 1514
6. Shi'a Kizilbaş ("red cap") rebels deported to Cyprus, 1578 onward

Main Shi'a and Kizilbaş uprisings

A. Shah Kuli, in Teke, 1509–12
B. Celali, in Bozk Sançak, 1520
C. Dhu'l-Qadar tribe, 1526
D. Kalenderoğlu, in Karaman, 1526–27
E. The "False Ismail," in Elbistan, 1578
F. Seyh Hayder, in Amasya, 1585
G. Kalenderoğlu, in Bursa, 1607

Beautiful scrollwork on a Persian cannon captured by Ottomans during the 16th–17th centuries.

further ten years of campaigning giving him control over most of Iran. A powerful and expansionist Shi'a state on their eastern frontier was a matter of concern for the Ottomans. Much worse was the claim of Shah Isma'il's followers that the Safavid leader had almost divine status in the extremist Shi'a *ghulat* tradition. Consequently his followers, especially the Turcomans whose red caps gave them the name of Kizilbaş "red heads," were often fanatical in their devotion to Isma'il as their religious and political leader. It was thus that Iran became overwhelmingly Shi'a Muslim. It was also a time of frequent wars between the Shi'a Safavids and the increasingly orthodox Sunni Ottomans, occasionally allied to the similarly Sunni Uzbek Turks of Central Asia.

Sultan Selim I's victory over Shah Isma'il at the battle of Çaldiran in 1514 has been described as the triumph of Ottoman logistics and firepower over traditional cavalry and the Safavids' faith in divine invincibility. The Ottomans used large numbers of guns, some mounted in wagons as a form of field artillery or even tank, plus massed and disciplined Janissary infantry armed with handheld firearms.

In the wake of this victory, the Ottomans annexed Kurdistan and tried to take Azerbaijan but were never able to hold it for more than a few years at a time. This left substantial Shi'a-dominated regions inside the Ottoman sultanate. The most troublesome of these were the Turcoman tribes of eastern Anatolia, where Kizilbaş sympathies were strong and resistance to central government control traditional. Kizilbaş empathy was strong among the peasants and even in some towns, resulting in frequent rebellions. These were crushed, and in many cases the people involved were forcibly transported to other parts of the Ottoman state. The early 17th century suffered several major rebellions, not only in southeastern Anatolia but also in the center and southwest, followed by trouble in Syria with the Druze (originally an extreme Shi'a sect that then broke away from Islam altogether). Then a powerful governor from Erzerum in northeastern Anatolia gathered various disaffected groups around him, followed by a series of Janissary revolts in the Ottoman capital.

In this atmosphere of near anarchy, the Safavid Shah Abbas (1587–1629) regained Azerbaijan and conquered most of the Caucasus, where Iran would remain the dominant power until the Russian conquests of the 18th and 19th centuries. In 1623 Abbas even occupied Baghdad. However, Ottoman fortunes were restored by a new sultan, Murat IV, who came to the throne as a child but took the reins of power nine years later in 1632. He crushed revolts and invaders with merciless ferocity. Baghdad was regained in 1638 and the following year peace was signed with Iran at the Treaty of Kasr-i Shirin. The agreed frontier is essentially that between Turkey and now independent Iraq on one side and Iran on the other. The Shi'a minorities within the Ottoman sultanate had by now largely accepted Sunni rule and would no longer be a major focus of discontent, though smaller scale disturbances remained common.

House of Osman (Ottomans)
Sultans from 15th to 17th centuries

(Interregnum, 1402–1413)

1413–21	Mehmet I
1421–44	Murat II
1444–45	Mehmet II
1445–51	Murat II *(second time)*
1451–81	Mehmet II *(second time; the Conqueror)*
1481–1512	Bayezit II
1512–20	Selim I *(caliph from 1517)*
1520–66	Süleyman I *(Kanuni; the Magnificent)*
1566–74	Selim II
1574–95	Murat III
1595–1603	Mehmet III
1603–17	Ahmed I
1617–18	Mustafa I
1618–22	Osman II
1622–23	Mustafa I
1623–40	Murad IV
1640–48	Ibrahim I
1648–87	Mehmet IV
1687–91	Süleyman II
1691–95	Ahmed II
1695–1703	Mustafa II

CHAPTER SIX: OTTOMANS IN THE EAST

Ottoman Syria

Syria was one of the wealthiest regions in the sultanate and although now only a provincial capital, 16th-century Damascus benefited from the improved security of an efficient if sometimes ruthless Ottoman system of government. The employment of two distinct types of troops insured against rebellion by an over-ambitious governor and fostered competitive spirit between the forces. The troops could, of course, be turned against each other if the occasion arose. Originally, however, the system was intended to avoid military units developing strong local loyalties while at the same time giving at least some role to indigenous communities who might otherwise indulge in banditry.

This system declined later, but for many years it served well. The troops consisted of the *kapı halkı* who were the governor's own units, and the sipahi cavalry organized on a quasi-feudal basis in the countryside. The latter had originally been more numerous, as the similarly organized provincial cavalry of Mamluk times had been, but from the late 16th century onward the numbers of salaried soldiers paid directly by the government, central or regional, increased in proportion. These salaried troops included both Janissaries and assorted mercenaries hired by the governor.

Ever since the initial Ottoman conquest, the so-called *yerli kulları* provincial Janissaries had been an increasingly significant force. A two-tier system appeared, consisting of locally resident Janissaries, no longer recruited through the *devşirme* system but either inheriting their military status or simply purchasing it. These men naturally had strong local loyalties—sometimes very localized. Then there were "imperial Janissaries" consisting of units sent from the Ottoman capital to ensure the presence of troops loyal to the central government. For reasons which are not entirely clear, but which may reflect the geographical proximity to Turkish Anatolia, there was only one corps of Janissaries in the northern Syrian city of Aleppo. As the generations went by, the yerli kulları were increasingly assimilated into the local largely Arabic-speaking population, very soon entering local crafts and businesses and becoming known in Arabic as Dawlat Dimashq, the Power of Damascus. During the 16th century there was also a reverse process, with local merchants and craftsmen purchasing entry into the Janissary Corps in order to enjoy its significant tax and other privileges. To reassert the sultan's control, new Janissary units were sent to garrison the citadel of Damascus and the city gates after 1659. There were usually two ortas of these regular soldiers, referred to as kapı kulları, as they would have been in the Turkish heartlands. Occasional clashes and street brawls between the two forms of Janissary became a feature of life in and around the city.

The declining willingness of troops in Damascus to muster for the sultan's campaigns on distant fronts was just one sign that the system was beginning to fail. The 1732 campaign against Persia seems to have been the last occasion where they

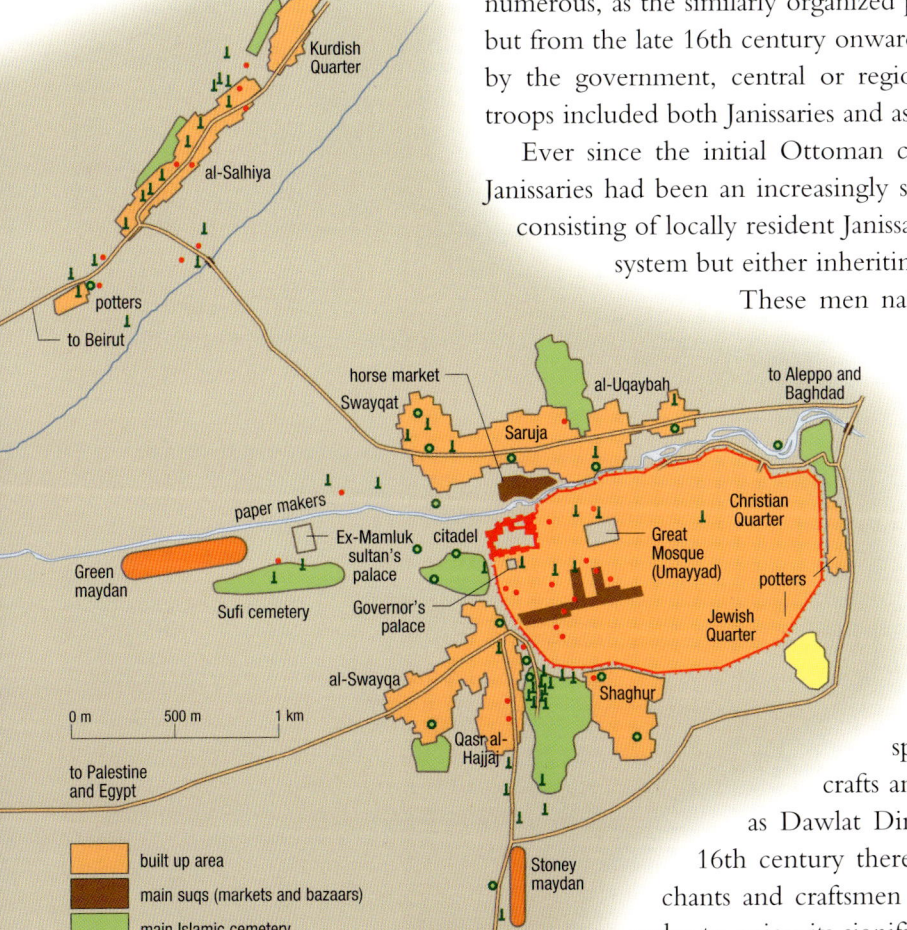

Ottoman Damascus

The Arrival of the Venetian Ambassadors at Mamluk Damascus by the School of Bellini underlines the value of the trade in spices and silks between Mamluk lands and Venice in the 15th century, and the potential threat the Ottoman conquests represented to future Venetian prosperity. Venetian ambassadors are being received in Damascus by the Mamluk governor, seated on a low divan, wearing a horned headdress as a mark of his high rank.

served outside their own region, except as paid mercenaries. One way or another, the Janissary regiments in Damascus became a serious headache for the Ottoman government during the 18th century.

The irregular or mercenary units in Damascus eventually included *delis* (light cavalry), *levents* (marines), *mağribis* (North Africans) and *sekbans* (literally "dog handlers"). The sekbans in the Ottoman army had been recruited from wandering peasants who had lost their land in late-16th century eastern Anatolia. They were then attached to the households of various provincial governors, including those in Syria. In addition to the North African Arab and Berber mağribis and the east Anatolian sekbans, a slightly later group were the *tüfenkcis* or musketeers, largely recruited from among the Kurdish tribes. Given the tendency for such units to come from one distinct ethnic or linguistic groups, it is not surprising that they also developed a strong sense of *'asabiyya*, an Arabic word meaning "group loyalty." This aided unit cohesion but it tended to divide one ethnic unit from another, each having their own style of costume, organisational structure and barracks, even quarter of the city. Meanwhile the shaykh or leader of each group was directly responsible to the local Ottoman governor.

Although they no longer took part in long-distance campaigns, these assorted troops did have military duties. Indeed, in the economic crisis of the late 17th and early 18th centuries, they demanded specially paid roles because inflation was undermining the value of their salaries. One of the most important tasks was to garrison the forts that the Ottomans built to defend the long and highly vulnerable hajj pilgrimage routes to Medina and Mecca. Janissaries would also receive special payment for escorting the pilgrim caravans to Arabia. On the other hand, underemployed and underpaid Janissaries sometimes joined *sofa* gangs of similarly idle local young men. When things got out of hand, the government would step in to disband redundant or otherwise useless Janissaries, withdrawing their privileges and declaring them to be among the *raya* demilitarized people. Sometimes when this happened, soldiers would disappear into the countryside or the mountains, hoping to return later. Worse, there were periodic outbursts of factional fighting between these armed groups. Between 1740 and 1746 the central government seemed to give up and disbanded the kapı kulları, leaving the defense and policing of Damascus to the turbulent local troops. Otherwise the Ottoman government did little more than tinker with this complicated and inefficient system until the sweeping reforms of the 19th century.

The Ma'n of Lebanon

To the west of Damascus, on the other side of the Anti-Lebanon range and Beqaa Valley, lay the autonomous region of Lebanon, centered on Mount Lebanon. Here a powerful Arab Druze clan, the Ma'n, had won widespread local power under Ottoman suzerainty following Selim I's conquest of the area in 1516. Their power-base had been the Shuf region of southern Lebanon but they formed occasional alliances with the Christian Maronites of Mount Lebanon itself, even with some European powers.

The greatest of the Ma'n emirs, Fakhr al-Din II (1585–1633), eventually dominated most of Syria, as far as the desert oasis of Palmyra and the Anatolian foothills in the north. Such an extension of power by a vassal inevitably provoked the sultan to react, eventually defeating and killing Fakhr al-Din. Most chronicles described the great Ma'n emir as a bloodthirsty tyrant, but he was credited with improving trade and agriculture as well as laying the foundation for a tradition of cooperation between the Druze and Maronite communities of Lebanon. For this reason, many modern Lebanese see Fakhr al-Din II as the founder of their country.

For over a century after his death, Fakhr al-Din's successors ruled much of what is now Lebanon, though as Ottoman vassals. In 1697 the last Ma'n emir, Ahmad Ibn Mulhim, died and power was handed over to a related clan, the Banu Shihab. These were Sunni Muslims rather than Druze, but they governed largely through the same leading Druze families as before. In this later period there was increasing factionalism and fighting between religious groups, and the Christian Maronites similarly increased in power at the same time. The conversion of some of the ruling emir's sons to Christianity caused huge and widespread scandal. One of them, Yusuf Ibn Mulhim, became the first Maronite emir (1770–88) and the Shihab emirs remained autonomous rulers of Lebanon until 1842. The Ottomans then imposed direct rule as part of a thoroughgoing attempt to modernize their state.

The Great Mosque of Damascus, seen from the fortifications of the Citadel.

CHAPTER SEVEN

The Golden Age

To the sultanate's greatest extent... before Vienna

Most of the gains in Ottoman territory and influence, as outlined in the previous chapter, were made by Süleyman II. Known in Europe as "the Magnificent" and called Kanuni, "the Lawgiver," by Turks and other Muslims, he was the son of Selim the Grim and ruled from 1520 to 1566; the second longest reign in Ottoman history. Although this period was undoubtedly magnificent, Süleyman's primary claim to fame lay in the way his government consolidated the work of its predecessors. This was also a time of enormous achievements in the arts and, to a lesser extent, the sciences.

Süleyman II was a determined and enthusiastic military commander, leading 13 campaigns and entrusting several others to his most senior officers. In the east Süleyman advanced beyond the frontier city of Erzerum to conquer territory as far as Kars in Armenia, despite the Safavids' scorched earth campaigns. Uprisings by Shi'a groups in Anatolia were contained, but the persistent Safavid Persians could not be put down. Süleyman and his senior commanders repeatedly found it necessary to lead armies deep into what is now western Iran. In 1534, for example, one campaign captured Tabriz, from where Süleyman led a remarkable march through Kurdistan into Mesopotamia, which he then conquered. While there, Süleyman undertook a pilgrimage to the holy cities of Hilla and Karbala. Under Safavid rule the Sunni Muslims of Mesopotamia had been persecuted by the Shi'a, but once the Ottomans were in power it was the Shi'a who suffered, a state of affairs that would last almost unchallenged until the 21st century. Although Ottoman occupation of Tabriz and eastern Kurdistan in what is now northwestern Iran was short-lived, another war with the Safavids led to a further occupation of Tabriz. This time a more permanent peace was agreed in 1552. Again the Ottomans withdrew from Tabriz, but they retained the greater prize of Mesopotamia.

It was clear that Sultan Süleyman had a deep interest in eastern affairs and the associated wealth from trade. In 1538 a small Ottoman army had been sent down the Red Sea coast of Arabia to annex Yemen, including the strategic Indian Ocean port of Aden. A fleet also campaigned across the western part of the Indian Ocean, defeating the Portuguese in some minor confrontations off the coast of India. However, despite the importance of containing Safavid and Portuguese threats in the east, European affairs probably remained Süleyman's top priority, in keeping with Ottoman tradition. Süleyman had fought his first campaign in Serbia, capturing the vital Danube fortress city of Belgrade in 1521, which had held out long after the Ottomans had occupied the rest of Serbia and Bosnia.

Süleyman was able to take diplomatic, military, and trading advantage of deep divisions within Catholic central and western Europe, where conflict between France and the vast Habsburg-ruled realms would last for centuries. After suffering a major defeat in 1525 at the hands of the Habsburgs at Pavia in northern Italy, Francis I of France (1515–47) formed a strategic alliance with Süleyman—the Unholy Alliance, as it was known to a shocked Europe. Partially in consequence, the Ottomans

A 16th-century Ottoman manuscript illumination shows Süleyman the Magnificent receiving János Sigismund Szapolyai at his court. The Transylvanian noble was Süleyman's preferred candidate for the vacant Hungarian throne to keep the Habsburgs out.

107

The Ottoman Golden Age: central regions and Balkans, 16th to mid-17th centuries

- Ottoman empire at accession of Süleyman, 1520
- territory conquered by Süleyman by 1566
- territory conquered by Süleyman, then lost
- Ottoman vasal, 1566
- campaign of Süleyman
- other Ottoman campaign

invaded Hungary and in 1526 won a resounding victory at Mohács, where Louis II of Hungary was killed. Although Süleyman occupied the Hungarian capital of Buda (now the western half of Budapest, Pest then being a separate town on the east bank of the Danube), the sultan did not try to take control of the entire huge kingdom of Hungary.

A divided Hungary

The battle of Mohács was nevertheless a highly significant victory, removing a Christian state that for centuries had been regarded as Catholic Christendom's bastion against the Muslim Turks. The surviving Hungarian nobles were divided between those who wanted the Habsburg Ferdinand I of Austria (1503–64, subsequently emperor from 1558) to become their king and those who preferred one of their own number, János Szapolyai (1487–1540), who had opposed a Habsburg takeover for over 20 years. Naturally, Süleyman lent his support to Szapolyai—he didn't want the powerful Habsburgs to take control of a strategically important state on his northwestern frontier. Initially in 1273 then successively from 1438, the Austrian Habsburgs had also been the ruling dynasty of central Europe's Holy Roman Empire, which developed from the Frankish kingdom of Charlemagne, who had revived the title of western emperor in 800.

Civil war between the two Hungarian claimants came to an unsatisfactory and unstable end with a peace agreement in 1538. It was during these prolonged and confusing campaigns that the Ottomans attempted their first siege of Vienna in 1529. The fighting flared up again when János Szapolyai died in 1540. Ferdinand

CHAPTER SEVEN: THE GOLDEN AGE

invaded, prompting Süleyman to do the same. By the time the fighting ended, Hungary was divided into three parts. Ferdinand ruled so-called Imperial Hungary in the west, the Ottomans ruled the great central plain of Hungary and a new state gradually emerged in the northeast. This would become the Ottoman vassal state of Transylvania.

While Ottomans and Habsburgs were locked in prolonged and bitter conflict in

Sultan Süleyman's campaigns

1521 (May 18–September 19): Siege and capture of Belgrade.

1522 (June 16)–1523 (January 31): Siege and conquest of Hospitaller-ruled Rhodes.

1526 (April 23–November 13): Defeat and partial conquest of Hungary (Mohács on August 29).

1529 (May 10–December 16): Invasion of Austria and unsuccessful first siege of Vienna.

1532 (April 25–November 21): Further conquests in Hungary.

1534 (June 11)–1536 (January 8): Invasion of western Persia; pilgrimage to Hilla and Karbala.

1537 (May 17–November 22): Unsuccessful attack on Corfu.

1538 (July 9–November 27): Campaign to restore Ottoman domination over Moldavia.

1541 (June 20–November 27): Further conquests in Hungary.

1543 (April 23–November 16): Further campaign in Hungary.

1548 (March 29)–1549 (December 21): Further campaign in Persia.

1553 (August 28)–1555 (July 31): Further campaign in Persia.

1566 (May 1–September 6): Final campaign in Hungary. Süleyman dies immediately after the capture of Szigetvár.

Left: Silahdar military hat, c1550.

Right: The Battle of Mohács depicted in a 16th-century Ottoman manuscript.

Ottoman forces of Süleyman I prepare for the final assault on the Hospitallers' stronghold of Rhodes in 1523, from a 16th-century European manuscript.

central Europe, Süleyman's armies conducted a number of remarkable land-sea operations in the Mediterranean. The most successful was against the strongly fortified island of Rhodes in 1522–23, only a year after the Ottomans' similarly dramatic capture of Belgrade. The bastion of the crusading Military Order of St John, better known as the Knights Hospitallers (and sometimes as the Knights of Rhodes), the fall of Rhodes to the Ottoman Turks sent shockwaves across Christian Europe. The Hospitallers soon withdrew to another Mediterranean island, Malta, which the Order was granted in 1530 by Charles V, the Spanish-Habsburg emperor, and which they again made into a powerful fortress. Then, as now, Malta's midway position between Sicily and the North African coast made it strategically important and Charles hoped the Hospitallers would provide a bulwark against Ottoman expansion

CHAPTER SEVEN: THE GOLDEN AGE

into the western Mediterranean. The rent for this valuable possession was one live Maltese falcon, the bird presented annually to the emperor's viceroy in Sicily. The symbolism is apparent—the knights were birds of prey, protecting Christendom.

During the long years of his reign Süleyman spent over ten of them on military campaigns. It is interesting to note that his European campaigns were relatively short, each being completed within one year, whereas some of his invasions of Safavid territory in Persia took over 18 months. This reflects the very different military circumstances that the Ottomans faced when operating beyond the sultanate's western and eastern frontiers; but in both areas Ottoman troops won an astonishing series of victories.

Süleyman the Magnificent has been criticized for allowing the home fleet based in and around Istanbul to decline during the first part of his reign. It was clearly unable to prevent a Habsburg fleet under Genoese Admiral Andrea Doria (1467–1560) from ravaging the coast of Ottoman-ruled Greece in 1532, so Süleyman was obliged to summon the provincial squadrons of North Africa—the corsairs of the "Barbary Coast," regarded by Europeans as nothing more than pirates. They defeated the Habsburg fleet but were diverted by European attacks on their own bases in North Africa. In 1537 Süleyman attempted to repeat his success against the Hospitallers at Rhodes with an assault on the Venetian-ruled island of Corfu. It was not a success, though several Venetian overseas territories including Crete were raided the following year.

A Venetian portrait by Titian of Süleyman the Magnificent, who threatened to bring central Europe to its knees, but ironically helped the Protestant cause by his harassment of the Catholic Habsburgs—the Spanish by sea, the Austrians by land.

The most famous and unsuccessful of the Ottoman naval assaults was against the new Hospitaller base of Malta in 1565, occasioned after the seizure of an Ottoman treasure galleon in the Adriatic by a Hospitaller "pirate." Led by the Ottoman admiral Piyale Paşa, and North African corsair commanders Turgut Reis and Uluç 'Ali, the Ottomans withdrew after four months of bitter fighting, leaving an estimated 30,000 dead behind them. But even this setback did not seriously damage the sultanate's naval power in the Mediterranean and the following year a fleet captured the island of Chios, the last Genoese outpost in the Aegean Sea. The Aegean did not become an Ottoman lake like the Black Sea had done, but the Ottoman navy was now the dominant power in this region and would remain so for many years.

Just under five years after the conquest of Chios, the now aged Süleyman died while on campaign. He had been urged out of retirement by Sokullu Mehmet Paşa, his grand vizir, who insisted that Ottoman forces must capture the Hungarian fortress of Szigetvár in order to counter increasing Habsburg border raids. The fortress was duly taken by Sokullu Mehmet, as the sultan was too ill to command his troops, and just over a week later the most famous of all Ottoman rulers died.

The Ottomans' northwest frontier

When Yugoslavia fragmented in the late 20th century, many Westerners were surprised to discover that northern Bosnia was home to a substantial Muslim majority population. This enclave around Bihać was barely 186 miles from Venice but 1243 miles from the old Ottoman capital of Istanbul. The region had only been added to the Eyâlet of Bosna (Bosnia) after the death of Süleyman II in 1566, but it became a vital frontier zone and a base for Ottoman forces not only defending the Sultanate against Habsburg and Hungarian raids, but from which counter-raids were sent deep into enemy territory. For this reason the town of Bihać and its surroundings were settled by religiously-motivated frontier warriors, mostly converts from Slav regions of the sultanate. There was also substantial conversion to Islam among the local Bosnians.

Well before Ottoman regular forces took control of Bihać, the region had been subjected to numerous raids by the fearsome *akıncı* frontier light cavalry who did so much to pave the way for subsequent Ottoman conquest. The neighboring Christian kingdoms seemed unable to stop their depredations, which often penetrated an astonishing distance into Croatia, Hungary, Slovenia, Austria, and northern Italy. Their greatest successes had been in the late 15th and early 16th centuries, when their leader—insofar as the akıncıs recognized any single commander—was a member of the Mihaloğlu family, the "sons of Michael" descended from a 14th century Christian convert to Islam. However, the Mihaloğlu were normally based at Silistria on the lower Danube frontier in what is now Bulgaria. Other akıncı leaders included Malkoçoğlu Bâlibey, based at the strong Danube fortress of Smederovo

CHAPTER SEVEN: THE GOLDEN AGE

in Serbia, and İshak Paşa in Bosnia itself. There were many others, but senior frontier lord and follower of İshak Paşa's family Gürz Ilyas became the most popular hero of Bosnian-Islamic epic songs.

At first the majority of akıncı raids were across the Danube into the rich Hungarian heartlands, but as the defenses of these regions were strengthened during the 15th century, they directed their warlike enthusiasm to the northwest, into the slightly defended Habsburg provinces of Carinthia, Styria, and Carniola. Venetian territory in the Istrian peninsula and along the Dalmatian coast was similarly ill-protected and offered rich pickings, though the raiders did not yet reach the offshore islands of what is now Croatia. In addition to substantial booty, prisoners were taken for ransom or sale as slaves. The 1470s were terrible for the Christians of these regions, with akıncı attacks virtually every year. As had happened further south in the Balkans, persistent raiding resulted in the extension of Ottoman control across most rural areas; towns held out for longer. Coastal towns, which could be supported and resupplied by sea, rarely fell into Ottoman hands.

This northwestern frontier of the sultanate became more stable during the 16th century, most of the major campaigns and territorial expansion being to the northeast, into Hungary. Venice also adopted a peaceful policy on land, though not so much at sea, to avoid encouraging Ottoman aggression. In addition to paying tribute to the sultanate for Cyprus, the Venetian senate negotiated yearly renewals of a truce first agreed in 1503. This did not, however, halt occasional raids by Bosniak (Muslim Bosnian) akıncıs.

Remarkably detailed information about the structure and administration of the Ottoman provinces of Rumelia, including Bosnia, survives in a *defter* or property register drawn up for Grand Vizir İbrahim Paşa between 1523 and 1526. A century and a quarter later, the famous Turkish historian and writer Kâtip Çelebi wrote his *Cihannâma* or *Geography*, which contained updated information about the same areas. These show that Ottoman territory in Dalmatia, west of Bosnia, reached its maximum extent in the late 16th and early 17th centuries, between two wars against Venice. Even at this high watermark, the Venetians controlled most of the islands. Venetian territory on the mainland had shrunk to little more than a series of enclaves. Not until after 1721 did the Venetians begin to turn the tide, forcing the Ottomans and their Bosnian supporters into the coastal mountains. That frontier remained relatively unchanged for many decades,

Palmanova's heritage is clearly visible in this aerial photograph. Purpose-built in Friuli as a nine-point star fortress, the town was designed to defend Venice's eastern border against *akıncı* raids—and against the Republic's other enemy—the equally aggressive Habsburgs.

Lipova castle stood guard over the Mures valley east of Arad in what is today eastern Romania. "Lippa"—to the Ottomans—was a target for the hit and run *akıncı* raids.

113

One hint on the beginning dissolution of Ottoman power came on October 7, 1571 off the Greek coast near Lepanto (modern Naupaktos), when the Christian fleet of the Holy League commanded by John of Austria opposed the Turkish fleet under the command of Uluç Ali. The Christian fleet of about 200 Spanish, papal, and Venetian galleys was about evenly matched with the Ottomans, but this decisive Christian victory ended the myth of Turkish naval invincibility. It did not, however, affect Ottoman supremacy on land. Painting from the Venetian school of Tintoretto.

and is today more or less the border between the Croatian Catholic coastal province of Dalmatia and the mixed Muslim, Catholic, and Orthodox nation of Bosnia-Herzegovina.

Strength without covers up a weakness within

Several of the sultans who had reigned between Süleyman II and ruthless, reforming Murat IV, who acceded in 1623 were criticized for being dominated by their wives and mothers. This so-called "sultanate of the women" began during the reign of Süleyman the Magnificent's son, Selim II, known as Selim the Sot. It continued during the reigns of Murat III and his five brief successors when the grand vizirs wielded as much power as the sultans. In the Ottoman administration and bureaucracy, corruption was becoming endemic. War booty, official positions, commercial monopolies and the right to collect taxes were sold to the highest bidder. Most senior government officials were now of slave or captive origin, educated in the highly effective Ottoman governmental school system and dedicated to both the sultanate and Islam. But too many also regarded their position as a means of gaining

wealth and power. European voluntary converts to Islam now included many who did so largely as a means of advancement; most are said to have been of Italian, Bosnian, Greek, German, or Hungarian extraction.

In a way, this was a positive feature of Ottoman society, for unlike in western Europe, advancement depended on merit, ability, and ruthlessness. A man's social, ethnic and even religious origins were virtually irrelevant, as long as he had become a Muslim. The sultanate was thus a meritocracy. Meanwhile in Europe, noble ancestry, political connections, or sufficient wealth were needed before a man could rise in society, with ability counting for relatively little. At the same time, some of the high-ranking converts to Islam were accused of maintaining dubious links with wealthy non-Muslim financiers and Christian relatives outside the Ottoman state. Others of humbler status nevertheless proved their worth to the sultan by serving with distinction in both the army and navy. Such men would still be prominent at the time of the Napoleonic Wars (1803–15). Furthermore, the descendants of these converts became fully integrated and loyal Ottoman subjects, however superficial the conversion of their fathers may have been.

During a hard-fought war between the sultanate and the Habsburg-ruled Holy Roman Empire from 1593 until 1606 the Ottomans achieved a major victory at the battle of Keresztes in 1596. There had been many reasons for this war but the most immediate had been possession of the Hungarian principality of Transylvania; it ended with an Ottoman nominee ruling the region but Habsburg Emperor Rudolf II (1576–1612) was released from paying tribute for his small strip of so-called Imperial Hungary in the west. In the following few decades, the Habsburgs of Austria and many other European rulers were preoccupied with the Thirty Years War (1618–48), which pitted Catholics against Protestants for domination of Christian Europe. Meanwhile the focus of Ottoman attention again turned eastward, to the sultanate's longstanding dispute with the Safavid shahs of Persia, thus pitting Sunni against Shi'a Muslims. After suffering major setbacks, the Ottoman position was restored during the reign of Murat IV, concluding with the peace of Kasr-i Shirin in 1639.

By 1640 the Ottoman sultanate was approaching its greatest extent—Crete, a few central Aegean islands, and the Podolia region in what is now Ukraine would be added a few years later. Elsewhere some temporarily held regions in western Mesopotamia, the Caucasus, Arabia, and Africa had already been lost. After three centuries of expansion, the Ottoman state was set for a similar period of contraction, and despite straddling the Middle East, North Africa and much of eastern Europe like a superpower, several of its sources of strength were showing signs of decay. The elite Janissary regiments were no longer the finest infantry force in the world, and the ruthless but effective devşirme system of recruitment was no longer

Selim II the Sot or Drunkard, first Ottoman ruler of the "sultanate of the women," during whose reign the naval disaster at Lepanto occurred.

used. Though their commitment and enthusiasm remained very high, the Janissaries' tactics, equipment, and standards of training, not to mention discipline, had either declined or been surpassed by that of other troops. The sipahi cavalry were similarly becoming outdated, though again their dedication and individual skills largely obscured this fact.

In spite of the signs of decomposition within the higher levels of the sultanate, there were some successes during the 17th century. Crete, which had been held by Venice since the Fourth Crusade in the early 13th century, was taken by Ottoman forces in 1645, though its main city held out for a further 24 years. The perennial competition with the Habsburgs for control of Hungarian Transylvania led to war in 1660; this time the Austrians won a notable victory at St. Gothard near the Hungarian border in 1664. Nevertheless, the Treaty of Vasvár that brought this war to a close the same year was more favourable to the sultan than it was to Leopold I (1658–1705). Their next clash would not go the way of the Turks.

After a period of chaos north of the Black Sea, during which the Orthodox Christian Cossacks had divided into pro-Russian and pro-Polish factions, a new *hetman* or senior Cossack leader had emerged, Peter Doroszenko. He hoped to form an alliance with the Krim khan and Ottoman sultan in order to guarantee Cossack independence from both Poles and Russians. He even promised to recognize Ottoman suzerainty, but due to circumstances this never came to full fruition. Instead the Ottomans took advantage of a widespread Cossack revolt against Polish authority northwest of the Black Sea to seize Podolia in 1672. This was a substantial expansion of Ottoman territory, bringing them within a day's march of the vital Russian (now Ukrainian) city of Kiev. It also meant that for the first time the Ottomans and their Muslim allies controlled the entire coastline of the Black Sea and its northern offshoot, the Sea of Azov.

However, this would be a brief period of unchallenged supremacy and eventually led to war with Muscovite Russia. The Cossack Peter Doroszenko had recognized Ottoman suzerainty in 1672, but within a couple of years the famous Polish military leader Jan Sobieski broke the peace treaty signed at Buczacz by the late King John Casimir of Poland and invaded the Ottoman-held regions of Ukraine. This campaign brought him great prestige at home and was largely the reason why Sobieski was elected King Jan III of Poland-Lithuania in 1674. However, it also led Ottoman armies and their Krim Tatar allies to raid deep inside Poland in the following two summers.

This conflict ended with the signing of a treaty in October 1676, when Ottoman rule over Podolia was confirmed, along with the sultan's suzerainty over the rest of the Ukraine. It was the high watermark of Ottoman expansion in eastern Europe, and would not last. Cossack independence proved fleeting, and Poland regained Podolia in 1699. By then, the sultanate had made its final and disastrous attempt to destroy its Habsburg rival at the second siege of Vienna in 1683.

Ottoman sea power and the Barbary Coast

At the time of the Ottoman overthrow of the Mamluks in 1517, the last Mamluk admiral, Husayn, had been campaigning in southern Arabia in a final attempt to contain the Portuguese threat to Islamic trade in the Indian Ocean and Red Sea. It failed and resistance passed to local Arab naval powers, primarily Oman, then later the

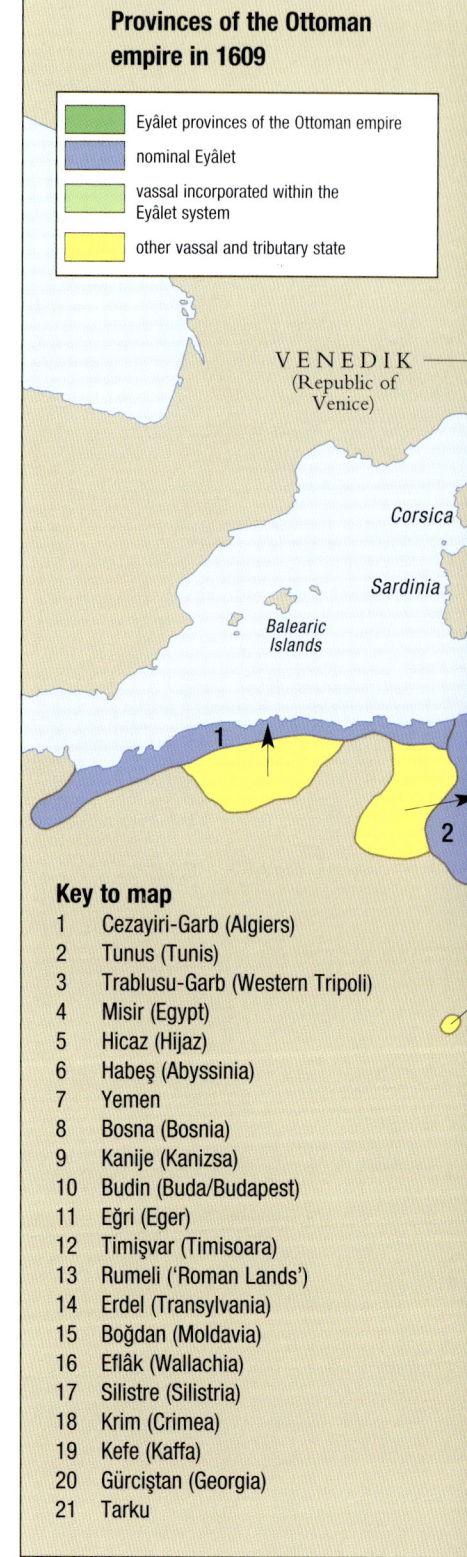

Provinces of the Ottoman empire in 1609

- Eyâlet provinces of the Ottoman empire
- nominal Eyâlet
- vassal incorporated within the Eyâlet system
- other vassal and tributary state

VENEDIK (Republic of Venice)

Corsica
Sardinia
Balearic Islands

Key to map
1 Cezayiri-Garb (Algiers)
2 Tunus (Tunis)
3 Trablusu-Garb (Western Tripoli)
4 Misir (Egypt)
5 Hicaz (Hijaz)
6 Habeş (Abyssinia)
7 Yemen
8 Bosna (Bosnia)
9 Kanije (Kanizsa)
10 Budin (Buda/Budapest)
11 Eğri (Eger)
12 Timişvar (Timisoara)
13 Rumeli ('Roman Lands')
14 Erdel (Transylvania)
15 Boğdan (Moldavia)
16 Eflâk (Wallachia)
17 Silistre (Silistria)
18 Krim (Crimea)
19 Kefe (Kaffa)
20 Gürcistan (Georgia)
21 Tarku

CHAPTER SEVEN: THE GOLDEN AGE

Inset: Woodcut of Hungarian hussar and an infantryman.

22 Trabzon
23 Sivas
24 Anadolu (Anatolia)
25 Cezayir ("The Islands," including southern Greece, all the Aegean islands except Venetian-held Tenos, plus the Gallipoli peninsula, and the Anatolian shores of the Sea of Marmara and of the Bosporus)
26 Karaman
27 Kibris (Cyprus)
28 Adana
29 Dulkadir
30 Halab (Aleppo)
31 Trablusu-Şam (Syrian Tripoli)
32 Şam (Syria)
33 Urfa (formerly Edessa)
34 Diyarbekir
35 Erzerum
36 Çildir
37 Kars
38 Van
39 Şehrizor (Shahrazur)
40 Musul (Mosul/al-Mawsil)
41 Bağdad (Baghdad)
42 Lahsa (al-Hasa)
43 Basra
44 Ragusa (Dubrovnik)

Ottomans. The Hijaz region of western Arabia had acknowledged the Ottoman sultan as suzerain immediately after the fall of the Mamluks. This gave the Ottomans control of most of the eastern coast of the Red Sea but there were no significant attempts to challenge the Portuguese in the Indian Ocean until Süleyman II became sultan in 1520, when a garrison was installed at Suakin on the western shore of the Red Sea and at Zayla on the Somali coast. Zayla appears to have been abandoned 20 years later and in 1524 the first Ottoman expedition was sent to support the Muslim ruler of Gujarat. Others would follow in 1530 and 1538.

Contrary to the view expressed by some European historians, Süleyman did not hope to extend Ottoman domination as far as the Islamic states of India. His ambitions in these eastern waters were more modest and were clearly stated in the orders he wrote for his admiral, Süleyman Paşa, before the latter's fleet sailed in 1538: "You will make preparations in Suez for a jihad, and having equipped and supplied a fleet… cutting off the road and blocking the way to Mecca and Medina you will avert the evil deeds of the Portuguese infidels and remove their flags from the sea." Ottoman naval expeditions of the 16th century were intended to remove the Christian threat to Islamic shipping, particularly in the sea lanes which carried pilgrims to the holy cities; beyond that, they wanted to restore Arab-Islamic domination of Indian Ocean commerce. In the latter they largely failed. According to a letter sent from Mecca to the vizir of Gujarat in 1539, Süleyman criticized his admiral for exceeding orders: "I sent you to drive the Europeans out of Diu and to help the ruler of that city, not in order that you might tyrannize the Muslims of India."

A manuscript illumination depicts a naval battle between Turkish galleys and European cog sailing ships.

Subsequent attempts to combat the Portuguese in the Indian Ocean similarly achieved little. In the Red Sea the Ottoman position was strengthened by their occupation of the Dahlak Islands, Masawa and part of the Eritrean coast. In 1581 another Ottoman admiral, Mir Ali, sacked Portuguese-held Muscat in Oman and then twice led his squadron down the East African coast, attacking Portuguese-held ports. Mogadishu, Brava, and Jumbo in what is now Somalia; then Petta, Lamu, Malindi, Kilife, and Mombasa in Kenya were forced to abandon Portuguese suzerainty. However, Mir Ali was then trapped between an African insurrection and a Portuguese fleet and forced to surrender. For over a generation, Portuguese domination was almost unchallenged on these coasts until the early 17th century when a new Islamic naval power arose from Oman in eastern Arabia. The Ya'rubid dynasty reestablished the thousand-year link between Oman and East Africa, but were themselves supplanted by the Al-Bu Sa'id in the mid-18th century, by which time the Ottomans were no longer a naval power in the eastern seas.

In 1775 the Ottoman governor of Basra in Iraq asked for Omani naval support against his neighbors. The Omani sent ten modern square-rigged European-style warships and over a hundred smaller vessels to break the Persian siege of Basra. The

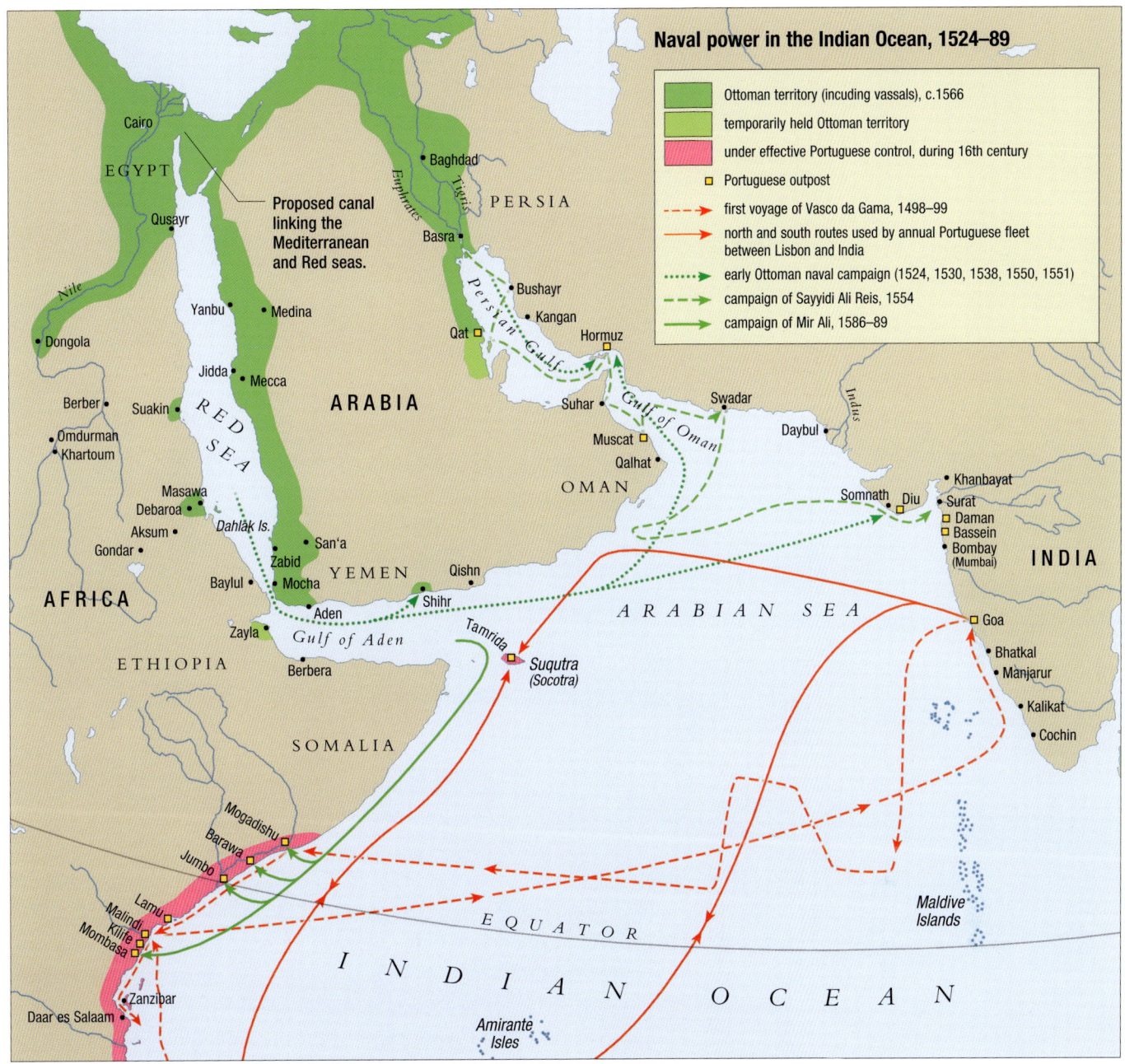

Persians had stretched an iron chain and floating boom across the river to prevent ships relieving the city. According to the Omani chronicler Ibn Raziq, "When they reached the river of al-Basra and saw the iron chain suspended across it, they forced the ship called *Al-Rahmani* [the Omani flagship] against it and broke it. Then the Arabs, sword in hand, fell upon the Persians and routed them."

The exploits of Ottoman sailors in the Indian Ocean remain much less well known than those of commanders like Hayrüddin Barbarossa and Uluç 'Ali in the Mediterranean. However, the eastern seas were sufficiently important for a special command to be established in 1525. While the *kaptan paşa* was responsible for the Mediterranean, Aegean and Black Sea, the first *Mısır kaptanı* (captain of Egypt) or *Hind kaptanı* (captain of India) was Selman Reis. His successors included Süleyman Paşa and Piri Reis, the latter best known for his map of the world, which is the

Corsair power in the Mediterranean, 16th century

- Ottoman territory, c.1466
- Ottoman gains by 1518
- other Muslim territory
- Christian territory, 1518
- Spanish Habsburg territory, c.1560
- major sack or siege by corsairs

Djerba — The Barbarossa brothers' early base, the island changed hands frequently

Malta: 1530 to Knights of Malta (previously "Knights of Rhodes," also known as the Knights of St. John or the Knights Hospitaller)

Tripoli: 1530 to Knights of Malta / 1551 to Ottomans

earliest surviving to show the east coast of the Americas. Sadly his career as a commander was less successful and he was executed in 1554 following a failed campaign against the Portuguese.

Ottoman North Africa or the Barbary States, as they became known, tend to be viewed as havens of fanatical corsairs who swooped on peaceful European coasts to seize fair maidens for sale in slave markets. The reality was rather different. During the 16th century Ottoman power was at its apogee at sea as on land. The sultans' armies had conquered Syria, Egypt, most of the islands of the eastern Mediterranean, and much of the shore of North Africa. Nevertheless here in the Maghrib (western lands), as they had long been known in Arabic, the Turks held only a narrow coastal strip. It consisted of three provinces or regencies: Tripolitania or Western Tripoli (to distinguish it from Tripoli in Lebanon), Tunis, and Algiers. Further to the west, powerful Arab-Islamic Morocco remained outside Ottoman control.

The three regencies were more or less governed by vassal potentates. However, the degree of Ottoman control varied considerably and was, for lengthy

CHAPTER SEVEN: THE GOLDEN AGE

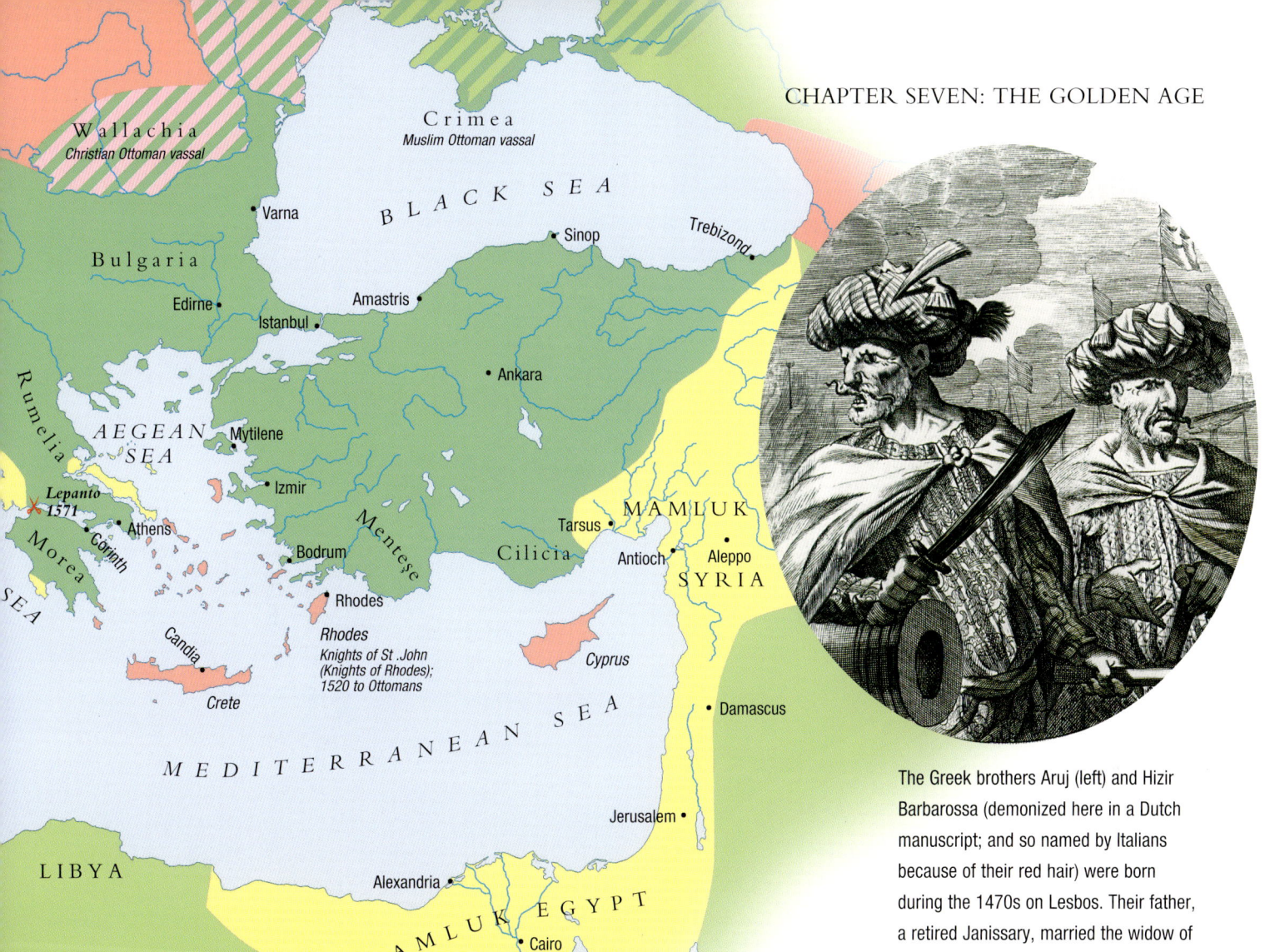

The Greek brothers Aruj (left) and Hizir Barbarossa (demonized here in a Dutch manuscript; and so named by Italians because of their red hair) were born during the 1470s on Lesbos. Their father, a retired Janissary, married the widow of a Christian priest. The brothers terrorized the Tyrrhenian Sea and Gulf of Liguria from their bases in Djerba and Algiers, and Hizir in particular—known to the Turks as Hayrüddin (Gift of God)—became a major naval commander for the sultan.

Opposite: *Spanish Men of War engaging Barbary Corsairs;* detail from a Dutch painting. By the early 16th century, the Ottomans were relying on North African galleys for their naval strength in the western Mediterranean. The Europeans called them pirates, but several corsair captains (*reis*) became senior officers, even admirals, in the Turkish navy.

periods of time, merely nominal. Each also had to deal with different strategic, political, military, economic, and indeed geographical realities. Tripolitania (now the western part of Libya) was certainly the most vulnerable, having the most limited human and natural resources as well as the fewest good harbors. It was also exposed to European naval attack while its main city and port, Tripoli, was the easiest to bombard from the sea. East of Tripoli lay Barqa, or Cyrenaica as it was known to the ancient Romans and more recent Europeans. Historically a bone of contention between the major North African power centers of Egypt and Ifriqiyah (Tunisia), Barqa lacked large sheltered harbors. Like the rest of Ottoman North Africa it became part of the sultanate during the reign of Süleyman II.

The regency of Tunis had been the heartland of the Hafsid dynasty (1229–1574) but the last three rulers of this long-lasting family had been vassals of the Ottomans since the first conquest by the sultan's great admiral Hayrüddin Barbarossa in 1534. A second conquest had been required in 1569 by another famous Ottoman admiral or corsair commander, Uluç Ali, with a final reconquest by Sinan Paşa after Tunis had been seized by Don John of Austria. Thereafter it was never entirely free from European interference. Algiers was very different. Widely referred to as Jazair al-maghazi, "Warrior Algiers" and "the redoubtable republic," it earned a fearsome

121

reputation as a thorn in the side of Christian naval powers. The city of Algiers, the capital of the Ottoman regency of Cezayiri-Garb and the residence of the provincial *deys* (autonomous governors) and their *diwan* government, became the center of a naval jihad. With its magnificent harbor and fertile mountainous hinterland of Algeria, Algiers was a fortified bastion and base from which fleets sailed to confront the most powerful Christian navies in the Mediterranean. At first the armed forces of these distant provinces were essentially the same as those of the rest of the sultanate. However, by the start of the 18th century the much-decayed Janissary units of Algeria were supplemented by European voluntary converts to Islam. Even this source of manpower seems to have been drying up later that century. Oddly, the greatest rivals to the Janissaries who arrived from the Ottoman heartlands were their own offspring, the Kuloğlıs or "sons of slaves."

The sipahi cavalry remained a highly effective force in this distant outpost, while those of central regions declined almost to irrelevance. Eventually the indigenous Baladi, whom Europeans knew as Moors, were allowed to play their part, primarily in the Algerian navy. Berber tribesmen from the interior served as auxiliary cavalry, as they had done ever since the arrival of Islam in North Africa.

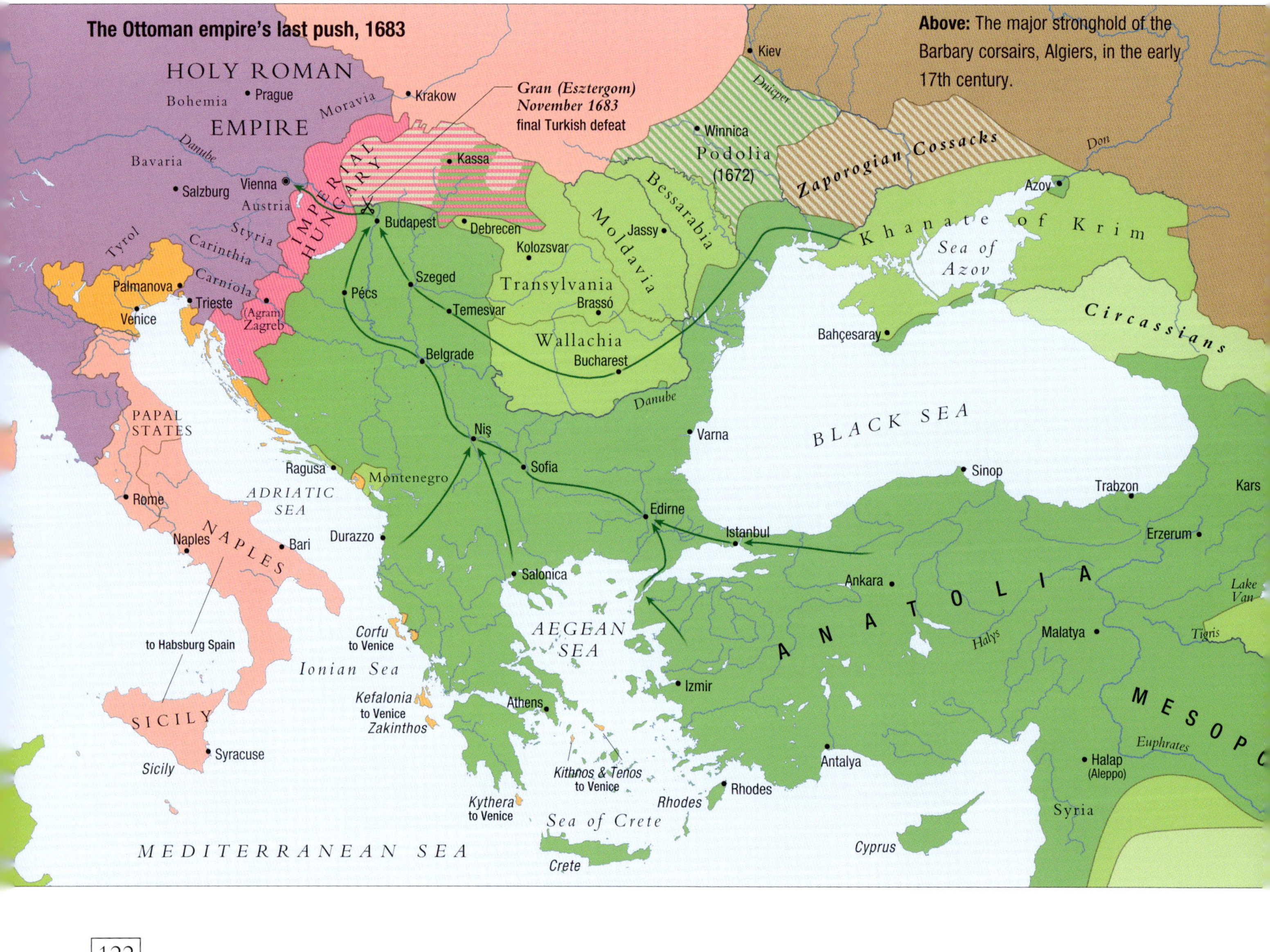

Above: The major stronghold of the Barbary corsairs, Algiers, in the early 17th century.

CHAPTER SEVEN: THE GOLDEN AGE

A separate infantry force known as Zouaves developed, usually commanded by officers with Berber names. These light infantrymen greatly impressed the invading French army of the 1830s. The French soon created Zouave regiments of their own; Italian and American Zouave regiments followed. Paradoxically, the army of 19th century autonomous Egypt also raised elite light infantry Zouave regiments. Despite being dressed in baggy trousers, embroidered waistcoats, sashes, and fezzes, these soldiers were inspired by the Zouave regiments of France, not the soldiers of Algeria or Turkey.

Siege of Vienna—the turning point

The defeat of a substantial Ottoman army outside the walls of Vienna in 1683 is widely seen as one of the turning points in European history. In reality its importance was more symbolic than geopolitical or even military. Furthermore, this particular Ottoman failure was only one step in a long process of decline; a process that still had centuries to run. The idea that the siege of Vienna was also the last occasion in which Christian western Europe was threatened by conquest by an external power is similarly misleading. More of a European state than an Asiatic or African one, the sultanate was no longer "external." The fact that it was Islamic-European rather than Christian-European was, of course, a different matter. It would therefore be more accurate to say that the second siege of Vienna marked the victory of Catholic or Latin Europe over an Islamic one, with the new Protestant Europe standing uncomfortably on the sidelines. Orthodox Christian Europe was similarly sidelined, either as a subjected element within this Islamic Europe or, in the form of czarist Russia, preoccupied with its own affairs far to the east. When seen in this light, the story of Ottoman Europe has remarkable parallels with the story of al-Andalus (Islamic Spain and Portugal), Sardinia, Sicily, and parts of Italy in the Middle Ages. Here, on the southernmost parts of medieval Europe, Islam had similarly challenged the continent's existing Christian civilization.

The Vienna campaign of 1683 was nevertheless on an epic scale. It had been triggered by events in Hungary where war with the Habsburg dynasty's Holy Roman Empire seemed so inevitable that Ottoman grand vizir Kara Mustafa Paşa had been willing to sign an unfavorable treaty with Russia just to be able to focus on the growing crisis in central Europe. A reluctant Sultan Mehmet IV did not want war with the powerful Holy Roman Empire but he was drawn into it by a significant revival of Hungarian nationalism, especially in western Hungary. This had taken on an anti-Habsburg, Protestant anti-Catholic, and anti-aristocratic character. The two most significant leaders of this movement were Nicholas Zrinyi and Prince Imre Thököly, who requested Ottoman support in return for becoming vassals; in this they were encouraged by the Habsburgs' arch-enemy France. Mehmet recognized Imre Thököly as king and in 1682 sent his army to conquer most of Upper or Imperial Habsburg Hungary.

Meanwhile, Leopold I had problems in the west where his Habsburg troops were fighting the French. French ambassadors and agents managed to convince Kara Mustafa that Vienna could be taken with relative ease, thus avenging a defeat which Süleyman the Magnificent had suffered beneath its walls in 1529. A huge army was assembled at Edirne under the grand vizir's command. Other Rumelian provincial forces headed toward the Serbian city of Niş, ready to join the main army as it

The Ottoman army employed numerous siege tactics—trenches, saps, and parallels—right up to the massive and modern fortifications of Vienna.

passed by on its way toward Vienna. For his part, Leopold drew together an impressive coalition of European Catholic powers. The most important of these, in military terms, was Jan Sobieski of Poland. Meanwhile the pope called for a new crusade against the Turks, and even sought support from the Safavid shah of Persia. Although France naturally continued to oppose this alliance, troops and money arrived from Spain, Portugal, and parts of Germany.

The Ottoman army moved out from Edirne in June 1683 and reached Vienna the following month. Large numbers of auxiliary Krim cavalry arrived from the vassal khanate. The subsequent struggle involved all of the Ottoman army's renowned siege tactics, including the advancing of trenches, saps, and parallels right up to the massive and modern fortifications of Vienna. A map of these Ottoman siege-works made immediately after their retreat shows something astonishingly modern; more like an aerial photograph of a particularly important section of the Western Front during the First World War than a battlefield dating from the late 17th century. Nevertheless, a series of Ottoman assaults failed and the arrival of King Jan Sobieski's cavalry finally raised the siege in September 1683.

The Ottomans had captured huge booty in a series of raids across Austria during the course of the fighting outside Vienna, but their retreat now meant that they had to abandon their heavy artillery and huge volumes of supplies. They tried to make a stand at the city of Gran in November but were completely defeated, after which their retreat degenerated almost into rout. Failure was rarely excused in the Ottoman court during this period, and the grand vizir Kara Mustafa was dismissed, then arrested and executed, which unfortunately left the Ottoman army in a state of near total disorganization.

If Mehmet IV's forces had prevailed at Vienna in 1683, there can be little doubt that the balance of power in central and western Europe would have been shattered. This would almost certainly have been of greater significance than any immediate territorial gains made by the Ottomans. The defeat highlighted increasing weaknesses within the Ottoman state, military, political, administrative, and economic. On the other side, despite the heroic role played by Jan Sobieski and his Polish troops in raising the siege of Vienna, it was the Holy Roman Empire that really benefited from the Ottoman failure. Fears of Ottoman-inspired uprisings in Habsburg-ruled western Hungary rapidly diminished and the Ottoman frontier was soon being pushed remorselessly back. The sultanate's position in Hungary had never been as strong and certainly not as deep-rooted as it sometimes seemed, its hold on directly ruled central Hungary weakening since the early 17th century.

Meanwhile Transylvania had developed into a substantial power in its own right, though usually recognizing Ottoman suzerainty. Under the Hungarian prince Bethlen Gábor its prosperity had doubled. Significantly, Bethlen Gábor had taken advantage of his position within the Ottoman fold to act as the protector of ultra-Protestant Calvinism within central Europe. This enabled Bethlen Gábor to project Transylvanian power and influence beyond its own boundaries and those of the Ottoman sultanate—most notably into Habsburg-ruled western Hungary where the Catholic counter-Reformation was not imposed as rigorously as in the rest of the Holy Roman Empire.

This period of virtual Transylvanian independence ended in 1657 when Bethlen Gábor's successor was killed while trying to become king of neighboring Poland. The Ottomans intervened in strength, imposing direct rule on several strategic parts of Transylvania. Things changed dramatically once more in the aftermath of the unsuccessful siege of Vienna, and by 1699 the Ottomans had been driven out of most of Hungary, while Transylvania fell under Habsburg domination. The Carpathian Mountains would remain the frontier between the Ottoman and Habsburg territory for almost two centuries, with largely Romanian-speaking Transylvania to the northwest of the Carpathians, and the autonomous but Romanian-speaking Ottoman principalities of Moldavia and Wallachia to the east and south respectively. Until 1878, changes in the frontier took place further to the west, and even these remained relatively minor.

The graceful arch of the Ottoman bridge which spanned the Neretvar at Mostar, some 34 miles from the Adriatic coast, in southern Bosnia. The original, pictured here, was destroyed in fighting between Bosnian Christians and Muslims in 1993 and rebuilt in 2003.

CHAPTER EIGHT

The Tulip Period

Artistic flowering, music, and the legal system

In many respects, the greatest work of Ottoman art has been the city of Istanbul itself. After extending Turkish influence to the grain-growing regions across the Black Sea to relieve the severe food shortages which were a consequence of Mehmet the Conqueror's policy of rapidly repopulating Constantinople–Istanbul, the city's population increased even faster during the 16th century. Its adornment matched in pace so that it glittered with new architecture, its quarters divided into distinct communities that reflected a mixed population.

New localities (*mahalles* in Turkish) were built in previously deserted or market garden areas. This was particularly noticeable close to the city's massive land-defenses and along some of the walls facing the Sea of Marmara. These newly populated areas required new civil and religious facilities, including large mosques, hamam public baths, *sibil* public fountains, madrasa schools, and markets. This was the period during which the famous architect Sinan was credited with an astonishing number of buildings. The most prestigious were designed by the great man himself, but many others were the products of his school, or more accurately the architectural business headed by Sinan.

In 1539 Süleyman the Magnificent ordered the construction of a massive new complex of religious, educational, public, and commercial buildings in the Aksaray area, close to the ancient Roman column of Arcadius. It was dedicated to his wife Hürrem Sultan, better known in Europe as Roxelana, and at its center stood a mosque, madrasa, hospital, and hospice. Its upkeep was financed by *vakıf*, specially dedicated tax revenues from a han or caravanserai for visiting merchants and others, a haman, timber-store, slaughterhouse for *halal* (correctly killed) meat, and various other shops and warehouses. The annual income from these commercial premises was estimated as 500,000 *akce*—a massive sum for those days. However, it is an architectural complex instigated by Süleyman later in his reign which still dominates the skyline of Istanbul: the Süleymaniyye. At its center towers the huge Mosque of Süleyman itself, often regarded as Sinan's finest achievement. It was built in 1550–57 and its 89-foot dome was surrounded by two mausoleums and the baths, schools, and soup kitchens traditional in Ottoman settlements. Destroyed by fire in 1660, the mosque has been rebuilt in a slightly different style.

Though the architectural wonders of Istanbul might continue to amaze the modern visitor, it was the city itself which became the economic and cultural powerhouse of the Ottoman sultanate. Great building projects brought in craftsmen and laborers from far afield; surviving documents show that they were

Opposite: The architect Sinan's Istanbul masterpiece was said to be the huge Mosque of Süleyman the Magnificent. Its present decoration, however, dates from the mid-17th century.

Constantinople as Istanbul, new capital of the Ottomans' empire; from a Turkish map created in about 1537.

managed with almost military discipline. For example, records of wages paid to men working on the construction of the Mosque of Ahmet I in the 16th century indicate that over a quarter came from Istanbul itself, half as many from "Rumelia and the Islands" (the European provinces), almost exactly the same proportion from Anatolia, while the origins of the rest were unspecified. Just over half were Christian, the remainder Muslim. The men who built the walls, did the ironwork, and constructed the sewers tended to be relatively unskilled Christians, while the more skilled stone-carvers, carpenters, painters, glass-workers, and leadworkers were usually Muslim. These fascinating financial records stated that over half of the workers were free men receiving normal wages, while 40 percent were *acemi oğlan* recruits for the Janissary corps and five percent were described as galley slaves.

The luminous glory of Istanbul, as seen in an anonymous painting from the early 18th century. The artist may have been an Ottoman trained in the European artistic styles.

Until the 17th century, almost all expansion of the residential and commercial quarters of Istanbul was inside the ancient fortified walls. This area of over seven square miles had not been entirely built over even at the height of Byzantine power and prosperity in the early Middle Ages. Thereafter the open areas within the walls had expanded considerably; a process only reversed after the Ottoman conquest of 1453. Many areas of cultivation, orchards, and even grazing land were present well into the mid-16th century golden age of Süleyman the Magnificent. These open spaces were dotted with the pleasure-gardens and fine houses of the wealthy Ottoman elite. This was especially apparent along the little Lycus stream and around the main gates through the still massive if now crumbling landside walls. During the 17th century, for example, the Yeni-Bahçe or New Garden area near the Edirne Gate was described by the Turkish writer Hezarfenn as a "vaste meadow with ten thousand horses grazing the grass." An exaggeration, perhaps, but it illustrates a pleasant rural setting inside the city walls.

Another significant feature of Istanbul in its days of Ottoman splendor were strict building regulations and the control of main streets in an effort to reduce the danger from fire, earthquake, and crime. In these respects, the Ottoman capital remained far in advance of most western European cities for centuries. Privacy and the sanctity of the harem domestic quarters of a household had been central to Islamic civilization from the beginning. Consequently, Ottoman urban or local government regulations paid considerable attention to this area.

Residential communities and local life were largely based on the *mahal*. This was a community, usually from one religious or ethnic group, within a small but defined area with its own religious building, be it a mosque, church, or synagogue.

CHAPTER EIGHT: THE TULIP PERIOD

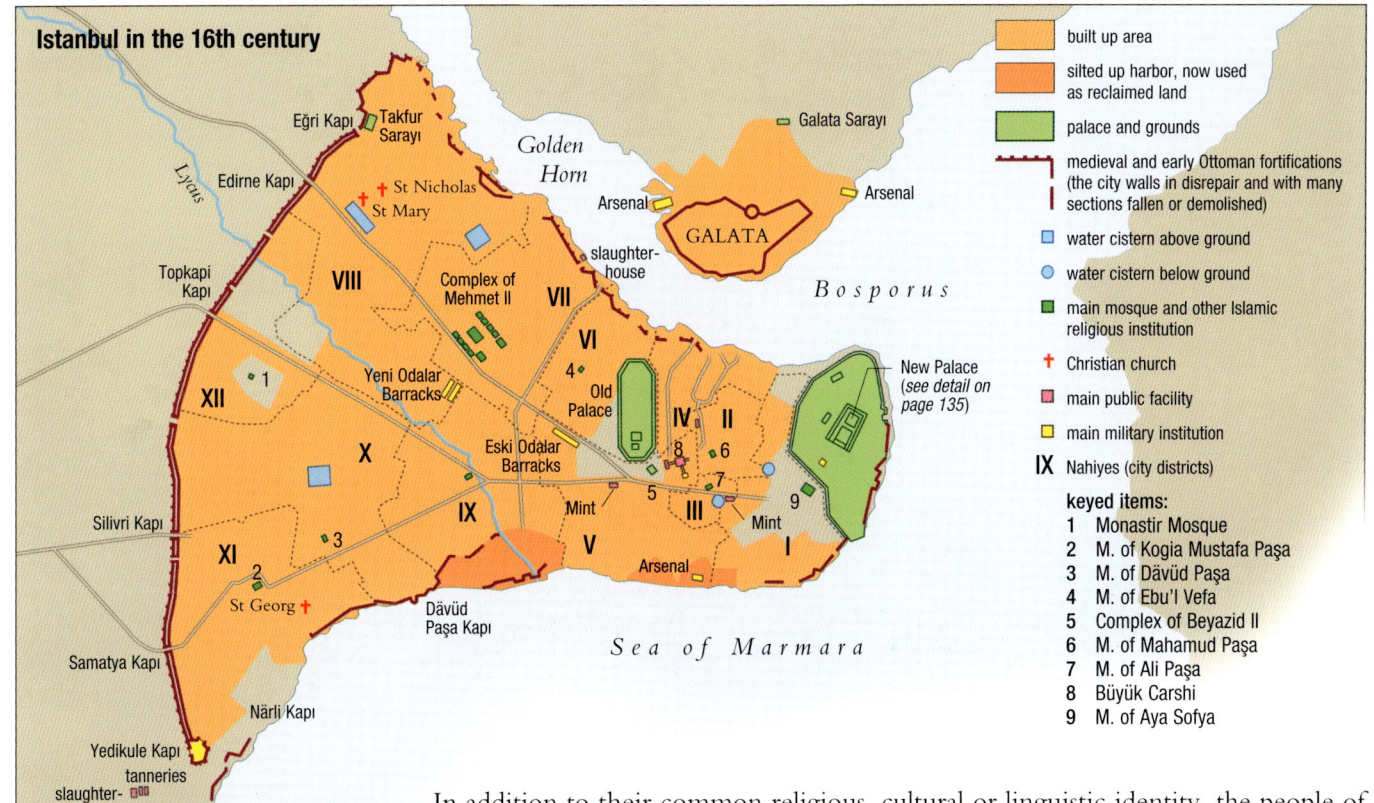

Istanbul in the 16th century

- built up area
- silted up harbor, now used as reclaimed land
- palace and grounds
- medieval and early Ottoman fortifications (the city walls in disrepair and with many sections fallen or demolished)
- water cistern above ground
- water cistern below ground
- main mosque and other Islamic religious institution
- Christian church
- main public facility
- main military institution
- IX Nahiyes (city districts)

keyed items:
1. Monastir Mosque
2. M. of Kogia Mustafa Paşa
3. M. of Dävüd Paşa
4. M. of Ebu'l Vefa
5. Complex of Beyazid II
6. M. of Mahamud Paşa
7. M. of Ali Paşa
8. Büyük Carshi
9. M. of Aya Sofya

The Sülaymaniye Mosque, from Galata.

In addition to their common religious, cultural or linguistic identity, the people of a mahal tended to have other shared interests that led to strong solidarity. Virtually every mahal had its own school, drinking fountain, and other public facilities provided by vakıf charitable foundations established by wealthier members of that community. In 1672 there were 253 Muslim mahalles in Istanbul, plus 24 Christian, Jewish or otherwise non-Islamic ones. Two centuries later these had increased to 284 Muslim, 24 Greek (Christian), 14 Armenian (Christian) and nine Jewish mahalles. By then, there were a further 256 such localities outside the city walls, beside the Golden Horn, along the European shore of the Bosphorus and on its Asiatic shore at Üsküdar (former Scutari) and Kadıköy (former Chalcedon).

In its dealings with the Ottoman authorities, each mahal was considered responsible for maintaining law and order within its own small territory, along with the correct payment of taxes and other obligations to the state. Taxes owed by those who had recently fallen on hard times or fled the area remained the responsibility of the mahal and were often paid out of a charitable or emergency fund established for that purpose. This fund could also provide loans to those in need or considered deserving. Each mahal had its own salaried night watchman. In the early days, this duty had often been carried out on a rota basis, but later on full-time watchmen were normally hired. In 1695 the government issued a decree which stipulated that each mahal should have two such *bekci* watchmen who must patrol the streets with lanterns in their hands, arresting any strangers found out of doors after evening prayer. Not surprisingly, the bekci entered local folklore and storytelling, soon featuring prominently in the hilarious shadow-puppet plays still seen in many traditional quarters of Turkish, Balkan and Middle Eastern towns.

Bringing the world to life

If the great age of expansion in the 14th and 15th centuries was an artistically modest time—producing few fine manuscripts, though characterized by original architecture and some superb ceramics—the Ottoman golden age from the later 15th through the 16th centuries was, in contrast, a time of astonishing creativity, awe-inspiring architecture and highly original literature, even though the latter remains little known outside Turkey itself. Nevertheless, during these decades most of the cultural output of the Ottomans and their subject peoples was embedded within existing traditional forms, whether Islamic or eastern Christian. Vigorous creativity continued during the 17th century but remained firmly traditional, with only minor influence from western European civilization.

The most visible characteristic of traditional Ottoman religious art was its very direct and almost naïve approach to the subject matter. Manuscript illustration was more sophisticated than that of the earlier Turcoman styles in Anatolia, western Persia, and northern Mesopotamia, yet it retained a typically Turkish piety alongside an occasionally earthy humor, quite unlike the sophisticated and elaborate "pleasure loving" art of neighboring Persia. During the late 16th century even the technical influence of Persian painting largely disappeared and gave way to a purely Ottoman style. Simple, direct compositions with bold colors and very little shading remained typical, although there was increasing variety in subject matter. At the same time, some influence from late-Byzantine and Balkan Christian art could be seen in the use of gilded backgrounds and in certain distinctive methods of arranging the subjects.

Another typical Ottoman trait was a profound interest in ordinary people. Real emotions, accurately represented buildings, crowded urban scenes, and everyday life were now included in what, to western eyes, might otherwise appear very fanciful paintings. These strong elements of present-day life went hand in hand with an intense interest in history, especially the history of the Ottomans themselves. There

Simple, direct compositions with bold colors and very little shading remained typical of a purely Ottoman style in the 16th century, as seen **below** in this detail from *Death of Bahram Pasha*, 1558. Some simple attempts at correct linear perspective may be observed in examples such as the manuscript illustration of a prince in discussion with a *kadi* (an Islamic judge), **below right**.

CHAPTER EIGHT: THE TULIP PERIOD

was little of the dreamlike quality that had become characteristic of Persian manuscript illustration and palace wall-painting. Portraits of real people—though almost invariably sultans and other senior members of the state hierarchy—were found in Ottoman art, as they were in the Islamic art of Mughul India, a century or so before such subjects commonly appeared in Persian art.

There were not many changes during the 17th century, though there was a decline in vigor and a further increase in the realism of illustrated architecture; even some simple attempts at correct linear perspective. The result was a sometimes odd mixture of eastern and western artistic traditions and values. The so-called Tulip Period began in the early 18th century and was named from the fashion for growing, collecting, and displaying tulip flowers which swept through the Ottoman cultural and political elites. The tulip became hugely popular as a decorative motif in almost all forms of art, from architectural carving to embroidery. Though very different in appearance to European Baroque art, this Tulip Period seemed strangely close to it in spirit. Suddenly, Ottoman art became playful and pleasure-loving, delicate as well as decorative. There was a significant increase in private forms of art, ranging from delightful wall-paintings for the private harem rooms, to erotic manuscript illustrations, which were very private indeed!

An astonishing array of crafts

Of all the Ottoman crafts or minor arts, textiles and carpet-making were clearly the most famous outside the sultanate itself. They were also economically important industries and were illustrated as luxury items in western European art, especially Italian, since at least the 15th century. However, Ottoman rugs and carpets remained very traditional, perhaps because their designs were so successful and their export so welcomed in the outside world. Furthermore, Ottoman weavers correctly believed that they had little or nothing to learn from western Europe, either in terms of design or of manufacturing techniques.

Examples—like the early 18th-century *Odalesche*, **left**—of an earthy humor are rare in Ottoman representation, and in most cases the icon-like composition and decorative background of late Byzantine art prevailed, as exemplified in this portrait **below** of Ahmet III (1703–30)

Two pages from a *surname* (Book of Festivals or Parades) of c.1583 showing members of the "kemha" weavers' guild.

Ottoman ceramics were almost as popular, though they rarely achieved the luxury status of Ottoman carpets. The origins of what might be called the Ottoman school of ceramics are not entirely clear, and in any case the sultanate covered such wide and culturally disparate regions that there were several differing centers or schools of pottery. Within the heartland of Anatolia, however, the first stylistic influences clearly came from Seljuq Turkish, Persian, Armenian, and Byzantine potters and glazers. The Ottoman industry was given a huge boost by a demand for the large-scale production of glazed and colored decorative architectural tiles for the massive mosque-building and repair program which characterized the early centuries of Ottoman history. This gave ceramics a head start, compared to other arts and crafts. Most of the earliest designs showed clear Mongol and even Chinese influence. A simple form of Ottoman ceramic called Miletus-ware had been known since the 14th century. It was a somewhat coarse red earthenware decorated with blue and green under a lead glaze, similar to some of the simple folk-ceramics of the Balkan peninsula. It led directly to the more famous Iznik-ware.

The town of Iznik (ex-Byzantine Nicaea) became the main center of Ottoman ceramics production in the late 15th century with a sudden outpouring of new styles of exceptional decoration, initially on a red ground. Later a fashion developed for naturalistic floral designs on a white ground, while the use of a rich and slightly embossed red glaze was characteristic of Iznik-ware from the late 16th century onward. Subsequently, an array of realistic motifs came into fashion, especially ships as well as symbolic plans of Islamic religious buildings.

Edirne was another, though shorter-lived, center of ceramics production, at first probably serving a religious building program in the newly conquered Balkans. Its most distinctive wares had their decoration on a gray ground. Then there was Kütahya, which rose to prominence in the 18th century, believed to be the result of greater artistic freedom being given to the Armenian and

Iznik-ware bowl with sailing ship motif, 16th–17th centuries.

CHAPTER EIGHT: THE TULIP PERIOD

Greek potters who dominated this center. Kütahya-ware was generally more refined and elaborate than that of earlier centers, with greater use of red, black, blue, green, and bright yellow glazes. It is, however, sometimes criticized for lacking the simple vigor of earlier Ottoman pottery.

Ottoman metalwork has never enjoyed the prestige or popularity of textiles or ceramics. It first appeared under strong Timurid Persian influence in the 15th century and most seems to have been made in the same eastern Anatolian centers which had been famed for metalworking for centuries. There was also an almost inevitable continuation of previous Seljuq Turkish styles and motifs. Ottoman metalworkers charged with highly expensive or prestigious commissions tended to inset numerous precious or semi-precious stones as a luxurious form of surface decoration. Many of these techniques survive in the traditional or folk-jewelry of Greece and the Balkans. Some prestigious weapons were also highly decorated, although their blades or working parts tended to be more business-like than those of neighboring Safavid Persia.

Little changed until the 18th century Tulip Period, when Ottoman metalwork reflected the same Baroque spirit as did most arts. This again included a clear European influence, alongside the Ottomans' tradition of delicate craftsmanship, especially in filigree and engraving.

Architectural tiles of the 15th century at a mosque in Bursa.

Topkapı Sarayı—home of sultans

The Topkapı Sarayı is one of the most remarkable complexes of buildings anywhere in the world. The main palace of the Ottoman sultans was built in the late 15th century but appended by subsequent rulers until it became an odd collection of buildings. Unlike most European palaces it does not consist of one great building, nor did it ever have one dominant structure. Instead it is a somewhat rambling array of low structures, mostly linked to one another, surrounded by gardens and incorporating several courtyards, some of which are also gardens in their own right. Though a fortified wall surrounds the area, it cannot in any real sense be described as fortified. The Topkapı gives the impression of having been designed for pleasure, ease of mind, and practicality, rather than to impress foreigners or even the citizens of Istanbul outside the palace walls.

When Mehmet II conquered Constantinople in 1453 none of the existing late Byzantine palaces was considered suitable for the ruler of such a powerful and ambitious state. So Mehmet ordered work to begin on the construction of an entirely new palace at the northern end of what had been the Forum of Theodosius, now Beyezit Square. When it was completed in the winter of 1457–58 Mehmet moved in

Sultan Selim II receiving ambassador at the Gate of Felicity (**9 in the plan following**), Ottoman, early 19th century.

The Topkapı harem garden and quarters, tranquility in the midst of government.

Below: the kitchen ranges and the baths of Selim II face out onto the Bosporus. Topkapı Sarayı finally ceased to be the sultan's residence in 1853, when Abd'l Mecid moved into the Dolmabahçe Palace, a newly constructed, much more modern and largely westernized imperial residence on the western shore of the Bosporus, north of Istanbul.

from his old capital at Edirne. Yet he was not satisfied and instead decided that the acropolis of the ancient city of Byzantium, on a hill overlooking the Bosporus strait and the entrance to the Golden Horn, was more appropriate. It was a magnificent location which could also be isolated from the rest of the city by adding minimal fortifications to the existing Byzantine sea walls.

Construction of the two distinct sections of what became the new Topkapı Sarayı ("gun-gate palace") began in 1462. Mehmet II's original buildings consisted of delightful summer pavilions close to the water's edge, largely destroyed during the building of a railway in the late 19th century, plus a winter palace on a ridge overlooking the city. The first of a series of courts included an imperial armory, housed in what had been the Byzantine church of St. Irene, plus hospitals and barracks. The second court had a reception hall and a treasury on one side with kitchens on the other. A third court served as the palace school while the fifth largely consisted of pavilions and flower gardens.

The harem or private quarters of the sultan and his family was to one side, closer to the bustling city of Istanbul and beyond the barracks of an elite guard unit of

CHAPTER EIGHT: THE TULIP PERIOD

halberdiers. The harem was divided in sections, including those for eunuchs, laundry and other service areas, the queen mother's own series of rooms, the chambers of the ruling sultan and his women (he was not married in the usual sense of the word). There was also a sacred chamber which housed religious relics such as the Robe of the Prophet Muhammad.

Thereafter Mehmet the Conqueror's successors continued to add kiosks, private apartments, libraries, mosques, barracks, offices, and stables. The result was a huge but far from coherent complex which not only served as a public and a private palace for the ruler, but also housed the central administration and government of the Ottoman state—the "Porte," as it became known. In addition to the vizir's council chambers there were financial offices, central and provincial administrative offices, plus archives. Widely known as the Südde-i Seadat or Threshold of Bliss, the Topkapı palace was in some respects a small, self-contained, and closed city; mysterious to the ordinary citizens and occasionally terrifying to its Christian neighbors. By the end of the 17th century it was a place of extraordinarily brutal and bloody events, including the assassinations of Osman II and Ibrahim I.

The mehterhane—music to the ears of marching men

The Ottoman state was the first in Europe to have a permanent military music organzation in the form of the *mehterhane*. The military band corps was a distinctive feature of the sultanate in its days of greatness and emphasized the percussive and rhythmic elements we associate with military music today; European composers were influenced by the Turkish pieces. Military music has ancient roots among the

The Topkapı Palace
Key to numbered items
1. women's dormitory
2. laundry
3. Mosque of the Black Eunuchs
4. Mosque of Beşir Aga
5. barracks of the Black Eunuchs
6. Kubbealti; halls and offices of the Divan (government)
7. Inner Treasury offices
8. quarters of the White Eunuchs
9. Bab-üs Saadet (Gate of Felicity)
10. Arz Odasi (Throne Room)
11. Ahmet III library
12. Agalar Mosque (school mosque) with Harem mosque attached
13. rooms of the Robe of the Prophet
14. tulip garden
15. Abd'l Mecid kisok
16. Physician's Tower
17. Mustafa Pasha kiosk
18. Revan kiosk (Yerevan kiosk)
19. Boating Pool
20. sultan's quarters (throne room, hamam, dining rooms, and bedchambers, etc)
21. Osman III terrace and kiosk
22. Valide Court

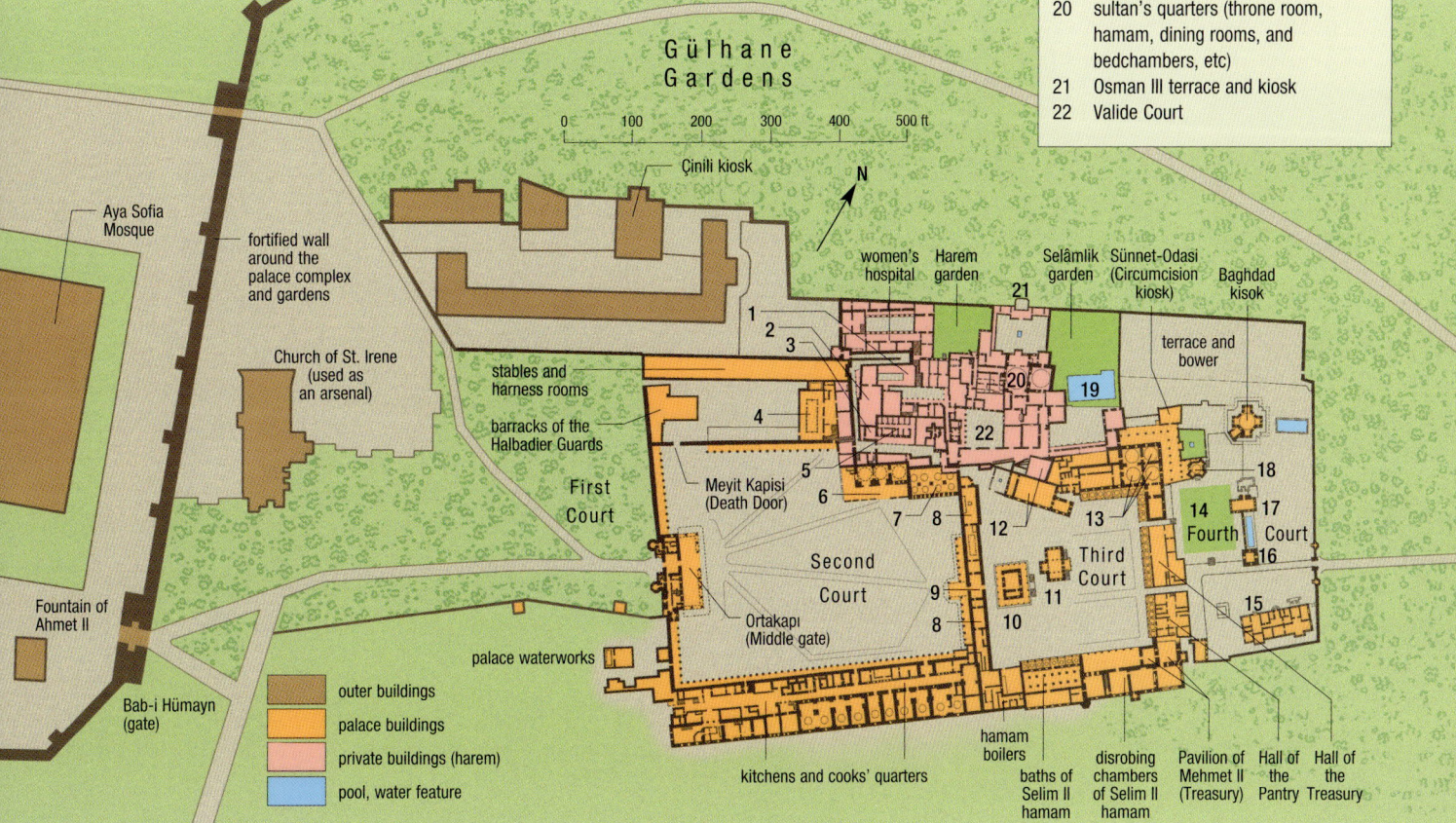

One of the *zurnazen* playing a *kaba zurna*, the clarinet-like instrument which gave the mehterhane its characteristic sound. It is made of plum or apricot wood, has seven holes, and is remarkably similar to the medieval French *chalumeau*.

† Chama-Pur was a traditional foe of Alexander the Great.

Central Asian Turks, while in the Middle East music played an important role throughout Islamic history.

The origins of the mehterhane are, however, lost amid the legends which surround the creation of the Ottoman sultanate itself. One story maintains that it began when the Seljuq sultan of Rum recognized Osman Gazi, the founder of the Ottoman state, as an autonomous emir late in the 13th century. Part of this recognition ceremony entailed sending Osman various insignia of authority, including a large *kös* war-drum, *nekkare* small double kettle drums, and a *çevgen* set of bells mounted on a staff. The sultan also sent musicians to play them, their first concert supposedly held at Eskişehir (Byzantine Dorylaeum) where, to show his respect for the sultan, Osman Gazi remained standing while the musicians played.

All subsequent Ottoman rulers stood when the mehter band played until Mehmet the Conqueror, declared that "One should not stand in respect to a ruler who has been dead 200 years. This sort of respect does not suit the magnificence of the great Ottoman sultanate," and abolished the custom. The band was then known as the Tabl-i Ali-i Osman, the Great Ottoman Band. It was reorganized in the 16th or 17th century and came to an end with the abolition of the Janissary Corps in 1826. By then, however, every regiment and most garrisons had some kind of military band.

In the 17th century the mehterhane had played "tunes of Afrasiyab," meaning Persian military music, and according to the Turkish traveler Evliya Çelebi writing in 1638, "…five hundred trumpeters raised such a sound that the planet Venus began to dance and the skies reverberated… All these players of the drum, kettle-drum and cymbals marched past together beating their different kinds of instruments in rhythmic unison as if Chama-Pur's army† was marching by." Forty-five years later the Ottomans were besieging Vienna and, of course, there were mehter bands with the army. Their role was graphically described by one Turkish observer, Silahtar Fındıklı Mehmet Ağa: "Toward the middle of the afternoon the Grand Vizir's mehterhane started to play first. Then the bands of the provincial governors and the bands of the right wing all started to play together. Thus, after the evening prayer until dawn the sound of drums, clarinets, kettle-drums, and cymbals joined from every side the rumble of cannons and gunfire, the whole countryside echoing to these sounds."

Turkish bands influenced the music of the rest of Europe, tunes written alla Turca were particularly popular in the 18th century. Around 1780, composers like Mozart, Haydn, Beethoven, and Glück began to imitate the "Janissary music" used by the fearsome Ottoman infantry of the same name. Some Turkish instruments were eventually adopted, most obviously the Turkish Crescent, popularly called a Jingling Johnnie, which was an elaborate version of the Ottoman *çevgen* with which the leader of a mehter band kept time.

A Mehter band was built up of *kats* or "folds," each normally consisting of a drum, double kettle-drums, clarinet, trumpet, and cymbals. The size of the resulting band varied; the sultan's mehterhane had nine folds, that of the Yeniçeri Ağası, commander of the Janissary corps, had seven. A band was led by its *mehterbaşı* or conductor and each group of instruments was headed by an *ağa*, the leader of the drum section being the chief mehter ağa.

Wind instruments consisted of two kinds of seven-hole clarinet made from plum

CHAPTER EIGHT: THE TULIP PERIOD

or apricot wood, the low-pitched *kaba zurna* and the higher *cura*. The *kurenay* or *boru* Turkish trumpet was a relatively simple brass instrument used only for keeping rhythm. Mehter *düdüğü* or whistles sometimes completed the wind section. *Nekkare* double kettle drums or tom-toms, *zil* cymbals, *davul* two-sided drums and the massive *kös* bass drum formed the percussion section. Traditionally the kös players were a separate musical organization only employed by the sultan himself. There were several sizes of kös; those carried on horseback, a middle-sized drum for a camel, and the largest mounted on an elephant, though all could be placed on the ground to form the final piece in a full mehterhane. The *çevkâni* singers who are now such a striking feature of the revived mehter band were only added in the late 18th century.

Mehterhane normally stood in a crescent formation, with only the kettle-drummers sitting. The kös player stood slightly forward, like the star within the crescent of a Turkish flag. Before the band started to play, a junior sergeant would step forward and call out, "Attention! mehterbaşı ağa, it is time for fun and enjoyment," while the nekkare played a three-time drum-roll. The conductor and his musicians then saluted each other before the mehterbaşı conductor told the audience what his band were going to perform. The concert would then begin with the mehterbaşı shouting, "Haydi, yallah!"—"Attention, let's go." Most of the performances consisted of battle songs and marches but some were based on the music of sufi Islamic mystics or dervishes. However, the names of the composers and lyricists remain unknown to the vast majority of western listeners. In addition to their distinctive music, the mehter band also had their own peculiar form of marching. This was almost a dance-step, having the rhythm 1, 2, 3-4, 1, 2, 3-4, right-left-right-pause and half turn right, left-right-left-pause and half turn left, etc.

For almost a century after the original mehterhane was abolished in 1826, the only military bands in the Ottoman empire were based on the European pattern. Then in 1914, during a wave of patriotic fervor which accompanied the outbreak of the First World War, a traditional mehter band was recreated. This lasted until 1935, when it was again abolished. The third reincarnation of the mehterhane came in 1952 with the setting up of a six-"fold" band, based at the Military Museum in Istanbul, and its first big performance marked the 500th anniversary of the Turkish conquest of Constantinople on May 29, 1953.

The mehter reenactment band in concert. The *köszen* or bass drummer plays a pair of large camel-skin copper drums. These same *kös* drums can be mounted on each side of a special horse-saddle. Behind stands a soldier in Janissary uniform with the band's four-horsetail *tuğ*, a characteristic Ottoman banner.

Ottoman Law—the quality of mercy

Ottoman law and its enforcement was based on Şeriat Islamic law but was not quite the same as the legal systems of earlier Islamic states. Although all inhabitants of the Ottoman empire were subject to the sultan's laws, or *kanun*, each *millet* or religious group was also governed according to its own religious and customary laws. Where Muslims were concerned, this involved the local or provincial *kadis* or qualified Islamic religious judges who interpreted Şeriat law and pronounced judgments. In practical terms, a kadi's employees investigated criminal cases, arrested and interrogated suspects, summoned witnesses, and punished the guilty after the kadi had made his final judgment. These legal officers were also aided by the local sancak bey, or provincial military governor, but he was often away on campaign so it was the local *subaşı* or police chief who played a more visible role in identifying and catching suspects. The subaşı also had authority to arrest suspects on his own initiative, though not to try or condemn them. Judgment had to be carried out in the presence of local witnesses to ensure fairness, while the trials themselves relied on the testimony of witnesses, both to the litigant's character and to the facts of the case.

The legal profession had developed early in Islamic history and at its heart were the *ulema*. These men were recognized religious scholars qualified to interpret Şeriat law in its practical as well as theoretical forms. They advised the kadis who were also recruited from their ranks. The science of jurisprudence, or *fıqıh*, was studied at a madrasa or religious college. *Fetvas* (fatwa) or judgments were pronounced on the basis of şeriat law and were not normally the death sentence. Those qualified to serve as legal consultants, roughly equivalent to solicitors, were usually called *fakihs* or *muftis*. There was at least one such properly qualified man in every town or district. Different schools of Şeriat law demanded different degrees of evidence before a guilty verdict was passed. A condemned person had to be of sound mind or the individual could not be considered responsible for their actions. Punishments were varied and occasionally ruthless.

A prisoner brought before the sultan for judgment, in a 16th century Ottoman manuscript.

The concept of compensation rather than vengeance was central to şeriat law, although the Old Testament Biblical idea of "an eye for an eye" remained. As a result, murder was punishable by death or a substantial fine, paid to a victim's family as a form of recompense for their loss of a productive member of the community. The ultimate choice remained theirs. Adultery was theoretically punished by stoning to death, but was only deemed proved if there were four eyewitnesses to the act, thus few were found guilty. Persistent theft could result in the whole or partial amputation of the offender's hand; in practice, physical mutilation as a form of punishment was far less frequent under Islamic Ottoman rule than had been the case in the previous Christian Byzantine empire.

Fornication was punishable by one hundred lashes and banishment from the community for a year, while drunkenness in a public place was punished with 80

CHAPTER EIGHT: THE TULIP PERIOD

The sancaks of the European and western Anatolian provinces, mid-17th century

1. Sancak of the Kaptan Paşa; also called the Sancak of Gelibolu, and often considered part of the Eyâlet of Cezayir. Note the separated additional territory west of the Sancak of Selânik (5 below)

Sancaks of the Eyâlet of Rumeli
2. Kırkilise
3. Vize
4. Silistre
5. Selânik
6. Tirhala
7. Eğriböz (previously considered part of the Eyâlet of Cezayir)
8. Mora (previously considered part of the Eyâlet of Cezayir)
9. Inebahti (previously considered part of the Eyâlet of Cezayir)
10. Karli-eli (previously considered part of the Eyâlet of Cezayir)
11. Yanya
12. Delvina
13. Avlonya
14. Elbasan
15. Dukagin
16. Iskenderiye
17. Ohri
18. Üsküp
19. Köstendil
20. Sofia
21. Nigbolu
22. Çirmen
23. Vidin
24. Smederovo
25. Alacahişar
26. Vulçitrin
27. Pirzerin

Sancaks of the Eyâlet of Bosna
28. Bosna
29. Izvornik
30. Kirka
31. Kilis
32. Hersek (the southern part of Hersek was sometimes considered to lie within the Eyâlet of Rumeli)

Sancaks of the Eyâlet of Cezayir
33. Biga
34. Midilli
35. Sakiz
36. Sugla
37. Rodos
38. Koca-eli

Sancaks of the Eyâlet of Anadolu
39. Hudavendigâr (note the separated additional coastal territory between the sançaks of Karasi and Saruhan)
40. Karasi
41. Saruhan
42. Kütahya
43. Sultanönü
44. Aydin
45. Menteşe

46. Eyâlet of Egri
47. Eyâlet of Kanije
48. Eyâlet of Budin
49. Eyâlet of Timisvar

Note that the Imperial capital cities of Istanbul and Edirne were outside the normal Sancak system

lashes. All such physical penalties had to be carried out in public to show that justice was being done and to ensure that nothing more that the legal punishment was inflicted on the guilty person. One of the most important Hadiths or sayings of the Prophet Muhammad, stated: "Let there be neither injury nor vengeance for that injury." This statement, when taken with the numerous Koranic verses which advocated mercy, ensured that the maximum penalty was normally only exacted in the most serious or persistent of cases.

The ancient Persian tradition that a ruler should do all in his power to win the loyalty of his subjects had been adopted by Islamic ruling elites from the beginning. It, and Islamic legal tradition, probably accounted for the advice seen in several pre-Ottoman books of advice for rulers. These normally advocated the forgiveness of trivial offences and minimum punishments elsewhere. The Turks did introduce some punishments based on their central Asian pre-Islamic traditions, which had much in common with Chinese legal practice. Some could be violent and even sadistic, including strangling, hanging, impalement, and other vicious punishments. However, these were normally only used in political cases involving members of the political or military elites who were seen to have not only broken the law, but to have betrayed their ruler.

CHAPTER NINE

Restoration or Reform?

Fragmentation and dissolution during the 19th century

At the close of the 18th century, the Ottoman sultanate with its centralized administration in Istanbul—the Porte—was still an enormous state with huge potential. In administrative and political terms, it remained a complex structure of military provinces, autonomous regions, and virtually independent regencies. Each province had a *paşa* or governor supported by a large staff, including numerous military officials. This local administration was, however, largely concerned with the Islamic population, while the Christian and Jewish minorities were effectively self-governing, unless their affairs impinged on those of the Ottoman state.

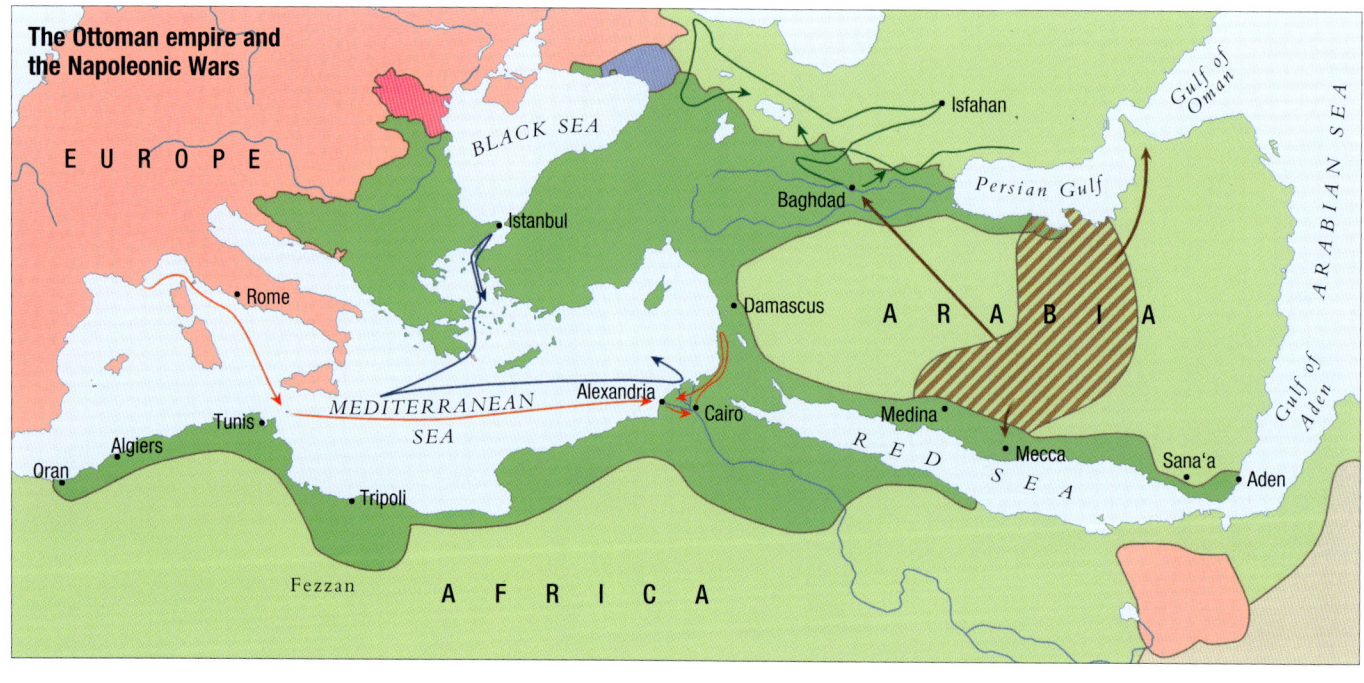

- Ottoman territory (inc. vassals), c.1812
- Mingrelia, Imereti and Guria conquered by Russia, 1803–04
- Bessarabia conquered by Russia, 1812
- Wahabi heartland, expanding since 1757
- other Islamic territory
- Christian territory
- Persian invasions of Nadir Shah to 1746
- Wahabi raids from 1801
- Napoleon's invasion of Egypt and Palestine, 1798–1801
- unsuccessful British attacks on Istanbul and Egypt, 1807

Some regions were of more strategic significance than others, generally those on the frontiers. They included the constantly threatened Danube valley, which had once served as a major channel for Ottoman raids into central Europe but now formed a vulnerable opening through which the Christian Habsburgs could invade Ottoman territory. In the reign of Francis II, the Holy Roman Empire collapsed and became Austro-Hungarian territory after 1806. Several outlying regions had already been lost, yet the massive reduction of territory which would characterize the final century of Ottoman history had barely begun. During the Napoleonic Wars of 1803–15, the Ottoman sultanate was only capable of raising 30,000 troops for a major campaign. Consequently the army had to rely on a defensive strategy and from 1806 initially served as a lesser ally of France against Russia and Britain. The latter's invasion of Egypt was defeated at Rashid (Rosetta) in 1807 and British and Russian attempts to control the Dardanelles failed.

Problems arose from the fact that the Ottoman empire had a larger population than its old-fashioned agricultural systems could support, which resulted in migration to underpopulated mountainous regions, widespread banditry on land, and piracy at sea. Within the sultanate's European provinces there were Muslim majorities in Albania, Bosnia, Herzegovina, Crete, parts of Bulgaria, and most of the cities. This Islamic population was now in relative decline, not least because it suffered disproportionately high casualties in a state where, officially, only Muslims served in the armed forces. Christian expansion was turning the Muslims into a threatened, though socially dominant, elite in many areas. Recent Ottoman defeats had resulted in the wholesale slaughter or expulsion of Islamic populations in lost territories. Such "ethnic cleansing" had not been seen before, but would remain an unpleasant feature of most Balkan Christian "national liberation" movements down to modern times.

The Islamic population of the sultanate was largely Sunni, though there were large Shi'a communities in eastern Anatolia, coastal Syria, southern Iraq, and Yemen. Non-Muslims were still categorized as members of one of the *millet* communities into which the population was divided; such as Armenian Christians, Orthodox Christians (mostly Greeks and Slavs), Catholic Christians, and Jews. In rural areas communities were ruled by their own "notables," who were responsible for law, order and relations with the Muslim elite. Greek Christians enjoyed a culturally and politically privileged position compared to other Christians, but until the rise of philhellene sympathy for Greek independence in the 1820s, most western European visitors tended to be dismissive of them and instead advocated alliances with the dominant Turks.

During the Napoleonic Wars, visiting western soldiers and diplomats had a clear appreciation of Ottoman strengths and weaknesses. General Koehler once told his superiors in London that Ottoman commanders showed no foresight and wrote

A Turkish "pepperpot" pistol with decorations of tin inlay, dating to the 19th century

The real power behind the sultanate: Officers of the Grand Seraglio, from a print of c.1800.

French Adjutant General Pierre Devaux leads a charge of Napoleon's cavalry against Egyptian regulars in 1799.

"What is expected from such troops, or rather mob thus commanded? Nothing but shame and disgrace, and yet they have fine men, excellent horses, good guns, plenty of ammunition and provisions, and forage; and in short a great abundance of all the materials required to constitute a fine army, but they want order and system, which would not be difficult to establish if their principal officers were not so astonishingly adverse to anything tending toward it."

The Ottomans remained confident and motivated by religious certainty. Their highly traditional attitude toward warfare was illustrated in a little-known poem by Wasif which commemorated the defeat of French invaders in 1801:

When the misbelieving Frenchman suddenly swooped on Egypt's land,
Thither was the army sent by the Great Sultan's command;
But soon the foe o'erthrew and defeated his luckless band.
Then you went and scattered the vile foe on every hand,
When they your lightning, life-consuming cannon scanned,
The hell-doomed misbelievers knew the vanity of all they'd planned.
Countless foemen your happy officers did withstand,
Three full years, day and night, they fought you brand to brand.
Wretched they fell at your feet and mercy did demand.
You do deserve in glory so to stand!
Bravo! Champion of the Age! Rending ranks in serried fight!
Now your sabre hangs o'er the fire, sparking like the stars at night.

CHAPTER NINE: RESTORATION OR REFORM?

Even while the Napoleonic Wars were being fought, major reforms were attempted, and continued long after Napoleon's defeat. Many proved successful, so the vast state which threw itself into the Great War a hundred years later had little in common with the ramshackle empire which once endured the scorn and loathing of European liberals. Most dramatic of these reforms was the Tanzimat, literally meaning "regulations." This program aimed to remodel the Ottoman administration, armed forces, economy, legal and educational systems, and thus enable the state to compete in a world dominated by European imperialism. The Tanzimat began in 1839, following the accession a new reformist sultan, Abd'l Mecid, and only ended with the cancellation of the 1876 Ottoman Constitution, a mere two years after it had been drawn up.

Murad Bey Paşa's Egyptian cavalry charges the French infantry at the battle of the Pyramids at Giza on July 21, 1798.

The history of the Tanzimat can be divided into two periods, the first beginning with an edict called the *Hatt-ı şerif* and the second in 1856 with the *Hatt-ı humayun* edict. Between the two came the Crimean War, when the Ottoman government faced more immediate problems. Both edicts attempted to improve the lives of the millet communities. In practical terms the Tanzimat consisted of a huge mass of often very detailed legislation, some of which had a serious impact but much of which seems to have had little effect. Western observers dismissed the reforms as merely cosmetic and designed to win European sympathy. Though they were genuine, the edicts were not always workable and the reformers faced considerable conservative opposition within the sultanate, even from the non-Islamic millets who might have expected to benefit from reforms. For example, while refusing to accept the new obligation of military service, Christians and Jews still seemed to expect the benefits of equal Ottoman citizenship.

Abd'l Mecid abdicated in 1861, and his successor Abdulaziz proved less willing or able to press ahead with the Tanzimat. During his reign European economic and financial penetration of the Ottoman system began on a massive scale, frequently marginalizing or even ruining local craft-based industries. In 1874 the Ottoman state's massive debts, not least to foreign bankers, led to a financial collapse. Nevertheless this period had witnessed an increasing assimilation of European ideas by the ruling class. In many respects the Tanzimat largely failed, but at least the Ottoman army was modernized and many of the administrative, educational, and other reforms subsequently carried out by the Turkish Republic under Kemal Atatürk in the 1920s and 1930s were rooted in the previous program.

There were other remarkable changes in the 19th century. Painting and literature, at least among the more educated sections of Ottoman society, were substantially westernized, though for the bulk of the population traditional arts and crafts remained central to their cultural identity. This was as true in Albania and Macedonia in the west as it was of Iraq and Yemen in the east. The ethnic folk arts of these disparate regions retained an extraordinary degree of similarity, the result of long centuries under Ottoman Islamic rule.

In the period of the Tanzimat a degree of weternisation took place—the classical influence is clear in this wooden house (early 19th-century) near Istanbul.

The Russian Bear advances

Of all the Ottomans' neighbors, Russia was the most threatening. Czar Peter the Great (1682–1725) significantly increased the power and effectiveness of the already huge Russian army. His ruthless combination of western technologies and traditional Russian autocratic power created a potential superpower in eastern Europe. Peter's defeat of Swedish invaders and conquest of a substantial stretch of the Baltic coast altered the balance of power in northern Europe. Meanwhile in the deep south, his campaigns began a process which would change the entire political, cultural, religious and even ethnic composition of a far larger part of Europe, and

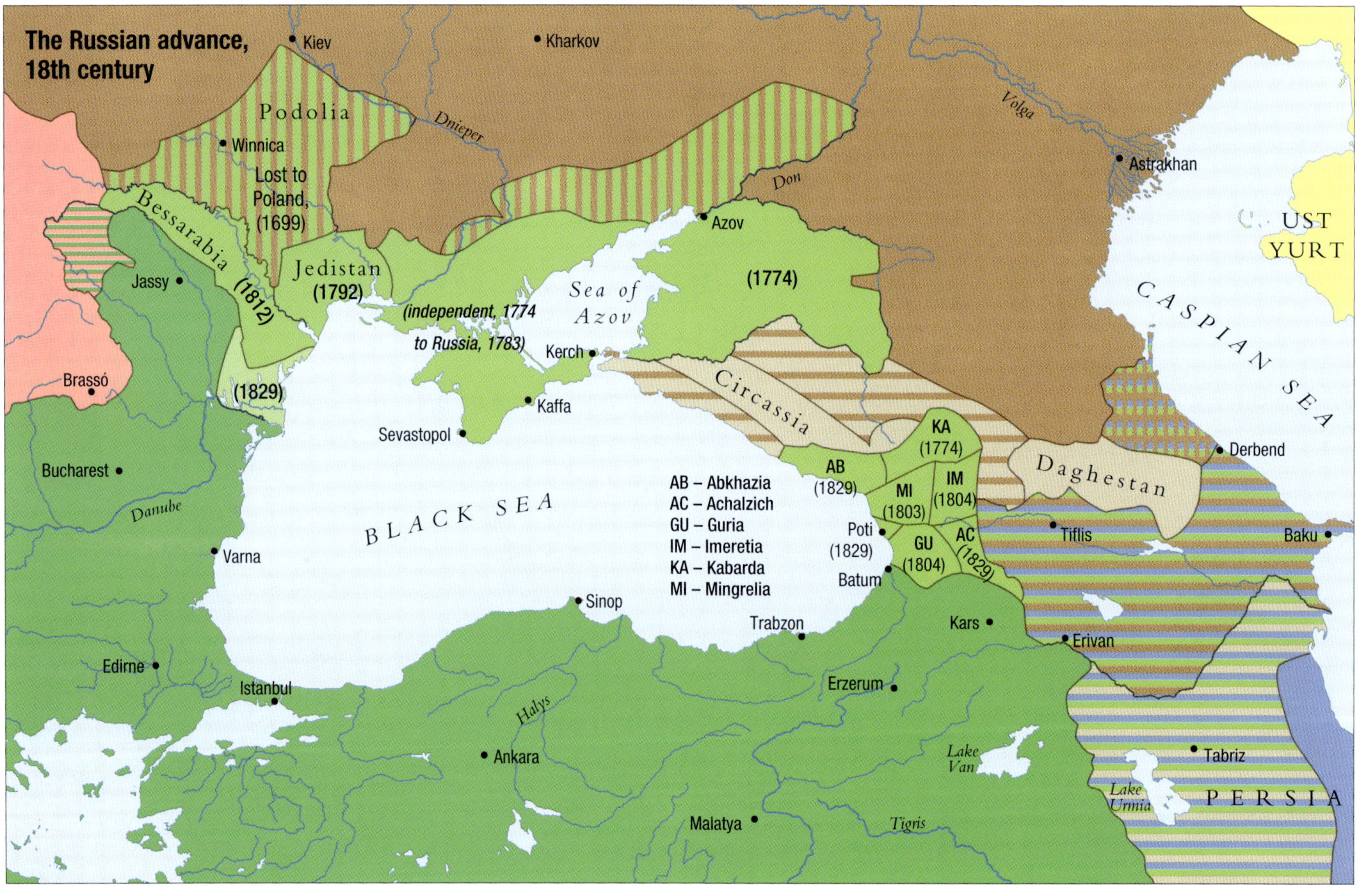

indeed part of Asia. In the short term, the rise of Russia seemed to stall when her army, defeated by the Ottomans, lost the strategic outpost of Azov on the Black Sea in 1711. The supposedly declining Turks also defeated an assault by the Habsburg empire of Austria and Hungary, and regained much recently lost land under provisions of the Treaty of Belgrade in 1739.

But by then things were no longer going so well for the Ottomans north of the Black Sea. Under the Treaty of Belgrade, Russia regained Azov and the lands of the Zaporogian Cossacks who had previously been autonomous vassals of the sultanate. Another Russian-Ottoman war erupted in 1768, during which the Russians gained further territory in and around the Crimea. Even more ominous, the Treaty of Küçük Kaynarca which ended this six-year war in 1774 allowed the czar some rights and duties to "protect" Orthodox Christian inhabitants of the Ottoman state. It was to cause, or be an excuse for, many problems in the future.

CHAPTER NINE: RESTORATION OR REFORM?

The frontiers between the Ottoman sultanate and czarist Russia altered considerably over the following decades and during the Napoleonic Wars, with Russia seizing areas from the Ottomans in what are now southern Ukraine and the Caucasus mountains. The increasingly archaic Ottoman armies performed notably better during another conflict with the Habsburgs in 1788, borders restored with the agreement of Peace of Svishtov in 1791.

The most dramatic Russian advances in the Caucasus were at the expense of previously independent or autonomous Islamic and Christian peoples, with the sultanate and particularly the once-dominant shahs of Persia ceding territory that their predecessors had either ruled or claimed. The ancient state of Georgia soon began to feel the effects of Ottoman-Russian rivalry and in 1722 King Wakhtang VI (1711–24) formed an alliance with Peter the Great. Persia later regained control, though in 1783 the ruler of Georgia once more became a vassal of Russia. The Russians later withdrew most of their forces to face Napoleon, but Georgia remained nominally part of the czarist empire, while the Ottomans ruled Kars to the west plus the coastal region of Abkhazia and the Black Sea enclave of Poti, though the latter two would be lost in 1829.

By the late 18th century it was clear that Russia was determined to dominate the largely Orthodox Christian Balkans and wanted control of the Bosporus and Dardanelles straits. The British feared this Russian ambition, as it threatened their own communications with British-ruled India. Consequently Britain tended to support the Ottomans—though not invariably so. In 1792 the Peace of Jassy ended war between Russia and the Ottomans, and the Dniester which now forms part of the Ukraine-Moldova border was agreed as the frontier, but by 1806 the sultanate would ally with Napoleon's France against Russia and Britain, and a treaty of 1812 would cede Bessarabia (now Moldova) to the Russians.

The behavior of the new Russian authorities in the Crimea, the western Caucasus and coastal regions of the eastern Black Sea led to a massive emigration of Muslims. There was a less well-known migration into Ottoman territory by Christians and Jews fleeing religious, cultural, and political oppression in both Russia and the Habsburg domains. Many of these immigrants settled in Ottoman cities but others became farmers and farm managers on agricultural estates being established by great landowners, thus relieving food shortages felt in many parts of the sultanate. Large numbers of refugees from the Caucasus also settled in disturbed regions of what are now Syria, Jordan, Lebanon, and Palestine as loyal subjects of the sultan who could be relied on to control the rebellious Bedouin tribes.

Commander of the Naked Sword volunteers from the *Fenerci Mehmed Album* (an illustrated compendium of Ottoman uniforms), 1811.

Egypt's bid for independence

Conquered by the Ottomans in 1517, by the end of the 18th century Egypt paid little heed to the Porte in Istanbul. Before Napoleon invaded Egypt in 1798, the country was ruled in way that differed from practically all other provinces of the Ottoman empire. A revival of Mamluk power resulted in the Neo-Mamluk Household System whereby Egypt was dominated by autonomous military leaders who owed only nominal allegiance to the sultan. Despite Napoleon's overwhelming victory over the Mamluks at the Battle of the Pyramids, the Ottomans now allied with Britain and Russia and he was defeated offshore by Nelson; Napoleon's

Bakrwali House in Rashid (Rosetta), Egypt dates from the mid-19th century.

House of Osman (Ottomans)
Sultans from 18th to 20th centuries

1703–30	Ahmed III
1730–54	Mahmut I
1754–57	Osman III
1757–74	Mustafa III
1774–89	Abdul Hamid I
1789–1807	Selim III
1807–08	Mustafa IV
1808–39	Mahmut II
1839–61	Abd'l Mecid
1861–76	Abdulaziz
1876	Murat V
1876–1909	Abdul Hamid II
1909–18	Mehmet V *(Reşad)*
1918–22	Mehmet VI *(Vahdeddin; deposed)*

attempt on Syria was deflected at Acre (1799). The Turkish attempt to retake Egypt failed in 1800 but the French agreed to return it to the Porte at the Peace of Amiens in 1802.

However, Ottoman rule was not firmly reestablished and there was widespread confusion until a powerful new governor emerged in the person of a Turco-Albanian officer named Muhammad Ali, initially with no more than the title of *kaymakam*, sub-governor and commander of Ottoman forces in Egypt. The first and unexpected threat he faced came from a sudden British invasion. Outside Rashid (Rosetta) in 1807, Britain suffered a little-known defeat of the Napoleonic Wars at the hands of Ali's motley army. Four years later, Muhammad Ali consolidated his position by banning the immigration of Mamluk slave recruits into the country and slaughtering the existing Mamluk leadership. Some surviving Mamluks accepted his victory and entered Ali's service, but many more migrated south into the Sudan, where they were to cause problems for years to come.

During these chaotic years Egypt was home to an astonishing variety of soldiers, including Scottish captives taken at the battle of Rashid, German engineers from Napoleon's Tyrolean battalions, French soldiers who had converted to Islam, Greek artillerymen from passing Ottoman armies, and Italians recruited for an American blockade on Tripoli in neighboring Libya (1803–05). As Muhammad Ali's fame spread, many Albanian and Bosnian comrades from his early days as an Ottoman *yol ağa* or road commander in Macedonia joined him in Egypt. In 1820–21 a small number of Americans were among the foreign troops who fought for Muhammad Ali during his invasion of Nubia, or northern Sudan. George Bethune was a Bostonian born in England who converted to Islam and adopted the name Muhammad Effendi. As a *topcı başı* he commanded the artillery. Alongside him an American from New York similarly converted to Islam and took the name Halil Ağa; a third American, name unknown, died of disease during the same Nubian campaign. These may have been the first Americans to fight for Egypt, but they were far from the last. More common foreign recruits came from France and Italy. Like many Asian and African rulers, Muhammad Ali and his grandson Isma'il believed that the only way to resist western imperialism was by a wholesale adoption of western technology and military systems.

The history of 19th-century Egypt reflects the fortunes of its rulers, first styled *paşa* and subsequently raised to the semi-independent status of *khedive* (viceroy). If a graph were drawn, an unexpected rocket to success would be followed by a rapid but not too serious fall, then a long and steady revival before a second and catastrophic collapse. In 1823 a French emigré officer named Captain Sève, known locally as Süleyman Paşa, set about creating a disciplined and uniformed Egyptian army. Muhammad Ali had already failed to force his fellow Albanian warriors into a European military mold; a subsequent attempt to create a medieval-style slave army from the human resources of Muhammad Ali's expanding empire in the Sudan similarly faltered, as the paşa's slave soldiers died faster than they could be trained. Muhammad Ali's answer was revolutionary for Egypt. He decided to conscript the tough, hard-working and patient though traditionally unwarlike Egyptian *fellahin* peasantry. The desperate acts of self-mutilation many used to avoid conscription indicate the unpopularity of this development.

Many other European instructors offered their services at this time. Italians were

CHAPTER NINE: RESTORATION OR REFORM?

involved in Egypt's new navy, Spaniards in the artillery and Poles in the cavalry. Nevertheless, Muhammad Ali put greatest emphasis on the considerable infantry forces required to garrison an ever-expanding empire within Egypt, the Sudan, and Arabia. The first duty of this *Nizam al-Jadid* or New Army was internal security, with small units stationed in villages and each quarter of every city as local police. A chance for the Nizam al-Jadid to show off its military capabilities to the European powers came in Greece during the Greeks' battle for independence when, in 1821, transported Egyptian troops virtually crushed the rebellion that the Ottoman sultan's forces had been unable to defeat. Egypt was officially no more than another province of the Ottoman state and in return for the help given in Greece,

The Turco-Albanian Muhammad Ali, born in Kavála, Greek Macedonia in 1769, founded the dynasty that eventually took Egypt out of the Ottoman sphere of influence. This contemporary engraving—in common with most portraits of the Egyptian viceroy—displays the genial appearance that disguised his brutal ruthlessness.

A motley crew of European and American military adventurers flocked to the Egyptian banner of Muhammad Ali and helped build him a modern military system. This lithograph shows Muhammad Ali with a certain Colonel Patrick Campbell and French engineeers.

Muhammad Ali requested governorship of Syria and Palestine, in addition to that of Egypt, newly conquered Sudan, and much of Arabia. This was refused by Mahmut II, a sultan motivated by the failures of overthrown predecessor Mustafa IV, who himself had seized Selim III's throne. A resulting quarrel led to hostilities in which Mahmut's tough but disorganized troops lost several battles to the properly equipped and disciplined soldiers of Egypt. When it was over, Muhammad Ali controlled virtually all the Middle Eastern Arab provinces of the Ottoman state, with the notable exception of Iraq.

In the following years modernization and westernization continued in Egypt, while Ottoman forces were similarly rebuilt, often along Prussian lines with Prussian advisors. When the quarrel between the Egyptian governor and Ottoman sultan flared up again, the troops ranged against each other were advised by Frenchmen and Germans respectively. At the main battle of Nezib in 1839, Muhammad Ali's eldest son Ibrahim Paşa commanded the Egyptians, supported by General Beaufort d'Hautpoul; Ottoman commander Hafiz Paşa facing him had a young Prussian named Helmuth von Moltke (1800–91) on his staff. At Nezib the French-advised Egyptians were victorious, but d'Hautpoul and von Moltke would meet again in the Franco-Prussian War 32 years later with a very different outcome.

Somewhat shortsightedly, perhaps, most European powers preferred to see a weak Turkey rather than a strong Egypt in the Near and Middle East. So Russia, Britain, and Austria-Hungary invaded the eastern Mediterranean at the sultan's request. The Lebanese coast was seized and, in the

CHAPTER NINE: RESTORATION OR REFORM?

The Crimean War (1853–56) was the first conflict in which photography played a part. Pioneer newspaper photographer Roger Fenton's plate shows Ahmad Manliki, commander of the Egyptian contingent that fought alongside British, French, and Turkish forces, taking a break for a pipe of tobaccco.

subsequent Treaty of London in 1841, Muhammad Ali was obliged to reduce his army to a mere 18,000 men. Egypt's hard-won empire was returned to direct Ottoman rule, even including the Eritrean enclaves on the Red Sea, though Egypt retained control of the Sudan. In return Ali and his family were given governorship of Egypt in perpetuity.

In 1848 Muhammad Ali died, to be briefly succeeded by his soldier-son Ibrahim, who died that same year. Ali's more peaceful and conservative grandson Abbas Hilmi became paşa and it was not until Abbas was succeeded by his uncle

A 19th-century watercolor of a bugler in Muhammad Ali's army. In contrast to the slightly later uniform shown on page 150, this dress—especially the pantaloons— looks as if it comes from a previous era.

A blundering waste of French, British, Russian and Turkish lives, the Crimean War paved the way for a more modern Ottoman Turkish state to emerge over the next century. This 19th-century painting shows French forces battling for Malakov, a hill fort overlooking Sevastopol.

149

Muhammad Sa'id in 1854 that Egypt returned to the modernizing and expansionist policies of Muhammad Ali. However, Sa'id did not seek independence. Instead he proved to be a loyal servant of the Porte, sending a crack force of Egyptian troops to fight alongside the sultan's British, French, and Piedmontese (Italian) allies in the Crimean War (1853–56) against Russia. Such was the reputation earned by these Egyptians, most notably in defense of Eupatoria, that France later asked Sa'id Paşa to provide a battalion to help in Mexico. This extraordinary expeditionary force, commanded by Yabrit Allah, sailed from Alexandria in 1862. A handful of survivors returned to be wildly fêted in Paris before landing back in Egypt on May 28, 1867, where they were reviewed by their new sovereign, Isma'il, who had been promoted by the Ottoman sultan to the status of khedive.

Fragmentation in the Balkans

While loyalty to the Ottoman empire came and went and came again in the Middle East, revolts and financial crises had weakened the Porte's hold on all of the Ottoman provinces. The Turks' first European possessions in the Balkans were among the first to shake loose. In the late 18th to early 19th centuries, the sultan faced disobedience in widespread though small-scale revolts and through the economic decline that undermined his government's ability to finance defense and administration. The impoverishment of existing military groups meant that a large proportion had to find alternative means of making a living, some becoming so desperate that they turned to banditry.

While the sultan's authority had declined in the late 18th century, local Muslim leaders or *ayans* had risen to power in many provinces. The most successful assembled private armies that were often more numerous, better paid and better equipped than those of the official Ottoman governors. Some of these ayans, such as Ali Paşa of Janina (Ioánina), established highly effective regimes with considerable support from the local population. Regular Ottoman troops were even thinner on the ground in traditionally autonomous regions of the Balkans such as Wallachia and Moldavia. Within Anatolia the sultan controlled only a few provinces, the rest having been in a state of rebellion for decades, to a greater or lesser extent. As one European visitor

A captain in the Egyptian battalion which served with the French in Mexico poses for the new-fangled camera in 1867.

Uniforms of the First "New Army" of Sultan Mahmud II, after 1826. By contrast, Egyptian uniforms, with the influence of European advisors, were looking distinctly more modern (**right**); mid-19th century French drawing of a bugler of the Egyptian Artillery.

CHAPTER NINE: RESTORATION OR REFORM?

▓ (green)	Ottoman territory, c.1840
▓ (yellow)	Greece, c.1840
▓ (orange)	Ionian islands and Cerigo (Kythera)
▓	Russia
▓	gained by Russia, 1829
▓	Habsburg Austrian empire
▓	other Christian state
Ottoman vassals and autonomous territory	
▓	Montenegro, autonomous since 1600s
▓	Serbia, autonomous from 1817
▓	territory ceded to Serbia, 1833
▓	Crete under Viceroy of Egypt, 1824–40
▓	Moldavia & Wallachia from vassal to autonomous status. 1829
▓	Danubian enclaves ceded to Wallachia, 1829
▓	Chios and Samos autonomous from 1832

wrote, "It is governed by independent *ağas*, or chiefs of districts, revolted from oppression, every man asserting and maintaining his own." A concerted effort by Mahmut II reimposed the sultanate's authority in much of Anatolia in 1812–17.

The fragmentation and weakening of Ottoman authority in the Balkans was one of the most noticeable aspects of 19th century eastern European history. Some historians have even described it as a key factor in destabilizing Europe as a whole after the defeat of Napoleon. The process was complicated and embittered by the fact that Balkan nationalism developed in a part of Europe where national, linguistic, religious, and supposed ethnic identities were far less clear-cut than in western or even central Europe. Communities overlapped and intermingled to an astonishing degree, which led to frequently savage competition for territory—or even for survival.

The peoples of western Europe generally had much greater sympathy with the nationalist aspirations of the region's Christian peoples than for the Muslims. In contrast, governments were far less concerned, as the international priorities of the period were peace and stability at almost any price. Popular European sympathies were above all aroused by the Greeks, the supposed heirs of Classical civilization, and their increasing desire for independence. This Greek-loving philhellene movement was particularly strong among artists, poets, and other cultural leaders, the most famous of whom was Lord George Byron (1788–1824), who died in Greece while trying to unify local forces against the Ottomans.

Yet it was the Romanian-speaking and traditionally autonomous provinces of Moldavia and Wallachia which were the first to revolt against Ottoman rule in 1821, encouraged by the Russian czar's Greek minister, John Capodistria. This uprising failed but was rapidly followed by the much more successful Greek War of Independence (1821–29). After a weak start, Ottoman efforts to crush this rebellion were effective, largely thanks to the presence of the modern Egyptian army of Muhammad Ali, as mentioned above. However, the combined Ottoman fleets of Turkey, Egypt, and Tunisia were obliterated by a mixed British, French, and Russian navy at Navarino on October 20, 1827, which eventually ensured Greece the independence she had failed to win on the battlefield. It would, however, be many decades before central Greece and most of the Aegean islands were incorporated into the new Greek kingdom, while Crete and northern Greece were not won until the early 20th century. Rhodes and the Dodecanese islands had to wait until after the Second World War.

Serbia's 13 years of revolt against the Ottomans ended in 1817 when they were

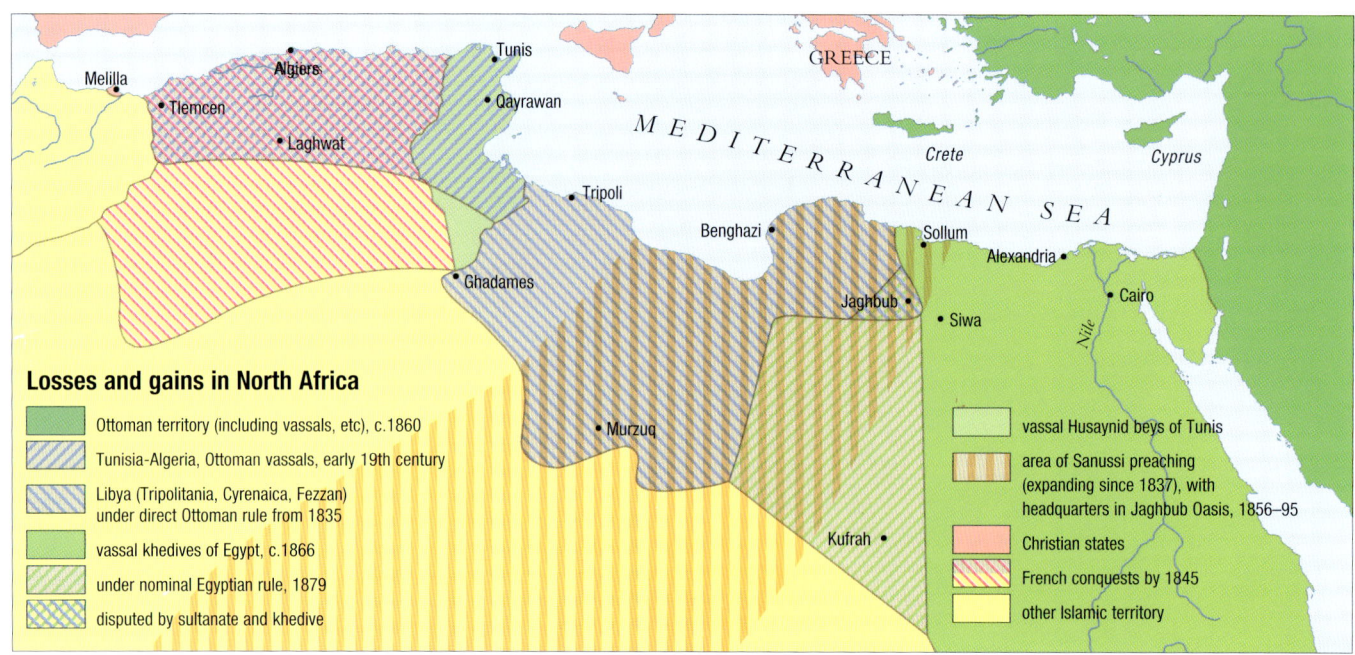

Losses and gains in North Africa
- Ottoman territory (including vassals, etc), c.1860
- Tunisia-Algeria, Ottoman vassals, early 19th century
- Libya (Tripolitania, Cyrenaica, Fezzan) under direct Ottoman rule from 1835
- vassal khedives of Egypt, c.1866
- under nominal Egyptian rule, 1879
- disputed by sultanate and khedive
- vassal Husaynid beys of Tunis
- area of Sanussi preaching (expanding since 1837), with headquarters in Jaghbub Oasis, 1856–95
- Christian states
- French conquests by 1845
- other Islamic territory

given autonomy, followed by Moldavia and Wallachia 17 years later. In 1861 the latter two merged as the United Provinces, the forerunner of modern Romania, but Serbia remained confined to a small area, despite some limited territorial gains. All, including tiny Montenegro to the west, remained autonomous within the Ottoman sultanate until the major upheavals of the 1870s.

Gains and Losses in North Africa

For hundreds of years, the sultans had delegated authority along the Barbary Coast to the regencies of Tripolitania, Tunisia, and Algeria. However, in each North African area the paşas, beys, deys, and other governors controlled little more than a narrow coastal strip. The military and administrative capabilities of each regency also differed considerably. For example, in Tripoli the senior officials included a guardian *başı* or chief of the palace, a *kâhya* or paşa's lieutenant with an assistant, five administrative ministers, plus a unit of Turkish soldiers and a general in command of local Arab cavalry. Traditionally, the paşa's eldest son commanded the army as a whole. The paşa also had an elite guard of extremely loyal *hampas*, black African soldiers recruited as slaves and armed with short blunderbuss muskets. Among an array of other exotic military units were the *Kuloğlıs*, described as the offspring of Turkish Janissary fathers and local Libyan mothers. In reality most Kuloğlıs were merchants and craftsmen who felt more akin to the indigenous Arabs or Berbers than to the ruling Turks.

Strange as such defensive forces may have looked to westerners at the start of the 19th century, they remained disciplined and skilled, though admittedly old-fashioned. When an American fleet attacked the so-called pirate haven of Tripoli in 1803, the Janissaries and Kuloğlıs of the garrison fought back in an orderly manner under heavy fire, while their religious leaders stood on the parapets reading from the Koran. Subsequent efforts to modernize Tripoli's forces had some success and enabled Yusuf, the greatest of the local Karamanli dynasty, to dominate the northern parts of the trans-Saharan trade routes. Further south the Saharan oases collectively

A Kuloğlı soldier of Tripoli.

known as Fezzan had been under the sultan's authority several times.

To the east, the more tribal and anarchic province of Cyrenaica had become the headquarters of an Islamic reformist movement, the Sanussi, though still under nominal Ottoman rule, while to the west the French occupied Algiers in 1830, ostensibly to suppress piracy. Thereafter, French forces moved inland and eventually conquered most of the Sahara Desert. The Ottomans immediately responded to this penetration of lands which had been Islamic since the Middle Ages, and in 1835 a naval expedition reimposed direct rule on Libyan Tripolitania. Fezzan was occupied in 1842, Ghat in 1875, and the Tibesti mountains in 1879, deeper into the Sahara than the Porte's authority had ever extended before.

To some degree the Ottoman sultanate, like its vassal the khedivate in Egypt, was simply responding in kind to the 19th century European empires' scramble for African territory, and as late as 1910–11 the Sanussi and other independent Saharan tribes called for the protection of the Ottoman flag. Within months, however, Italy invaded Ottoman Libya with the tacit approval of most European powers. Squeezed between Ottoman Libya and French-ruled Algeria was Tunisia, whose ruling paşa also had a small and at one time effective army. This originally included Janissaries recruited directly from Anatolia, the Greek islands, and the Balkans. Sometimes Janissaries on their way to serve in Algeria were persuaded to jump ship and join the Tunisians who offered better pay and modern weapons imported directly from western Europe.

While the French invasion of Algeria prompted a consolidation of Ottoman rule in Libya, it also led the autonomous governor of Tunis, Husayn Bey, to establish a new army of what were called Nizami troops, trained and organized along European lines. French missions played a major role in creating this new force but the results were never satisfactory. By the time of the unopposed French occupation of Tunisia in 1881, the Tunisian soldiers were described as unpaid, wearing tattered uniforms, training for at best an hour a day and spending the rest of their time knitting stockings, making rugs, and repairing shoes to earn some money. The French occupation was transformed into a protectorate of France two years later, after which the beys ruled as little more than puppets of a French resident-general.

Above right: Sidi Husayn, the Bey of Tripoli

Right: An Algerian cavalryman, painted by the French artist Géricault, 1820s.

CHAPTER TEN

Striving for Modernization

From the Hamidian Age to the skies

During the late 19th century, the Ottoman sultanate was widely regarded as The Sick Man of Europe. For 200 years the once-mighty Ottoman Turks had been losing territory to their European neighbors, while in more recent times large Balkan provinces had broken away to form the increasingly autonomous and in some cases independent states of Montenegro, Serbia, Romania, Greece, and eventually Bulgaria. The Ottoman empire was also wracked by internal problems. Muslims competed with Christians, Kurds with Armenians, reformists with conservatives, those who saw the Ottoman future in secular terms and those who retained a religious view. By 1900 these problems appeared to be tearing the sultanate apart, while old predatory neighbors like Russia and Austria-Hungary had been joined by a pack of Balkan states that had every intention of driving the Ottomans out of Europe entirely. Nor were the Asian and African provinces secure. Armenian nationalism was on the rise and there were even stirrings in some Arab provinces. Russia once again made no secret of its ambitions south of the Caucasus. France conquered most of North Africa and proclaimed a close interest in the fate of Lebanon's Christians. Britain occupied Egypt, the Sudan, Cyprus, and had seized the southernmost parts of Yemen with the strategic port of Aden, while Italy cast covetous eyes over Libya.

Yet in 1900 the sultanate remained vast. It stretched from close to Sarajevo in Bosnia to the Yemen, from the Persian Gulf to the oasis of Ghadames south of Tunisia. Other peripheral lands were still at least technically Ottoman, including the Austro-Hungarian protectorate of Bosnia-Herzegovina and the Anglo-Egyptian province of Equatoria in southern Sudan. The supposed sick man had tried to heal himself. Nineteenth-century Ottoman history included some notable military victories as well as better-known defeats. Some aspects of the economy were flourishing and communications were certainly improving, though from an exceptionally primitive starting point.

Surrounded by foes, modernization of the sultanate's bureaucracy and military had been given top priority since the early 19th century. Until the end of that century, concepts of democracy and national self-determination were seen as irrelevant but were beginning to surface, not only among subject Christian peoples such as the Greeks and Armenians, but also among Muslim Turks and Arabs who, with the Kurds, formed the great majority of the Ottoman population by 1900. The administration was quite unlike what it had been a hundred years earlier.

In 1876 a new sultan, Abdul Hamid II, came to the throne at the age of 34 with a reputation as a serious but dour young man. Two years later he shelved the new constitution and ruled autocratically. Popular opinion seemed happy with the return

Portrait of a tough-minded new ruler: the colored lithograph of "Abdul Hamid II Sultan of Turkey," which came from a set of carefully posed photographs taken in about 1880, was widely circulated and made his face as well known in the West as it was in the Orient.

of a strong-willed monarch determined to save the state from its many enemies, and the Hamidian period, as Abdul Hamid's reign came to be known, was one of increased centralization and considerably more continuity of policy. The sultan intervened more directly than predecessors had done for many years, and an elaborate secret service provided information directly to the palace. Abdul Hamid also took advice from unorthodox religious leaders, including members of dervish and sufi mystical sects. In response to Balkan Christian nationalism, a closer alliance developed between the Islamic establishment and the Ottoman government than had been seen for decades. Abdul Hamid's pan-Islamic ideology sought to contrast the toleration enjoyed by Christians within the Ottoman state with the oppression suffered by many Muslims in the newly independent Balkan states and in some European colonial empires.

Nevertheless, the sultan could not overcome Europe's deep-seated anti-Islamic prejudice that recognized him and his empire as protector of Muslims worldwide but also portrayed him as Abdul the Damned, persecutor of Christians within the Ottoman empire. This caricature became even more pronounced following disturbances in eastern Anatolia in the 1890s when Muslim refugees from Russia joined with local Muslim villagers to take revenge for the killing of their coreligionists by Armenian Hunçak terrorists and Dashnak revolutionaries. As a persecutor, Abdul Hamid was inevitably damned the most by circumstances in the Balkans. At the start of the 20th century the Ottoman empire still included Thrace, Macedonia, and Albania but they were bounded by recently independent ex-Ottoman provinces. Each side was fortified by its own tradition of martyrs and memories of massacre. In European mythology it was the Muslim Turks who massacred Christian Greeks, Bulgarians, and Serbs, though in reality the Muslims may have suffered more as ever-widening areas fell under Christian control. As a result, the remaining Ottoman territories were crowded with refugees, many of whom had been forced to migrate more than once. Muslim villages were frequently raided, officially or unofficially, from neighboring Balkan states, though rarely from Greece.

"Abdul the Damned (with blood on his hands)" became the iconic Wicked Turk in Christian European minds, excoriated in magazine lampoons like this one of 1901 by August Roubille.

The most backward of the remaining Ottoman areas in Europe was Albania. Almost three-quarters of its population were Muslim, inhabiting a poor and mountainous land where loyalties remained essentially tribal. A nationalist movement had flickered into life between 1878 and 1881, but this had been directed against Bulgarian, Serbian, and Montenegrin claims rather than Ottoman authority. In the early years of the 20th century Albania's nationalism was revived, with widespread disorder resulting in virtual autonomy being given to the four Albanian provinces. Nevertheless, Albanian leadership remained divided between those seeking independence with European support, most of which were Catholics, and those favoring a continued link with the sultanate.

The situation in Macedonia was even more confused. This was home to a population of Turks, Bulgars, Greeks, Serbs, Albanians, Vlachs (linguistically akin to the

Ruins of a mosque near Parakila, Lesbos; remains of the once-great Ottoman empire littered the Balkans and Aegean basin.

Opposite: Drums of the Egyptian Army's 11th Sudanese Regiment, dating from the late 19th century.

Romanians), Jews, Gypsies, those regarding themselves as specifically Macedonian, and others. None formed a clear majority. Greece, Bulgaria, Serbia, and even Romania laid some claim to this area, while the Muslim population, numbering almost half of the total, looked to Istanbul for protection against the persecution which had become a feature of Christian Balkan rule elsewhere. Macedonia's strategic location in the heart of the Balkan peninsula also ensured that the outside European powers took a keen interest in its problems. While neighboring Balkan states argued over the future of Macedonia, their territories served as bases for various secret societies that ravaged the province. The European press—which had enthusiastically embraced the joys of modern moralism, crusading against atrocity while parading its violence for the horrified facination of its readership—proclaimed the sufferings of Christians, virtually ignoring those of Muslims, and even blamed the Ottoman authorities for terrorist outrages.

An Ottoman reform program was answered by an uprising on the part of the Bulgarian-backed Internal Macedonian Revolutionary Organisation (IMRO), which was also the most violent of the dissident groups. This in turn prompted savage suppression by the Ottoman army. Thousands of terrified Christians fled to Bulgaria while thousands of petrified Muslims went to eastern Thrace, reinforcing the Islamic character of a Balkan region that had been intensively colonized by Turks since the late 14th century.

Two other areas of southeastern Europe remained theoretically part of the sultanate at the start of the 20th century: Bosnia-Herzegovina, an Austro-Hungarian protectorate from 1878 until its annexation in 1908, and the island of Crete, where almost half the population had converted to Islam under Ottoman rule. A savage massacre of Crete's Muslims in 1897 had been followed by Cretan autonomy under a Christian governor supported by a Greek militia. Nevertheless Crete remained technically Ottoman until its annexation by Greece in 1912. Changes within the overwhelmingly Muslim Turkish, Arab and Kurdish provinces of the sultanate would only come into focus during the First World War, a conflict destined to alter the entire shape of the Middle East and bring about the end of a sultanate which had endured for over six centuries.

A New Empire on the Nile

In 1867 Isma'il had been the first of his dynasty to enjoy the title of khedive or hereditary autonomous governor of Egypt. Khedive Isma'il had great ambitions for his country but was aware that the Egyptian army had declined considerably since the glory days of Muhammad Ali's 43-year governorship. A report drawn up by a Russian, Rostislav Fadeiell, convinced Isma'il that success depended on a Europeanized officer corps, while the uneducated rank-and-file should merely obey orders. The officer corps was in need of reform, suffering bitter ethnic rivalry between Turks, Circassians, Albanians, and officers of Arab-Egyptian origin. The paşa system meant that senior commanders regarded their regiments almost as personal property. They resisted outside interference and were often unwilling to delegate even minor tasks. There was widespread illiteracy so that even officers had to rely on Coptic Christian clerks.

Isma'il's first foreign mercenaries had came from Europe but in the late 1860s he and Napoleon III of France quarreled over the financing of the Suez Canal. Work

CHAPTER TEN: STRIVING FOR MODERNISATION

commenced on the canal late in 1858 and took 11 years to complete, opening for business in November 1869, by which time all but three French officers had been sent home. Isma'il was already interested in recruiting veterans of the American Civil War, and the U.S.A. had few political or economic interests in Egypt. New York was a good place in which to recruit since, in addition to ex-Union officers, many ex-Confederates had gone there to restore their fortunes. One such man named Derrick wanted to escape what he termed the "cursed tyranny" of the U.S. government, while another, Graves, compared himself to "Abraham and Lot, who sojourned in Egypt when the famine was grievous in their own country." Isma'il was aware of the potential culture clash and his senior Egyptian officers were told to be patient with these westerners. For example, Major Morgan departed in a hurry after accepting a rose from a member of the khedive's harem then being chased by the lady's eunuch guards.

Prejudice and racism were now added to the old ethnic rivalries in an officer corps that already included Turks, Albanians, Circassians, Egyptians, British, French, Italians, Germans, and Swiss. It was, however, the Americans who played the key role during the 1870s. Mott and Stone revived the defunct Egyptian General Staff while other Americans went to the War Office. A military library and map collection was established and Stone even supported the creation of a military museum. Americans also commanded some of the navy's few ships. Of greater long-term significance for Egypt and the Sudan was the exploration work carried out by American officers. According to one senior officer, Loring, "Egyptian general staff officers, between the years 1871 and 1878, explored and mapped in details more of unknown African territory than all the other explorers of the world."

In military terms, however, the 1870s were disastrous, with Isma'il and General Stone believing that Egyptian authority could be extended across the entire Horn of Africa. King Yohannis of Ethiopia (1872–89) was reestablishing central authority over his country in 1875, the year Isma'il decided to launch a full-scale invasion with the aim of imposing Egyptian regional supremacy. It involved

This engraving shows Egyptian troops under the command of Chaillé-Long attacked by Yanbari tribesmen in southern Sudan. Charles Cahillé-Long (1842–1917), a captain in the U.S. Army, arrived in Egypt in 1869 and was soon made a colonel and bey attached to General Loring's staff. In an adventurous eight-year Egyptian career, Chaillé-Long carried out long treks of exploration into Central Africa, paving the way for eventual Egyptian military campaigns.

assault from three directions under four commanders—three western mercenaries and a Turco-Egyptian. Only Muhammad Rauf Paşa succeeded, his small force striking inland from the Gulf of Aden to take the city of Harar. More remarkable, in light of Egyptian failures under western officers elsewhere, was the continued success of Egyptian troops under Muhammad Rauf's successors at a time when the khedive's authority was collapsing, not only in the Sudan but when Egypt was occupied by the British.

Egyptian soldiers under their own officers continued to perform well, most notably in 1877 when 30,000 fought alongside Ottoman troops against Russians in the Balkans. By then, Isma'il was tiring of American mercenaries and was looking elsewhere for replacements, but Egypt's mounting financial crisis meant that nothing came of his plans. Instead the Egyptian army was reduced drastically and in 1878 all Americans were dismissed, with the exception of General Stone who remained Chief of Staff until 1882. He remained loyal to Khedive Muhammad Tawfiq (1879–92) throughout the army rebellion led by Colonel Urabi Paşa, staying by his side when rebels surrounded Cairo's Abdin palace and when Britain occupied Egypt in 1882.

Young Turks and the Balkan Wars

The Tanzimat reforms of the 19th century had introduced many Ottomans to western political ideas, including the belief that modernization can only succeed if accompanied by social change. Supporters of these concepts came together as a loose coalition of political groups known as the Young Turks. The progressive Young Turks came from a wide variety of backgrounds and could be found in the civil service, military, and educational systems. Other individuals, frustrated by lack of progress, had gone into exile in Europe or British-occupied Egypt. The Young Turks included moderates as well as radicals, but all hoped to save the Ottoman state from western Christian aggression. A few were prepared to use European pressure and even to collaborate with nationalist minorities within the sultanate in the hope of forcing the pace of reform.

CHAPTER TEN: STRIVING FOR MODERNISATION

In 1902 the Congress of Ottoman Liberals was held in Paris, attended by reformers of all shades and by representatives of nationalist minorities. Unfortunately the aspirations of these varied groups differed too much and the congress broke up in disarray. Although Abdul Hamid's security apparatus kept the Committee of Union and Progress under close watch, the CUP's ranks were swelled by increasing numbers of educated young men, ironically many of them graduates of a school system established by the sultan. Unlike earlier reformists, this generation tended to come from humble backgrounds and were not members of the old Ottoman ruling class. They were also more inclined to use force to achieve political change, particularly in light of Ottoman failure to deal with nationalist terrorism and worsening corruption in a government dominated by the sultan's palace. Secret Young Turk revolutionary cells even developed within the Ottoman officer corps, among whom was Mustafa Kemal, who founded an organization that became known as the Ottoman Liberty Society. Mustafa Kemal's hometown of Salonika (Thessaloniki) became a major center for such activity and his group found many supporters within the Ottoman Third Army garrisoning Macedonia.

Contemporary engraving of Khedive Muhammad Tawfiq of Egypt.

The Congress of Reformists met in Paris in 1907. For a while it seemed that Young Turks and Armenian Dashnak revolutionaries would cooperate, but it was not to be. The Young Turk revolution, when it came, was an independent and rather haphazard affair. It was once thought that a widespread conspiracy led to the

Tailor's chart for the new-style khaki Ottoman Army uniforms, 1909–18.

Young Turk revolt of 1908. In reality, it seems to have been triggered by a series of unplanned responses by disaffected Third Army officers who feared a purge by Abdul Hamid's security forces. Trouble began when an officer named Niyazi, leader of a CUP cell, took to the hills of Macedonia and demanded the restoration of the 1876 Constitution. His call was taken up by mutineers and demonstrators throughout the region. Investigations, arrests, and fresh troops merely accelerated the revolt; many of the newly arrived soldiers joined the rebels.

The CUP in Salonika was caught unprepared by this sudden upsurge of revolutionary feeling and had not joined the revolt when, on 23 July, the sultan anticipated their action by recalling Parliament. Abdul Hamid declared that his original suspension of the indirectly elected assembly and the Constitution had been merely to allow modernization to take place. Now that modernization was underway, he declared, it was again time for Parliament to share the burden of saving the empire. Despite such claims, there was no doubt that the sultan had surrendered and that the Ottoman state

was changing from autocracy to some form of constitutional government.

The events of 1908 didn't quite add up to a revolution, but they did make one possible the following year when a coup overthrew Abdul Hamid. College-trained *harbiye* army officers benefited most from the change. Protests from *alaye* officers who had risen from the ranks, along with those of Islamic fundamentalists, were crushed, while the powers of the new sultan, Mehmet V, were severely curtailed. The Ottoman army now took precedence over all other aspects of the state, while the Young Turk CUP developed into a fully-fledged political party. It won a landslide in the 1912 election and seized complete power the following January. In many ways this was the first of those quasi-military coups that would become a feature of the Middle East for the rest of the 20th century.

In practical terms, the Young Turks continued with reforms that had been attempted earlier. Decentralization was rejected and all effort was directed toward concentrating power in the hands of the government, streamlining the administration, and strengthening the armed forces. A new emphasis was placed on economic development, while the Young Turks were less inclined to compromise with opponents than their predecessors had been.

Three political concepts competed for domination: traditional multi-cultural Ottomanism, a Pan-Islamic vision which sought to draw in all Muslims whatever their ethnic or linguistic heritage, and a narrower ethnically based pan-Turkish nationalism which envisaged some sort of union between the Turks of the Ottoman empire and those who lived further east. Yet there is little evidence that such intellectual speculation had much impact on the majority of Young Turks, who still had to govern a multi-ethnic, multi-faith empire. Nevertheless, the seeds of Turkish nationalism were planted and contact between the sultanate and the huge numbers of Turkish-speakers living under foreign, mostly Russian, rule gradually increased.

A 1906 American postcard makes offensive fun of sterotypes.

The German military mission that had operated in Turkey for many decades was having a steady influence on the Ottoman army, while British advisors had rather less impact on the navy. A fledging air force began in 1912, largely under French guidance (*see pages 165–66*), and there was a complete overhaul of the provincial gendarmerie. Most foreign observers were unaware of the depth of such changes and, following humiliating defeats at the hands of the Balkan states and Italy in 1911–12, the resilience of the Ottoman army during the First World War came as a great surprise to its French, British, and Russian enemies.

Throughout this tumultuous period, the sultanate's neighbors inevitably took advantage whenever they could. In 1908 Austria-Hungary formally annexed Bosnia-Herzegovina, and in 1911 Italy attacked Libya. There a tiny Ottoman garrison, vigorously supported by tribal and the Islamic reformist Sanussi forces, initially confined the invaders to a narrow coastal strip but could not alter the fact that the Ottomans were losing their last directly ruled African territory. The Italians also sent weapons to Montenegro, encouraged Albanian dissidents, seized Rhodes and the other

Dodecanese islands in the Aegean in 1912, and even threatened the Dardanelles. In October 1912, one week before peace was concluded between Italy and the Ottoman sultanate, Montenegrin forces marched into northern Albania. This was the opening campaign of the First Balkan War, in which the Ottomans were defeated by a coalition of Montenegro, Serbia, Bulgaria, and Greece. The Greeks promptly annexed Crete, while the outnumbered Ottoman army in Europe lost everything except part of Albania, a few besieged cities and a small area west of Istanbul.

Food shortages and hordes of refugees haunted the empire. The Bulgarians surrounded Edirne and, when an armistice expired without a peace agreement, bombarded the ancient city and starved it into surrender. They also began to violently expel the Turkish Muslim peasants of eastern Thrace. Peace was agreed at the end of May 1913 but it did not last long. The Christian coalition soon fell out over its spoils and in the brief Second Balkan War, which began on June 30, 1913, Bulgaria pitted itself against its erstwhile allies plus Romania. It gave the Ottomans a chance to regain Edirne and eastern Thrace, even including a small area west of the Maritsa river. Albania, meanwhile, was declared independent—though its neighbors still cast covetous eyes on this new and largely Islamic state.

A museum-piece locomotive at Istanbul's main station (top); only two incomplete sections through the Taurus Mountains prevented Muslim pilgrims from making the journey from Istanbul to Medina by railroad. Today, parts of the line are abandoned—a bridge fails to span the Yarmouk river between Jordan and Syria.

Peace was agreed on August 10 of the same year. Despite the regaining of Edirne, the Ottomans had suffered a huge disaster with the loss of 83 percent of their European territory and almost 70 percent of their European population.

Problems in the east

A third of Anatolia's people—around 17.5 million in 1912—were Armenian, Kurdish, Georgian, Greek, Iranian, and Arab minorities. As in the Balkans, the Ottomans struggled for identity and control here and in Mesopotamia, Arabia, and Syria. In the period between 1878 and 1914, western Anatolia and the northern coastal belt enjoyed a period of prosperity. As a result of refugee settlement there had been considerable extension of cultivation but also much social unrest. Existing Christian communities (17 percent of the total in 1912) often endured hostility from Muslim newcomers who had themselves suffered at Christian hands—largely in the Balkans—in the past. The indigenous population of Muslims and Christians was also increasing.

In eastern Anatolia the main population groups of Turks, Armenians, and Kurds were inextricably mixed. The Kurds traditionally resisted the reestablishment of Ottoman central authority, though they remained loyal to the sultan, while the Armenians now looked to Russia for support. Russian military successes raised Armenian political hopes but stimulated Muslim fears

CHAPTER TEN: STRIVING FOR MODERNISATION

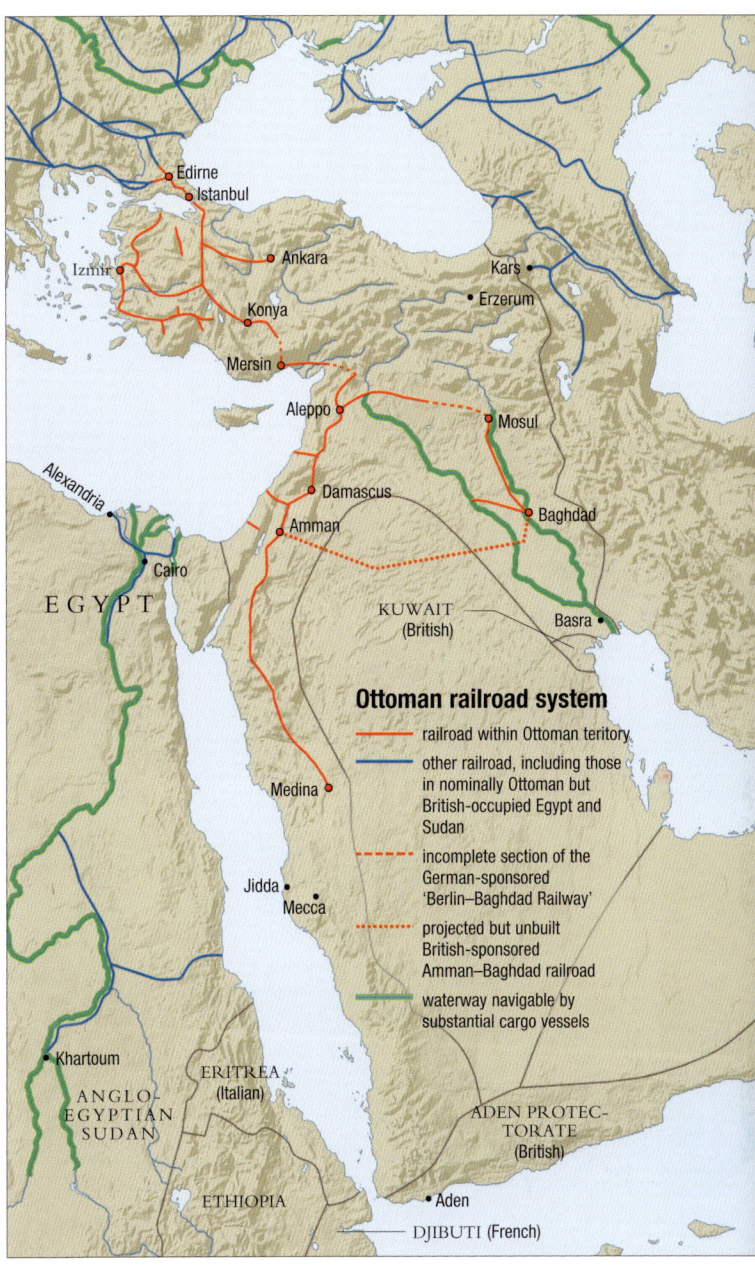

of their Christian neighbors. These factors had contributed to serious bloody clashes between Kurds and Armenians in the late 19th century. Some 860,000 Armenians lived in six eastern provinces that had earlier formed their medieval kingdom, but in none did they now constitute a majority. Nevertheless, there was a heightening political consciousness, partly as a result of improved education and greater contact with Armenian communities abroad. The main external Armenian nationalist groups were the pro-Russia Dashnaks and the Hunçaks, who were accused of terrorist activity within Ottoman territory. The Muslims, primarily Kurds, responded by attacking Armenian villagers.

British-occupied Cyprus, Egypt, and the Sudan theoretically formed part of the Ottoman sultanate until 1914, but in practical terms the Turks ruled only Greater Syria (now Syria, Lebanon, Palestine, Israel, and Jordan), Iraq, and most of the Arabian peninsula, while pro-Ottoman resistance continued in Libya. Syria was then, as now, a religious and confessional mosaic. Early stirrings of Arab nationalism were only one political strand among many and most remained loyal to the Porte. Only in predominantly Maronite Christian Mount Lebanon was there a tendency for some of the elite to look abroad for political solutions. Like western Anatolia, Greater Syria as a whole was enjoying increased prosperity as cultivation expanded, towns grew and the population rose to four million.

The situation in Mesopotamia was different again. This area consisted of culturally, economically, religiously and linguistically differing provinces. Though its population was overwhelmingly tribal, there had been a substantial decline in nomadism and a corresponding increase in agriculture. Education, again organized on confessional grounds, was spreading in towns, where an outward-looking Jewish community particularly prospered from increasing trade. In the late 19th and early 20th centuries there were considerable Ottoman efforts to improve communications. The construction of railroads was the most dramatic development and some modern

Above: The ornate facade of the terminal railroad station at the end of the Hijaz Line, at Medina.

Newly commissioned Ottoman Army officer-cadets pose proudly for the camera in 1913. The new "heavier than air" pilots were recruited from among the corps of cavalry officers.

Making do: the advent of aerial warfare forced several changes of plan, such as this makeshift anti-aircraft gun made from an up-ended Ottoman artillery piece, c.1914.

roads were built, though Asian provinces were still poorly served when the First World War broke out. Some ports were modernized and the telegraph had arrived, as had modern newspapers in various languages.

Not until the construction of the railroad from Damascus to Medina was Ottoman rule firmly reestablished in the Hijaz and Yemen. Control of Arabia's interior was mostly limited to playing one tribal group off against another. At the heart of the peninsula, Wahhabi Islamic fundamentalists reasserted themselves under the political leadership of 'Abd al-Aziz ibn Sa'ud, who later founded the kingdom of Saudi Arabia. Generally, the Arabian peninsula was divided between Ottoman and British spheres of influence, confirmed in March 1914 by an agreement which defined these zones as either side of an imaginary line between the Aden-Yemen frontier in the south and Qatar on the Gulf coast in the north.

The spread of literature and literacy naturally had an impact on the development of nationalist sentiments. The rebirth of Arabic literature has sometimes been ascribed to the Lebanese Christian community and western missionaries, but this appears to contradict the flowering of secular Arabic writing and printing earlier in the 19th century. Other forms of culture were less westernized in the Arab provinces than in the Turkish heartland of the Ottoman state. Artistic expression remained largely within existing Islamic forms. Though traditional, these were by no means static—essentially Turkish rug-weaving techniques spread to relatively isolated Arab areas, for example, while in Anatolia considerable migration and the arrival of refugee communities had a comparable impact on the repertoire of traditional decorative styles.

The Ottomans embrace aviation

As mentioned on page 161, the technology of powered flight arrived in the sultanate through the offices of the French. Although the circumstances in which the Ottoman air force was created were far from ideal, as part of a modernization process it enabled the ruling dynasty to briefly outlast its rivals and allies in Russia, Austria-Hungary and Germany. Aviation was not entirely new to the Ottomans. They had experimented in the 17th century and indulged in the ballooning craze of the late 18th and 19th centuries. As recently as 1909 the French balloonist Ernest Barbotte had ascended from Taksim Square in Istanbul. A kite balloon helped the besieged Ottoman garrison of Edirne during the First Balkan War; an airship purchased from Germany proved less successful.

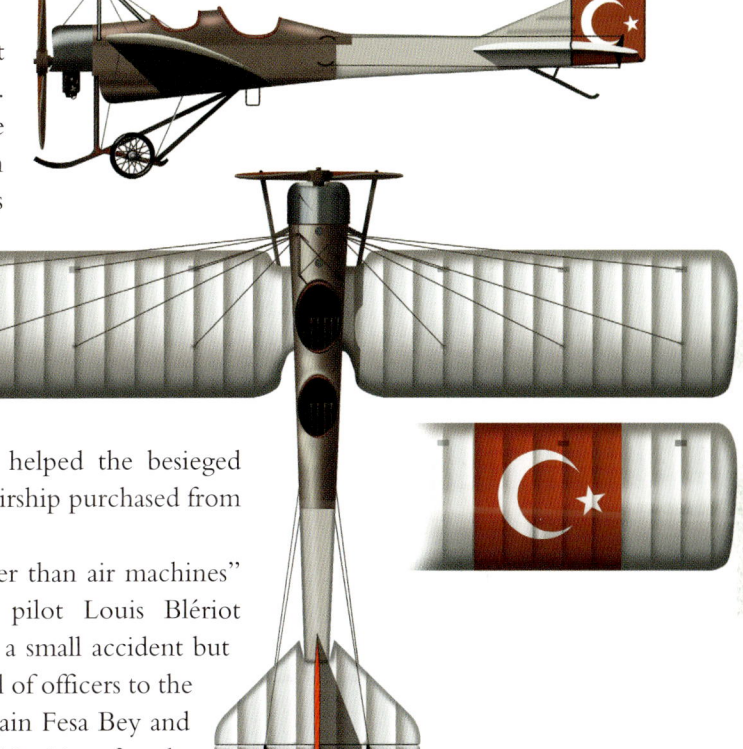

A two-seater Deperdussin TT named *Osmanli* first painted with the Ottoman-Turkish identification markings on the tailplane and the underside of the wings in 1913. Osmanli was one of the aircraft that took part in the propagandist flight from Istanbul to Alexandria in 1914.

The Ottomans concentrated on forming a unit of "heavier than air machines" and in November–December 1909 the famous French pilot Louis Blériot (1872–1936) flew over Istanbul. His aircraft was damaged in a small accident but the Ottoman army was sufficiently impressed to send a handful of officers to the Blériot Flying School near Paris. The first two, Cavalry Captain Fesa Bey and Engineer Lieutenant Yusuf Kenan gained their wings in 1911. Aircraft only played a minor role in Italy's unprovoked assault on Ottoman territory the same year, but before the Italian occupation of Libya and the Dodecanese Islands was complete, the Turks faced a joint invasion of remaining territory in Europe in the First Balkan War. The first Ottoman air force aeroplanes were also French, including a single-seater and a two-seater Deperdussin which arrived on March 15, 1912. Hangers were constructed over the next few months, a flying school established, and a public display put on by the little squadron. Other French, German, and British aircraft were purchased, and when the First Balkan War started the Ottoman pilots rushed home from France, bringing with them a handful of new machines. Nevertheless, there was little that they could do during that disastrous conflict.

The Second Balkan War went better, with Ottoman aircraft flying reconnaissance missions. The role of aircraft during the Balkan Wars had been sufficiently effective

Top: The Blériot *Ertuğrul* in Damascus with Fethi and Sadik posed at the group's center. Alas, disaster struck them down between Damascus and Jerusalem, but the pair were celebrated as heroes on postcards such as the one seen here, **above right** (Captain Fethi on the right, Observer Sadik on the left). After the further loss of the Deperdussin *Osmanli* off Jaffa, the replacement Blériot *Edremit* arrives in Cairo, **above**, with pilot Salim and his observer, Kemal, at the controls.

for a conference on military aeronautics to be organized in Istanbul by the French aviation writer Alfred Durand. This was followed by orders for additional French aircraft and an American Curtiss flying boat. The French government agreed to lend advisors to help establish a more effective Ottoman air arm.

Aircraft were also seen as a way to strengthen Ottoman prestige in the Arab provinces, as demonstrated by a checkered project of 1914. Previous flights between Istanbul and Alexandria in Egypt had been made in the winter of 1913–14 by the Frenchmen Jules Vedrine and Marc Bonnier, each taking 40 days. The Ottoman aircrew who followed in their flightpath were experienced men; pilots Captain Fethi and Lieutenant Nuri with observers lieutenants Sadık and Isma'il Hakkı. Fethi and Sadık flew a Blériot recently named *Ertuğrul*, while Nuri and Hakkı flew the Deperdussin *Osmanlı*. Such a long-distance and highly publicized flight was still very ambitious in 1914, especially for the Ottoman air arm with its limited technical support. The two aircraft took off with great ceremony on February 8, 1914. They flew separately and, though weather conditions and technical problems forced both machines to make unscheduled landings, they were greeted everywhere by enthusiastic crowds. Special stamps and postcards were printed and on February 10, 1914 Lieutenant Nuri made the first air postal service in Turkish history. He briefly broke the international altitude record of over 13,000 feet while crossing the Taurus mountains.

Then disaster struck between Damascus and Jerusalem, the Blériot crashing near Lake Tiberius, killing both Fethi and Sadık. Only a few days later the Deperdussin

CHAPTER TEN: STRIVING FOR MODERNISATION

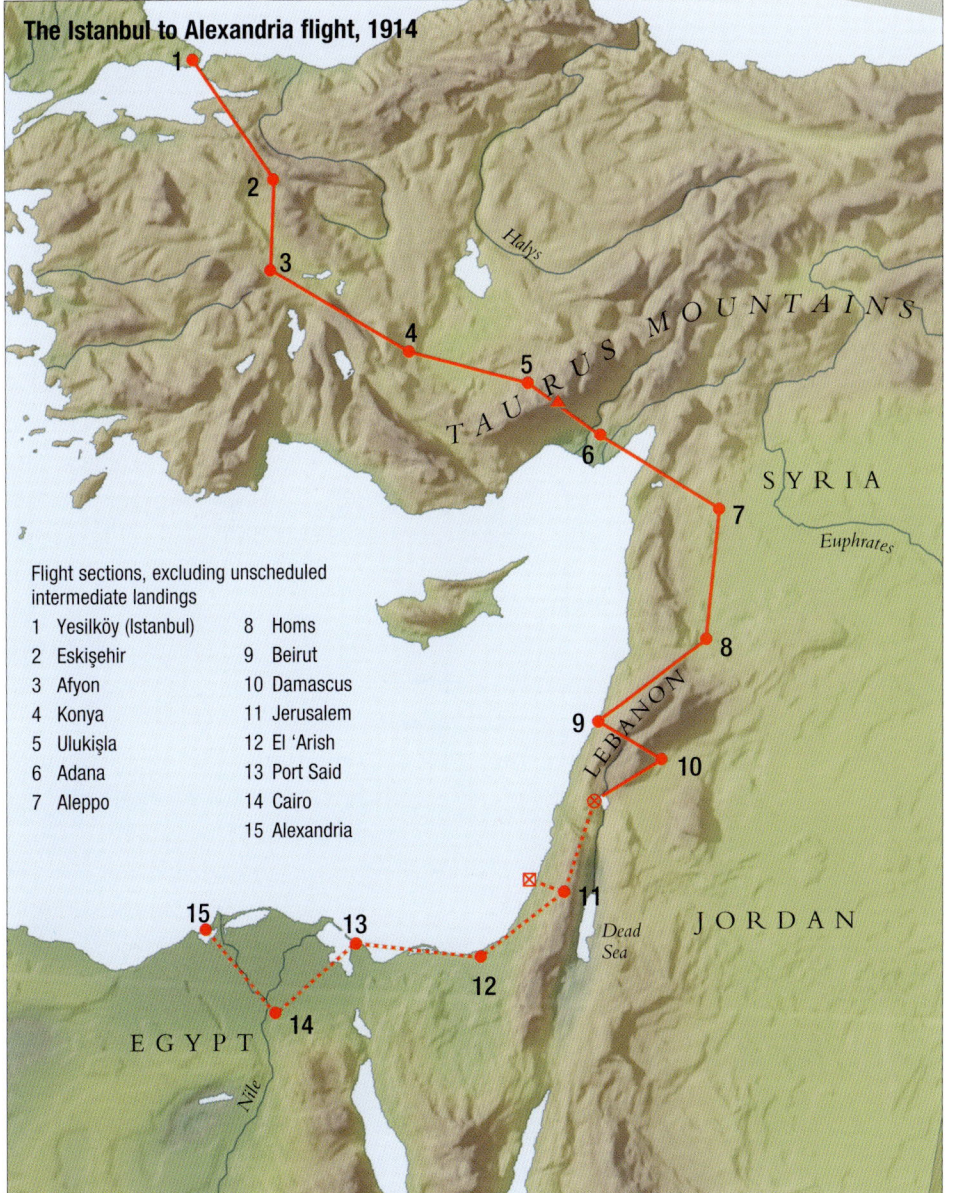

came down in the Mediterranean Sea near Jaffa; Nuri drowned but his observer Hakkı survived. The three dead officers were buried near the mausoleum of Saladin in Damascus, which had recently been restored at the expense of German Kaiser William II (1888–1918).

A second Blériot named *Edremit* was sent to Beirut by sea, and thence to Palestine to complete the final stages of the Egyptian flight. Flown by Captain Salim, with Captain Kemal as his observer, it reached Cairo on May 8, 1914 and Alexandria seven days later. *Edremit* was returned to Istanbul by sea. It remained in service until the Ottoman empire entered the First World War as an ally of Germany. The two badly damaged aircraft were repaired and also saw service during the Great War.

CHAPTER ELEVEN

Fall of the Ottomans

Disaster and redemption in the early 20th century

Enver Paşa, dominating the pro-war party in the Porte, soon had his militaristic way, taking the sultanate into the spreading conflict of the First World War on the side of the Central Powers.

Even today the reasons for the Ottoman sultanate's entry into the First World War are not entirely clear. German influence was by no means dominant and in 1914—given previous relations—Turkey even approached Britain and France as potential allies. In the event, Ottoman desire for protection against Russia and enthusiasm for a German alliance within a small group of politicians tied the state to the Central Powers. The declaration of war was greeted in Istanbul with deep gloom. Cavit Paşa was one of four ministers to resign in disgust, declaring, "It will be our country's ruin—even if we win." Casualties at Gallipoli validated his comment, even though the Turks won that battle.

During the first months of hostilities between Germany and France and Britain the Porte maintained a neutral stance but Enver Paşa, who dominated the pro-war minority within the Ottoman government, was able to propel the state into conflict after Britain commandeered two warships that had just been built for the Ottoman navy but not yet delivered. This caused widespread resentment, as they had been purchased using huge financial donations from the public. Enver and Cemal Paşa, the navy minister, then gave sanctuary to two German warships, *Goeben* and *Breslau*, which had been pursued by the British Royal Navy. In due course the ships and their crews were incorporated into the Ottoman fleet.

The significance of this seemingly minor event was later summed up in the colorful prose of Winston Churchill, then First Lord of the Admiralty, when he described the actions of the German admiral in command of the ships: "Admiral Souchon was cruising irresolutely about the Greek islands endeavoring to make sure that he would be admitted by the Turks to the Dardanelles. He dallied 36 hours at Denusa and was forced to use his telltale wireless on several occasions. It was not until the evening of the 10th that he entered the Dardanelles, and the Curse descended irrevocably upon Turkey and the East."

In October 1914 Enver and Cemal permitted the German captains of the two supposedly ex-German warships to bombard Russia's Black Sea naval bases,

Left: The German cruiser *Breslau* lies at anchor in 1915 in the Golden Horn on returning from the bombardment of Russia's Black Sea naval bases. The *Breslau* was joined by her sister vessel, the cruiser *Goeben*, **below.**

supported by several Ottoman vessels. Other members of the Ottoman government were furious, but by then the die was cast. The sultanate had a long and proud naval history, yet by the start of the 20th century its navy was a pale shadow of former glory and would play only a minor role in the Great War. It was neither designed nor intended to face the huge fleets of Britain or France. Considerable efforts had been put into strengthening the navy between 1909 and 1914, the reorganization supervised by a British rear admiral, but the foes envisaged were the Greeks and perhaps the Russians. In fact British influence was so strong that not only were Ottoman ships painted the same colors as those of the Royal Navy, but officer insignia also mirrored that of the British. And orders had been placed in Britain (as well as France) for new vessels ranging from battleships to gunboats, and local Ottoman yards at Samsun, Izmir, Beirut, and Basra competed to build the best small ships in the shortest possible time. The navy had only recently been a popular arm of service, with the exploits of the ex-American cruiser *Hamidiye* under Captain Husayn Rauf in the Aegean and Adriatic providing a much-needed boost to morale during the catastrophic First Balkan War.

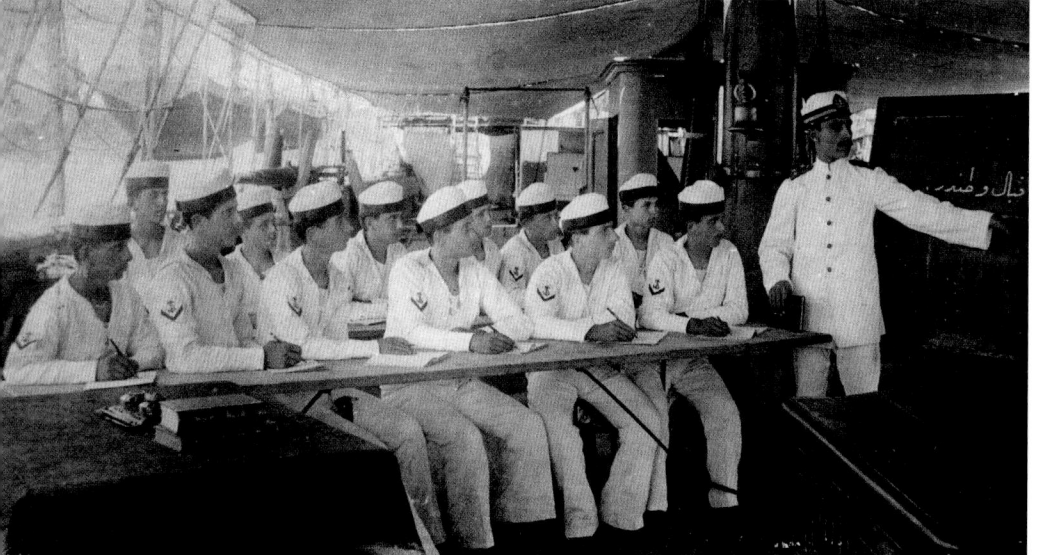

The navy was a popular arm of the sultanate's military. Here, Ottoman Naval midshipmen cadets in training in 1916 are wearing the new-style uniforms which were introduced in that year.

CHAPTER ELEVEN: FALL OF THE OTTOMANS

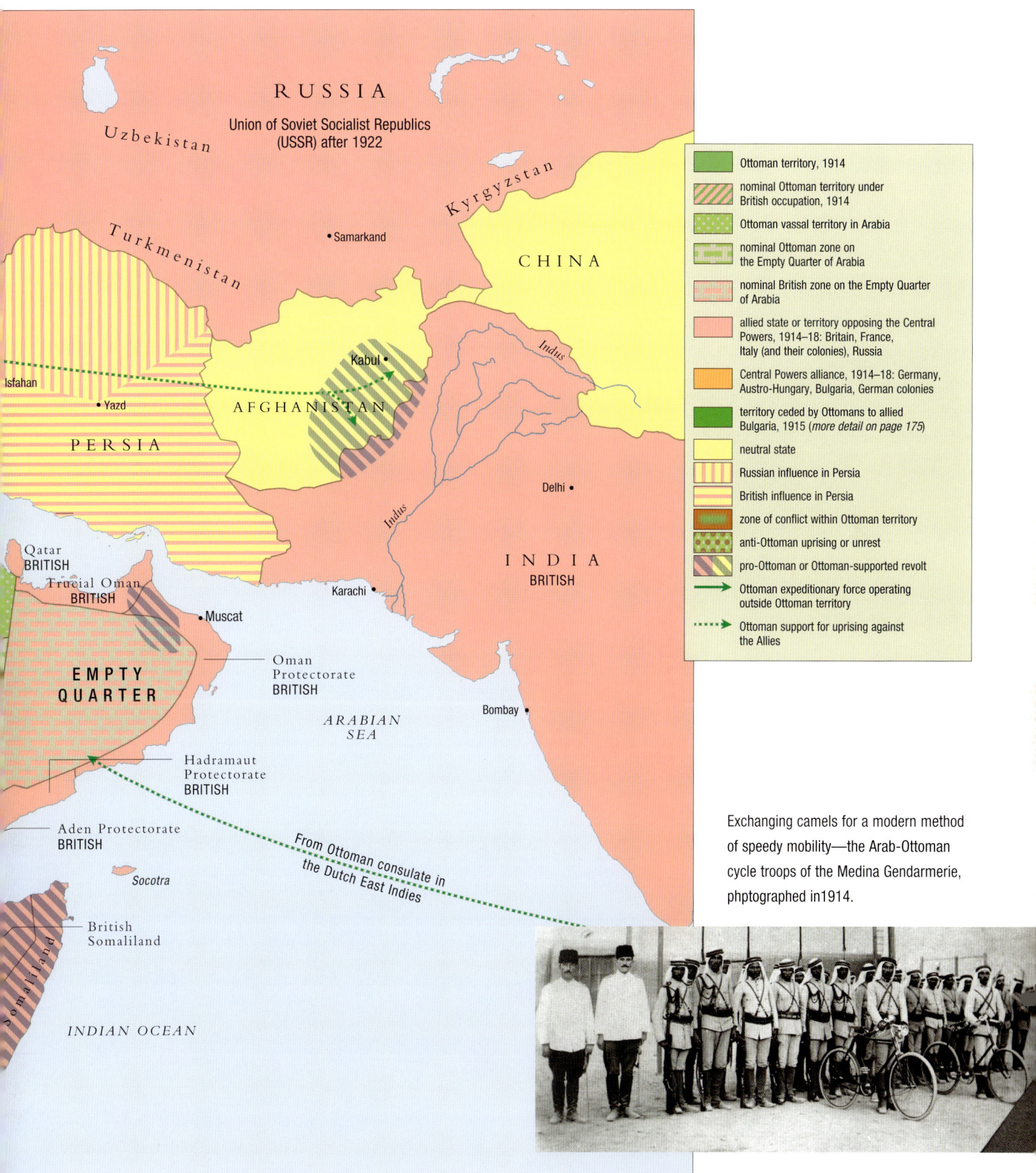

Exchanging camels for a modern method of speedy mobility—the Arab-Ottoman cycle troops of the Medina Gendarmerie, phptographed in1914.

British troops of the Middlesex yeomanry disembarking at Alexandria. They were to be tied up for months coping with the attack on the Suez Canal led by Djemal Paşa and in the Western Desert by the Ottoman-fomented Sanussi uprising.

In the face of overwhelmingly numerous enemies, the Ottoman navy attempted few offensive operations during the First World War, though the British HMS *Goliath* was sunk by the Ottoman torpedo boat *Muavenet Milli* under Commander Ahmet Efendi on May 13, 1915. The navy's main role was convoy protection, particularly in the Sea of Marmara. The second British submarine to enter this area, E-15, was captured by the Ottomans and the Australian submarine AE-2 was also destroyed by a torpedo boat, followed by the E-14.

The Ottoman navy's most serious losses were during coastal protection duties. The old battleship *Mesudiya* was torpedoed by submarine B-11 in the Dardanelles, and the *Hayruddin Barbarossa* by E-11 in the Sea of Marmara. By the end of the war the Ottomans had lost the ex-German light cruiser *Breslau* (renamed *Midilli*) to mines off Imbroz in 1918. The smaller cruiser *Mecidiye* had an extraordinary war service, having been sunk by a mine in the Black Sea in 1915, raised and repaired by the Russian navy only to be retaken by the Ottomans in 1918. The ex-German battlecruiser *Goeben*, renamed *Sultan Selim Yavuz*, survived to become the flagship of the post-war Turkish navy. She was decommissioned in 1960 and broken up despite widespread efforts to preserve this historic warship.

The destruction of Armenia

Before Britain's confiscation of the two undelivered warships drove the sultanate from its preferred peaceful status, the leading Entente powers of Britain, France, and Russia made little effort to keep the Ottomans neutral, believing that their participation would make little real difference. Yet in this they were wrong—the

Ottomans won some resounding victories and absorbed the attention of great numbers of enemy troops throughout the conflict. Only 300 Ottomans and few supplies sent to the Sanussi in the Sahara tied down an estimated 15,000 French, 60,000 Italians, and 35,000 British plus Egyptian troops in probably the most successful covert action of the First World War.

One of Sultan Mehmet V's first actions was to proclaim a jihad or holy struggle against the infidel foes, but this was widely regarded as a political ploy and few non-Ottoman Muslims responded. The tensions of war did, however, have an effect on Christian minorities. The Armenians of Anatolia were particularly exposed to Muslim resentment after Russian Armenians called on their Ottoman coreligionists to join the Russian army and "liberate" eastern Anatolia in November 1914.

Elsewhere, the Ottomans launched a daring but unsuccessful attack against the British-held Suez Canal, apparently in the hope of an Egyptian uprising. At the other end of the Red Sea, a tiny Ottoman force from northern Yemen overran much of the British-ruled Aden Protectorate (now southern Yemen) where they remained until the end of the war. To the east, neutral Iran was the scene of bitter fighting between Ottoman and Russian armies, and there was a brief conflict between British and Ottomans around the Iranian oil fields in Ahwaz, while German agents tried to foment anti-British and anti-Russian feeling even further east. Perhaps the most extraordinary effort at covert warfare was an attempt by the Ottoman consulate in the Dutch East Indies (now Indonesia) to provoke an anti-British rising in the Hadramaut region east of Aden. Meanwhile, the Ottoman commander outside Aden sent supplies to the so-called Mad Mullah's revolt against British, French, and Italian rule in Somalia.

For the Ottoman army, the main priority remained the Caucasus front, where large numbers of Armenians joined the Russian advance while preparations were made for an Armenian uprising behind Ottoman lines. The Russians also won a resounding winter victory at Sarıkamış in the snow-bound mountains of eastern Anatolia. In May 1915 Minister of War Enver Paşa imitated the Russian policy of emptying the zones behind the front lines and forcibly evacuated the Armenian populations of Van, Bitlis, and Erzerum in a badly organized operation that caused huge civilian casualties. Most rural Armenian minorities of Cilicia and northern Syria were similarly evicted in anticipation of a British seaborne invasion.

Armenians suffered both during and after the war. Photographed during the brief occupation of Maraş by French troops in June 1920, Armenian refugee children await the arrival of food relief outside Maraş in southern Turkey.

Dashnak guerrillas organized a revolt in Van, where Armenians formed almost half the population. A mixed Armenian irregular and Russian force reached Van on May 14, 1915 and attacked Muslim civilians. The Armenians declared their own state, to which their people flocked. In July, however, an Ottoman counter-offensive drove back the Russians and thousands of refugees along with them.

By the time the war ended the easternmost provinces of Anatolia had a minimal Armenian minority. The Allies claimed that over a million Armenians had been

Right: As Enver Paşa (left) discusses tactics with Winkler, the German commander of the army in Macedonia, his colleague Cemal Paşa does the same at his headquarters in Palestine, with his Chief of Staff, Colonel Ali Fuat Bey (**above**).

massacred; Ottoman documents indicated that around 400,000 were deported and 500,000 fled to the Caucasus with the Russians. Today, western historians put the Armenian genocide at around 600,000 dead; others estimate that 200,000 Armenians perished as a result of famine, disease, war action, and deliberate murder during a period in which a far greater number of Muslims perished.

Gallipoli—a disaster for the Allies

Despite Mehmet V's call for jihad, for the remainder of the conflict real power remained firmly in the hands of Enver Paşa, Talat Paşa, and Cemal Paşa. Enver ran the Ottoman war effort almost singlehandedly as a military dictator, Cemal took control of Syria and effectively became its independent ruler, while Talat concentrated on civil matters in the capital of Istanbul. Provincial governors ran their regions with differing degrees of autonomy and enthusiasm for the war. In Izmir, for example, Rahmi Bey behaved almost as if his region was a neutral zone between the warring states.

The anticipated British attack came not via Cilicia or northern Syria, as originally feared, but by way of the straits. Britain and France intended to knock the Ottomans out of the war by capturing the Dardanelles and threatening Istanbul

CHAPTER ELEVEN: FALL OF THE OTTOMANS

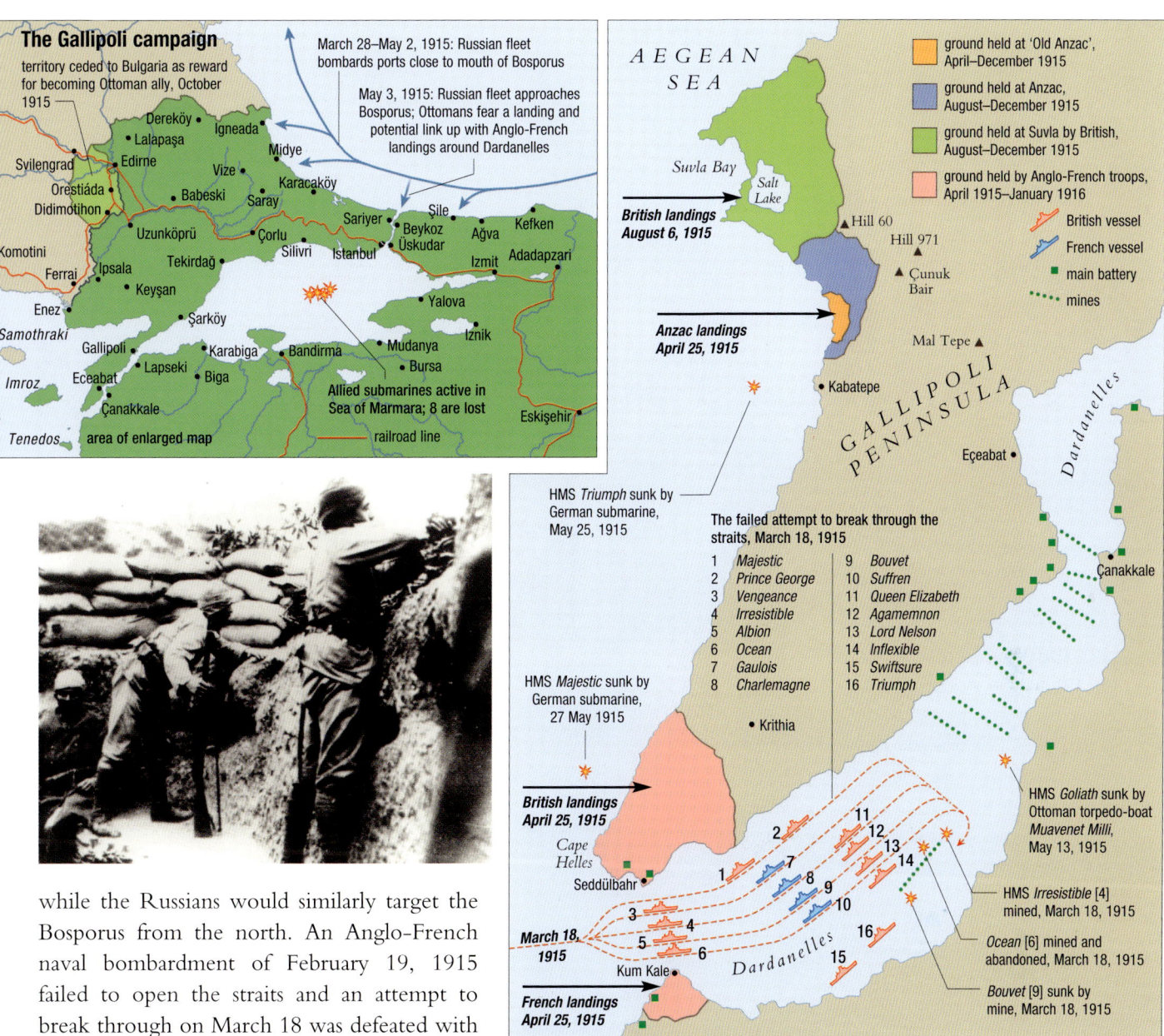

while the Russians would similarly target the Bosporus from the north. An Anglo-French naval bombardment of February 19, 1915 failed to open the straits and an attempt to break through on March 18 was defeated with several ships lost or damaged. It was down to the army. The first landings on the Gallipoli peninsula were made by British, Australian and New Zealand troops on April 25, 1915. A French force won a beachhead on the Asiatic side of the straits, but the Ottomans stood firm under the leadership of German General Liman von Sanders and former Young Turk, General Mustafa Kemal.

Amazingly, the morale of what even the most sympathetic modern military historian has called the "rugged but gimcrack Ottoman army" remained high almost to the end of the Great War. This was nowhere more apparent than on the Gallipoli front. Here the 57th Infantry Regiment, a Turkish unit, was almost wiped out while stopping an Australian advance from ANZAC Cove. What is less well known is that an Arab regiment then drove the Australians back to the coast.

Fighting dragged on at Gallipoli until January 1916. The British and ANZAC (Australian and New Zealand) troops made frequent frontal assaults, establishing an

Above left: Ottoman infantry in the Gallipoli campaign, 1915. The trench warfare in Turkey was every bit as harsh and wasteful as the better known battles of the Western Front in Flanders.

British forces hold Turkish prisoners behind their own barbed wire at Seddülbahr after the Anglo-French landings on April 25, 1915 at Cape Helles and Kum Kale.

additional bridgehead further north in August 1915. Yet throughout a year's fighting the Ottoman soldiers, who included Arabs and others as well as Turks, clung grimly to their defenses, consistently bringing Allied attacks to a bloody halt. Only massive reinforcements could hope to break the stalemate and these the British and French did not have. After suffering almost 214,000 British and imperial casualties plus those of the French—twice those of the defending Ottoman forces—the Allies withdrew and in January 1916 the Gallipoli campaign came to an end.

As a result, Russia remained largely isolated from her allies in the west, Ottoman morale was strengthened and the popularity of Mustafa Kemal (1881–1938) rose enormously as "the hero of the Dardanelles." As he later wrote, the greatest monument to this victory was Mehmetçik himself—Little Mehmet, the affectionate nickname given to the brave but unpretentious Ottoman infantrymen. The courage of Mehmetçik was recognized by allies and enemies alike. In the Middle East, where the Arab peoples had little reason to feel nostalgic about the final years of Ottoman rule, the Turkish soldier of the Great War was remembered as Abu Shuja'a, the Father of Courage, while his British opponent was remembered as Abu Alf Midfah, the Father of a Thousand Cannon. Most observers recognized that the uneducated Ottoman soldier was lost without good leadership. At Gallipoli commanders like Mustafa Kemal realized the capabilities of such men if their officers led from the front. There were many examples of silent pre-dawn attacks in which officers with drawn swords went ahead of troops who were ordered to charge only when they saw their officers raise their whips, and only to shout their battlecry of "Allahu Akbar!" when they reached the enemy's trenches.

The conflict on the sulatanate's eastern fronts

At first the majority of the sultan's Arab subjects remained loyal, though in January 1915 the standard of revolt was raised by the Idrisids of Asir, between the Hijaz and Yemen. The Sharifian Arab Revolt, proclaimed on June 5, 1916 by Sharif Husayn, the Hashemite ruler of Mecca, developed into a slow hard fight, with Egyptian help to contain Ottoman garrisons in western Arabia. By 1917 Ottoman armies were in gradual retreat on most fronts, which raised hopes of Arab independence. The Arab Revolt took on new life; a Northern Army under Emir Faysal, with some Egyptian troops and British advisors led by an obscure Arabist named T.E. Lawrence who was sent from Cairo to be the liaison officer, unexpectedly captured Aqaba and linked up with British forces in southern Palestine.

The British broke through Ottoman lines around Gaza and occupied Jerusalem on December 9, 1917, yet it was not until September 1918 that a restored Ottoman front was finally broken. British and Sharifian Arab forces then swept north to the Syrian-Turkish frontier. The Sharifians entered Damascus and raised the Arab flag. Emir Faysal was recognized by the British as Chief of OETA (Occupied Enemy Territory Administration) East.

Meanwhile, the Leninist revolution of 1917, which effectively pulled Russia from the war, had led to a reversal of Ottoman fortunes in eastern Anatolia. Turkish forces remained on the defensive while the crumbling czarist armies were replaced by local volunteers. In December 1917 the three major peoples of the Caucasus—Christian Georgians and Armenians and Muslim Turkish Azerbaijanis—formed a Federated Transcaucasian Republic and signed an armistice with the sultanate. Yet relations between the Caucasus peoples were bad from the start. Georgians wanted to throw off Armenian economic domination and allied with Germany. Armenians and Azerbaijanis were divided by territorial disputes, the latter looking to the Ottomans for support. When Armenians were accused of attacking the Muslim Turkish minority in the southern Caucasus, the Ottoman army took the offensive, swiftly advancing through Armenia and ex-Russian Azerbaijan to the Caspian Sea.

Ottoman ski troops on the Caucasus front in eastern Turkey, c.1918.

This dramatic success could not alter the outcome of a war that was costing the Ottoman state enormous losses in men and matériel. By 1916 the cost of living had risen by 2500 percent, leading to starvation in some areas. Some 325,000 soldiers had been killed, with 240,000 dying of disease, and there were an estimated 1.5 million deserters. Civilian losses were similarly enormous. The surrender of the Ottoman's ally and neighbor Bulgaria on September 29, 1918 left the way open to attack Istanbul. Germany was seeking peace. The Young Turk government resigned on October 8, and a week passed before Sultan Mehmet V could find anyone to take responsibility for making peace. Negotiations for an armistice were opened at Mudros on Lemnos island on October 27, 1918 and an agreement was signed three days later; but the Ottomans were forced to accept much harsher conditions than those imposed on their Christian allies in Germany, Austria-Hungary, and Bulgaria.

It had taken the Allied Powers considerable time to agree their aims in relation to the Ottomans, but by 1917 a rough arrangement had divided practically all Ottoman territory into areas of direct rule and zones of influence, with a rump Ottoman state surviving in northwestern Anatolia. Russia was to occupy Istanbul, the straits and northeastern Anatolia; Italy southwestern Anatolia; France southeastern Anatolia, Syria, Lebanon, and northern Mesopotamia; Britain southern Mesopotamia (Iraq) and Transjordan; while Palestine would come under international administration.

The fate of the Arab provinces

As the Great War had ground toward its bitter end, the significant shift in the political attitudes of the sultanate's Arab population had also raised the question for the Allies as to what should become of the Arab territories. As a total defeat of the Ottoman empire had started to look possible, British policymakers began envisaging small Middle Eastern states ruled by the Sharifian Hashemite family and effectively controlled by Britain. This appeared to be a realizable ambition as increasingly Arab nationalist sentiment replaced Ottoman solidarity and support grew for the Sharifian government installed in Damascus since 1918. The Arabs, however, faced much greater problems than did the Turkish nationalists. They lacked experienced senior military leaders—even Emir Faysal's entourage consisted only of captains and lieutenants—while there was a similar lack of knowledgeable administrators because the Ottoman senior bureaucratic hierarchy had consisted largely of Turks.

General Allenby, commander of British forces in Palestine, rides through the Jaffa Gate as part of his formal entry into the captured Jerusalem in January 1918. Edmund "The Bull" Allenby captured the city from Turkish forces on December 9, 1917. Before the city fell to the British, Colonel T.E. Lawrence (Lawrence of Arabia) lead many guerrilla raids on Ottoman forces east of Jerusalem.

Nevertheless, the Sharifian Hashemite family remained the only credible rallying point for nationalist feeling outside of Egypt, yet large sections of the Arab people had no wish to exchange Ottoman domination for Hashemite or British rule, and Syrians particularly had no wish to be ruled from a culturally backward province like the Hijaz. A parliament, called the General Syrian Congress, met in Damascus in June 1919 under the aegis of Faysal but his government appeared unable to control the OETA East. Clashes between Arab irregulars and French troops in OETA West (essentially Lebanon and the Syrian coast) grew more frequent. Meanwhile, Turkish nationalist successes in Anatolia raised Arab aspirations.

Faysal, though aware of French intentions and military power, was swept along by the radical demands of the General Syrian Congress, which offered him the throne of the kingdom of Greater Syria which had been proclaimed on March 8, 1920. Meanwhile Iraqis in Damascus had made 'Abd Allah, another member of the Hashemite family, king of Iraq. The Allied powers awarded France a mandate over Syria and Lebanon in April, but the climax came in July. Faysal accepted a French ultimatum but the French then merely increased their demands, brushed aside Arab defenses and occupied Damascus on July 25, 1920.

A little to the south of Damascus, another political cauldron was coming to the boil. Almost three years earlier—on November 2, 1917, in what became known as the Balfour Declaration—British Foreign Secretary Arthur Balfour had assured Lord Rothschild, a leading Zionist, that Britain would help establish a national home for the Jewish people in Palestine. It was hoped that an expression of support for Zionist settlement would win Jewish political support, especially in the USA, yet it had little impact on Jewish communities in America or Russia. Britain was not alone in attempting to win over the Jews—Germany had considered sponsoring a Jewish state in 1915–16. Earlier negotiations between Zionist leader Theodor Herzl and Abdul Hamid II had lasted from 1896 to 1902, before the Ottoman government excluded Palestine from intensive Jewish settlement. Nevertheless, there were at least 10,000 largely Zionist agricultural settlers in Palestine by 1914, plus larger, longer established Jewish urban communities. Jews represented about ten percent of the population, the balance being Arab.

Confrontation between Arabs and Zionists in Palestine had flared up as early as May 1918. The British military administration, recognizing the impossibility of reconciling Jewish and Arab aspirations, now opposed the more radical aspects of Zionism, though the government in London took little heed of their warnings. On April 4, 1920 severe anti-Zionist riots had broken out in Jerusalem just days before Britain was awarded a mandate over Palestine. When the British finally withdrew in 1948 Jews established the state of Israel, fragmenting the region with the West Bank and Gaza Strip regions. Israelis took eastern Jerusalem from Jordanians in 1967, beginning a bitter territorial conflict that continues to this day.

Territory east of the Jordan had formed part of Sharifian-controlled OETA East, but Britain would not let it fall to France after the collapse of Faysal's government in Damascus. Zionists wanted it to be opened for Jewish settlement while the British Foreign Office disliked the idea of Britain administering a huge region dominated

Faysal, son of Hussayn of Mecca, with his delegates and advisors at the Paris Peace Conference in 1919. Behind him are (left to right) his private secretary and fellow delegate Rustem Haidar; Brigadier General Nuri Said, of Baghdad; Captain Pisani of France; Col. T. E. Lawrence "of Arabia"; and Hassan Kadri

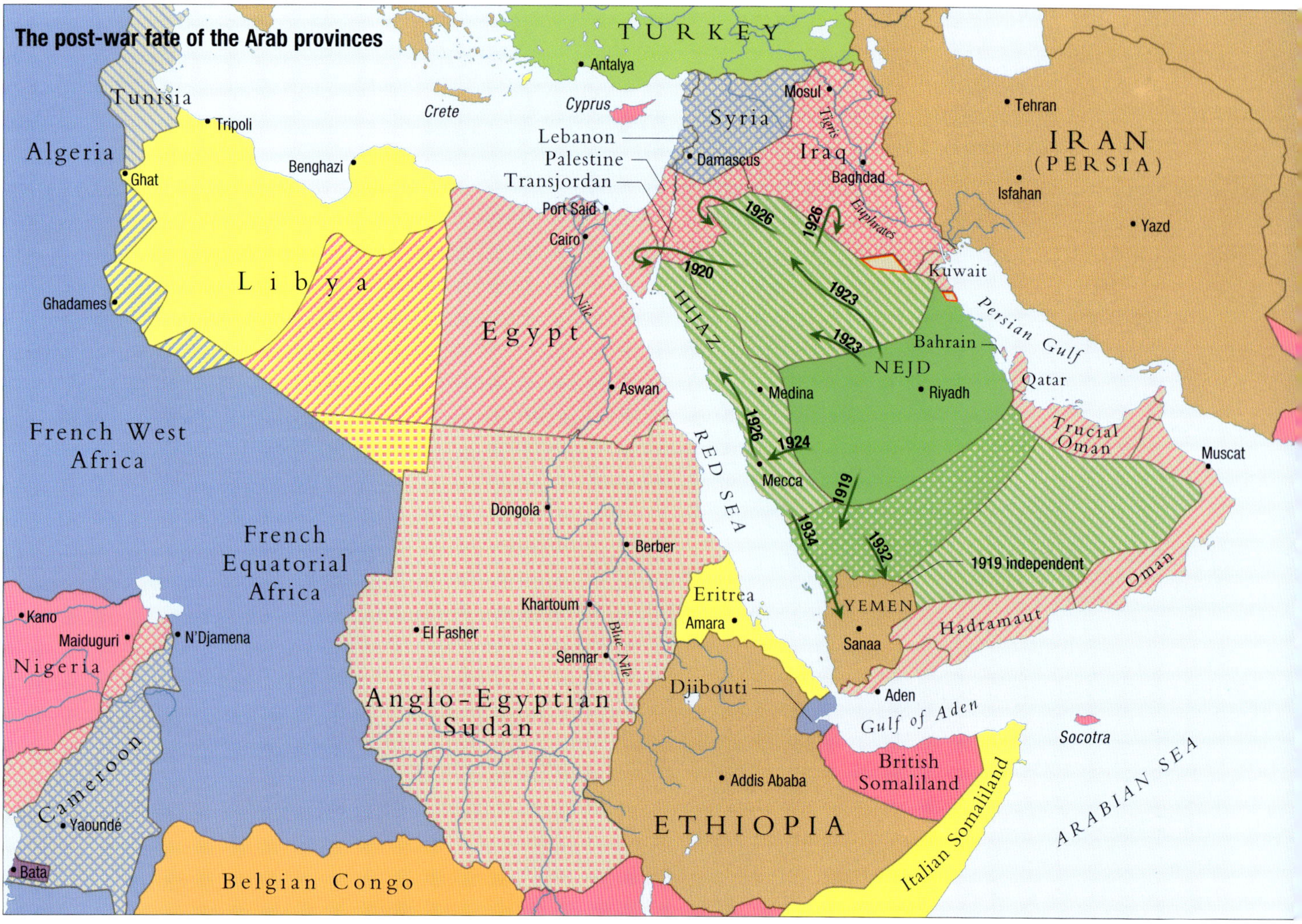

The post-war fate of the Arab provinces

▨	French colony
▨	French mandate
▨	French protectorate
▨	British colony
▨	British mandate
▨	British protectorate
▨	Anglo-Egyptian condominium
▨	Italian colony
▨	from French colony to Italian Libya, 1919
▨	from Egypt to Italian Libya, 1919
▨	from Anglo-Egyptian Sudan to Libya, 1925
▨	Belgian colony
▨	Spanish colony
▨	Turkey
▨	other independent state
▨	neutral zone

the expansion of Saudi Arabia's territory

▨ 1918	▨ 1920	▨ by 1926
→	Saudi campaign 1919–34

by powerful Bedouin tribes. In November 1920 a Sharifian army under Emir 'Abd Allah arrived in what became known as Transjordan from the Hijaz, intending to help Damascus resist French occupation. Britain offered 'Abd Allah a subsidy to govern Transjordan for a short while, though the emir still hoped to advance into Syria. Later, on the recommendation of Colonel T.E. Lawrence (by then for his exploits famously known as Lawrence of Arabia), this arrangement was continued indefinitely and Jordan was launched on the road to independence under the Hashemite dynasty that still rules the country.

British interest in Iraq was even more confused than elsewhere. The question of oil did not yet loom very large but factors of imperial prestige did. Some British administrators hoped that Iraq, despite consisting of three very different ex-Ottoman provinces, would prove a showplace of British imperialism. Such views ran counter to new concepts of self-determination as expressed at the League of Nations.

Many, too many, Arab affairs

At the end of the Great War Britain was by far the dominant power in the Arab world. The independence of what became the northern part of modern Yemen had been recognized and old ties were strengthened with rulers like the sultan of Muscat (Oman). Britain offered support to the Sharifians of Hijaz rather than to their rivals,

CHAPTER ELEVEN: FALL OF THE OTTOMANS

the Idrisids of Asir or the Saudis of the interior of Arabia (who only received a small subsidy until 1924). It was a major uprising late in 1920, part nationalist, part religious and part tribal in origin, that encouraged Britain to create a nominally independent Arab state requiring the minimum of British involvement. In 1921 Faysal was offered the crown of Iraq, partly as compensation for his loss of Syria but largely because he was capable of controlling this notoriously troubled region. But the British government clearly backed the losing side in the long quarrel between Sharifians and Saudis. British mediation failed and in 1926 Ibn Saud's forces seized the Hijaz, bringing the Sharifian kingdom to an end.

The First World War raised political consciousness in Egypt, where a massive British military presence merely stimulated a desire for self-determination. Britain's refusal to permit an Egyptian delegation to attend the Paris Peace Conference, despite the fact that Egyptian troops had fought alongside the British during the war, caused further resentment. A more significant role had been played, and far greater casualties suffered, by the long-suffering Egyptian Camel Transport and Labor Battalions without whom British successes against the Ottomans in Palestine and Syria would not have been possible.

In 1919 a virtual armed insurrection broke out in Egypt, though it lasted only two months. The trouble, particularly in the rural areas, was caused by a variety of factors but it was clear that British occupation could not continue in its present form. Anglo-Egyptian negotiations proved long and tedious because Egyptian nationalists regarded them as a step toward full independence, while Britain wanted an autonomous Egypt whose foreign affairs would remain under British control. The latter's interests would continue to be protected by a strong British garrison. Agreement was consequently impossible and on February 28, 1922 Britain unilaterally announced that Egypt would henceforth be an independent state subject to British control over its defense and foreign policy, security of the Suez Canal, and government of the Sudan. Civil unrest continued and in August 1924 the British *sirdar* or commander of the Egyptian army, Sir Lee Stack, was assassinated. Britain insisted on a further reduction in Egypt's armed forces and even tighter control over all modern weapons.

The shortsighted and racist disregard for Egyptian opinion was even

A Jewish Zionist settler, sheltering from Jerusalem's sun, strides past a Palestinian recruit for the Sherifian Regular Camel Corps (but still in Ottoman uniform), 1918. Troops of the Egyptian 1st Infantry Battalion march through Jerusalem (**below**) April 26, 1918, after the city's fall to the British.

more blatant in the way Britain forced Egypt to cede vast swathes of territory to the Italians in Libya. It was generally accepted among the Allies that Italy had suffered much but gained little from its participation in the First World War. As a result Egypt was alone in losing rather than gaining land as a result of fighting as an ally of Britain and France.

Britain suffered a comparable decline in Persia (Iran), where British interests had been dominant when the war ended. Russia returned to Iranian affairs in 1920, while inside Iran there was considerable opposition to overt British domination. Central government crumbled until, in February 1921, the British-organized Cossack Brigade under Colonel Reza Khan took control. This was regarded as one of the few effective units in the Persian army. While there is little evidence of a direct British hand in this coup, the new authorities included pro-British sympathizers. In 1925 Reza Khan overthrew the ruling dynasty and proclaimed himself shah, the first of the Pahlevi dynasty that ruled Persia-Iran until the theocratic coup of 1979.

Turkey, from sultanate to republic

The victorious powers of the Great War convened a Peace Conference which—among many matters, such as the level of German reparations—aimed to redraw the map of the Middle East. The ideal would be its division into numerous small states under varying degrees of western domination. Armenia, Syria, Iraq, Palestine, Arabia, and Kurdistan would be separated, and the Dardanelles placed under international control, while the Ottomans were to be confined to northwestern Anatolia. When the peacemakers gathered in Paris in January 1919 they faced an extraordinary array of claims, those of the Greeks being the most extravagant. Spurred on by the "Great Idea" of a restored Byzantine empire, Prime Minister Venizelos demanded southern Albania, all of Thrace, every island in the eastern Mediterranean, and most of western Anatolia. In May 1919 Greece pressed ahead unilaterally, sending troops to Izmir to forestall Italian expansion from the south. Greek atrocities did much to strengthen Turkish nationalist sentiment, as did the killing of Muslims by Greeks who hoped to establish a state on the northern coast of Anatolia.

America's president, Thomas Woodrow Wilson, declared that the Armenians should have a country to include Trabzon on the Black Sea, but neither America nor the other Allied powers were willing to help conquer this huge area. Kurdistan posed even greater problems as Kurds claimed, and inhabited, much of the territory awarded to Armenia. Nor was there a recognized Kurdish leadership. These competing claims seemed to be settled by the Treaty of Sèvres in August 1920, which allotted most of western and southern Anatolia to Greek control or Italian and French influence. Greek rule over Izmir was to last five years, after which in a plebiscite the inhabitants would choose between Greek or Ottoman sovereignty, an

The former Cossack commander Reza Shah Pahlevi, "shah of Persia," sits on his Peacock Throne after a coup which found much sympathy from the British.

arrangement that virtually invited the Greeks to replace the existing Muslim population with their own. Thrace would also go to Greece, though Istanbul would remain Ottoman.

Most Muslims were forced from public employment. State schools were reopened only for Christian pupils and missionaries in charge of major orphanages assumed all displaced children to be Greek or Armenian unless documentary evidence proved otherwise, while the killing of discharged Ottoman soldiers and Muslim civilians remained commonplace. In May 1919 the hero of the Dardanelles, Mustafa Kemal, was sent to eastern Anatolia to demobilize the only organized Turkish military forces. Once there he assumed command of the growing nationalist movement. Mustafa Kemal Atatürk, or Father of the Turks as he was known after 1934, became the founder of the modern Turkish Republic. Later generations of nationalists elsewhere in the Islamic world would try to emulate his westernizing reforms.

Large parts of Mustafa Kemal's country lay under foreign occupation and the existing Ottoman government was unable to save it from dismemberment. The nationalist movement was still weak, violence continued, and Allied forces consolidated their occupation of Istanbul. The nationalists responded by summoning a Grand National Assembly in Ankara that based its claim to authority on Islam and "the will of the people."

Hero of Gallipoli and the Father of Turks, Mustafa Kemal led the Nationalist uprising and fought for his country's rights in the international diplomacy arena.

Meanwhile they faced Armenians in the east, French in the south, Greeks in the west, a ragtag army sent by the sultan, and numerous tribal, conservative, and brigand disturbances. While defeating these forces at home, the nationalists abandoned their claim to most of the Arab provinces. An agreement was reached with Russia and a nationalist attack forced the Armenian Republic to sign a peace treaty late in 1920, though this was never ratified, as Bolshevik forces almost immediately took over what was left of Armenia.

Two Greek assaults in 1921 drove deep into Anatolia but were checked at the decisive battle of Sakarya. In August 1922 the Turkish Nationalists went on the offensive, the Greeks collapsed and panic reigned in Izmir as the local Greek minority struggled to escape before the nationalists arrived on September 9. Mustafa Kemal's troops turned north to the Dardanelles—the Turkish Straits—and Thrace, where they faced Allied forces. Bloodshed was avoided through the commanders' restraint, and the Greeks agreed to withdraw from eastern Thrace, except for a small area west of the Maritsa which had been regained by the Ottomans in the Second

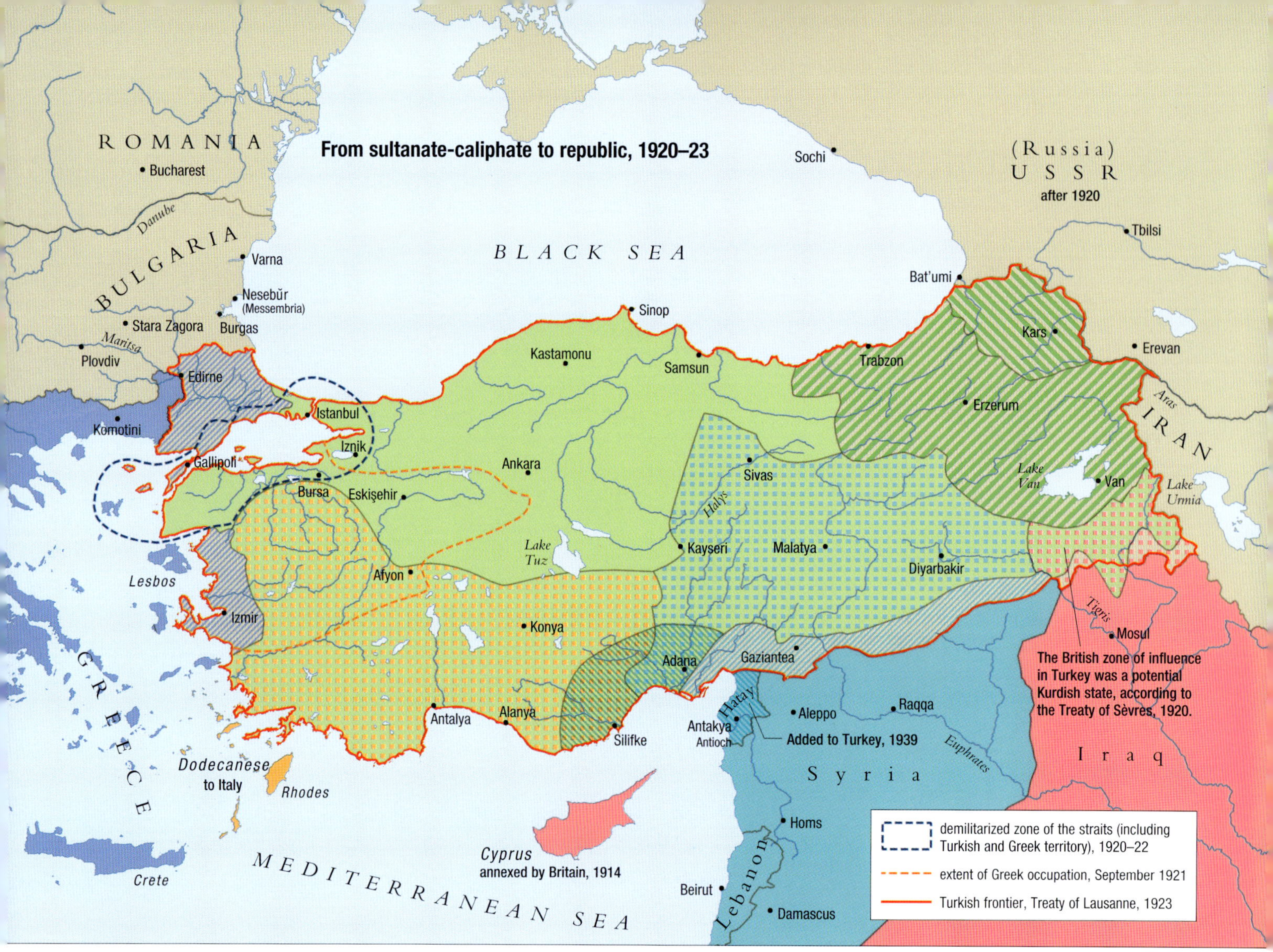

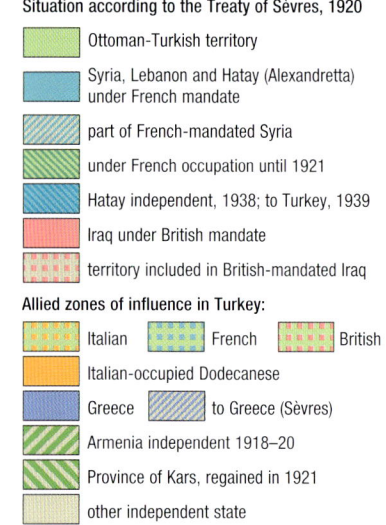

From sultanate-caliphate to republic, 1920–23
ROMANIA
Bucharest
Danube
BULGARIA
Varna
Nesebŭr (Messembria)
Stara Zagora
Burgas
Maritsa
Plovdiv
Edirne
Komotini
Istanbul
Iznik
Gallipoli
Bursa
Eskişehir
BLACK SEA
Sinop
Kastamonu
Samsun
Ankara
Lake Tuz
Afyon
Konya
Sivas
Halys
Kayseri
Malatya
Diyarbakir
Sochi
(Russia) USSR after 1920
Tbilsi
Bat'umi
Kars
Erevan
Trabzon
Erzerum
Aras
IRAN
Lake Van
Van
Lake Urmia
Tigris
Mosul
The British zone of influence in Turkey was a potential Kurdish state, according to the Treaty of Sèvres, 1920.
Lesbos
Izmir
GREECE
Antalya
Alanya
Adana
Gaziantea
Silifke
Hatay
Antakya Antioch
Added to Turkey, 1939
Aleppo
Raqqa
Euphrates
Iraq
Syria
Dodecanese to Italy
Rhodes
Cyprus annexed by Britain, 1914
Crete
MEDITERRANEAN SEA
Homs
Lebanon
Beirut
Damascus
demilitarized zone of the straits (including Turkish and Greek territory), 1920–22
extent of Greek occupation, September 1921
Turkish frontier, Treaty of Lausanne, 1923
Situation according to the Treaty of Sèvres, 1920
Ottoman-Turkish territory
Syria, Lebanon and Hatay (Alexandretta) under French mandate
part of French-mandated Syria
under French occupation until 1921
Hatay independent, 1938; to Turkey, 1939
Iraq under British mandate
territory included in British-mandated Iraq
Allied zones of influence in Turkey:
Italian
French
British
Italian-occupied Dodecanese
Greece
to Greece (Sèvres)
Armenia independent 1918–20
Province of Kars, regained in 1921
other independent state

Balkan War, then given to Bulgaria as a reward for entering the Great War as an ally. The Nationalists then turned to internal matters, marched on Istanbul, and abolished the Ottoman sultanate on November 1, 1922. The last sultan, Mehmet VI (Vahdeddin), and his family were declared *persona non grata* and exiled, leaving the country on the 17th. The caliphate was constitutionally abolished on March 3, 1924. (In 1974, the Grand National Assembly of Turkey granted descendants of the former dynasty the right to acquire Turkish citizenship.)

In a new peace settlement Turkey retained eastern Thrace, Edirne, the two northern Aegean islands of Imroz and Bozcaada, plus sovereignty over the Dardanelles, while the question of Mosul was referred to the League of Nations. The Republic of Turkey was officially declared with the Treaty of Lausanne, signed on July 24, 1923,which also paved the way for a massive exchange of minority populations. About 20 percent of the Anatolian population died in 1914–25; 10 percent had emigrated. In the Balkan states, 27 percent of Muslims died, over 60 percent had emigrated or been expelled. Bulgaria absorbed 250,000 refugees, while 380,000 Turks left Greece for Turkey. On the eve of the 20th century's second great conflict—Hitler's War—there was a last gain for the Republic when, in 1939, the Hatay (Antakya, Antioch region) became incorporated into Turkey, returning at least a part of the old sultanate's Syrian territory.

As to the Ottoman heritage, many Christian religious buildings were left to

CHAPTER ELEVEN: FALL OF THE OTTOMANS

crumble in Turkey, though many were converted into mosques or tourist sites. In the Balkans there was no comparable Christian tradition of reusing Islamic structures so the majority were demolished. A few survived, either reused as storage structures or—too well built—to simply crumble. Over 95 percent of Ottoman civic buildings were lost, including fine 14th-century monuments dynamited as late as the 1960s. Only in recent years have efforts begun to preserve the best examples of the Ottoman empire's grand architecture.

The prime minister Ismet Paşa (left), just returned from the Lausanne conference that confirmed modern Turkey's borders, and the president Mustafa Kemal Atatürk stand either side of Atatürk's wife Latifah, 19 October 1923.

The Süleymaniyye, silhouetted across the Golden Horn, seen from the old Galata Bridge in 1964, when the city's skyline still lacked tower blocks.

TABLES OF RULERS

Seljuq Turkish dynasties

Great Seljuq rulers
1037–1157
- 1037–63 Tuğril I
- 1063–73 Alp Arslan *(victor at battle of Manzikert, 1071)*
- 1073–92 Malik Şah I
- 1092–94 Mahmud I
- 1094–1105 Barkiyaruq
- 1105 Malik Şah II
- 1105–1118 Muhammad I Tapar
- 1118–57 Ahmed Sanjar

Seljuq rulers of Kirman (southern Iran)
1041–1187
- 1048–73 Ahmad Qawurd
- 1073–74 Kirman Şah
- 1074–85 Sultan Şah
- 1085–97 Turan Şah I
- 1097–1101 Iran Şah
- 1101–42 Arslan Shah I
- 1142–56 Muhammad I
- 1156–70 Toğrül Şah
- 1170–70 Bahram Şah *(1st time)*
- 1170–71 Arslan Şah II *(1st time)*
- 1171–72 Bahram Şah *(2nd time)*
- 1172–77 Arslan Şah II *(2nd time)*
- 1177–83 Turan Şah II
- 1183–87 Muhammad II

(Kirman as a separate state was conquered in 1187, probably by Ghuzz tribes)

Seljuk rulers in Syria
1076–1117
- 1078–95 Tutush I
- 1095–1113 Ridwan
- 1113–14 Alp Arslan al-Akhras
- 1114–23 Sultan Şah

(sultans/emirs of Damascus)

- 1076–78 Abaq al-Khwarazmi
- 1078–95 Tutush I *(of Syria)*
- 1095–1104 Duqaq
- 1104 Tutush II

Seljuq sultans of Rum
1077–1307
- 1081–92 Süleyman Ibn Qutalmïsh
- 1092–1109 Kilij Arslan I
- 1109–16 Malik Şah
- 1116–56 Mas'ud I
- 1156–92 Kilij Arslan II
- 1192–97 Kay Khusrau I *(1st time)*
- 1197–1204 Süleyman II
- 1204–05 Kilij Arslan III
- 1205–11 Kay Khusrau I *(2nd time)*
- 1211–20 Kay Ka'us I
- 1220–37 Kay Qubadh I
- 1237–46 Kay Khusrau II
- 1246–57 Kay Ka'us II *(as joint ruler, 1248–57)*
- 1248–65 Kilij Arslan IV *(as joint ruler, 1248–57)*
- 1265–82 Kay Khusrau III
- 1282–84 Mas'ud II *(1st time)*
- 1284 Kay Qubadh III *(1st time)*
- 1284–93 Mas'ud II *(2nd time)*
- 1293–94 Kay Qubadh III *(2nd time)*
- 1294–1301 Mas'ud II *(3rd time)*
- 1301–03 Qubadh III *(3rd time)*
- 1303–07 Mas'ud II *(f4th time)*
- 1307 Mas'ud III *(state absorbed by Il-Khans)*

Emirs of Lebanon

Ma'n emirs
- c.1516–? Qormaz I
- ?–? Ma'n I
- ?–? Ma'n II
- ?–1585 Qormaz II
- 1585–1633 Fakhr al-Din
- 1633–58 Mulhim Ibn Yunis
- 1658–97 Ahmad Ibn Mulhim

Shihab emirs
- 1697–1707 Bashir I
- 1707–32 Haydar
- 1732–54 Mulhim
- 1754–70 Mansur
- 1770–88 Yusuf
- 1788–1840 Bashir II
- 1840–42 Bashir III

House of Osman (Ottomans)

Pre-imperial heads of the House
- ?–1227 Süleymanşah *(bey)*
- 1227–1281 Ertuğrul *(bey)*

Imperial heads of the House
- 1281–1324 Osman I *(bey)*
- 1324–60 Orhan I *(bey)*
- 1360–89 Murat I *(sultan from 1383)*
- 1389–1402 Bayezit I

(Interregnum, 1402–1413)

- 1413–21 Mehmet I
- 1421–44 Murat II *(1st time)*
- 1444–45 Mehmet II
- 1445–51 Murat II *(2nd time)*
- 1451–81 Mehmet II *(2nd time; the Conqueror)*
- 1481–1512 Bayezit II
- 1512–20 Selim I *(caliph from 1517)*
- 1520–66 Süleyman I *(Kanuni; the Magnificent)*
- 1566–74 Selim II
- 1574–95 Murat III
- 1595–1603 Mehmet III
- 1603–17 Ahmed I
- 1617–18 Mustafa I
- 1618–22 Osman II
- 1622–23 Mustafa I
- 1623–40 Murad IV
- 1640–48 Ibrahim I
- 1648–87 Mehmet IV
- 1687–91 Süleyman II
- 1691–95 Ahmed II
- 1695–1703 Mustafa II
- 1703–30 Ahmed III
- 1730–54 Mahmut I
- 1754–57 Osman III
- 1757–74 Mustafa III
- 1774–89 Abdul Hamid I
- 1789–1807 Selim III
- 1807–08 Mustafa IV
- 1808–39 Mahmut II
- 1839–61 Abd'l Mecid
- 1861–76 Abdulaziz
- 1876 Murat V
- 1876–1909 Abdul Hamid II
- 1909–18 Mehmet V *(Reşad)*
- 1918–22 Mehmet VI *(Vahdeddin; deposed)*

Emperors of Byzantium

From the 11th century

976–1025	Basil II *(the Bulgar-slayer)*	
1025–28	Constantine VIII *(brother of Basil II)*	
1028–34	Romanus III *(son-in-law of Constantine VIII)*	
1034–41	Michael IV *(married widow of Romanus III)*	
1041–42	Michael V *(cousin of Michael IV)*	
1042	Zoe and Theodora *(daughters of Constantine VIII)*	
1042–55	Contantine IX *(married widow of Michael IV)*	
1055–56	Theodora *(restored)*	
1056–57	Michael VI *(chosen by Theodora)*	
1057–59	Isaac I Comnenus *(overthrew Michael VI)*	
1059–67	Constantine X Ducas *(chosen on retirement of Isaac I)*	
1068–71	Romanus IV Diogenes *(married widow of Constantine X; the loser at Manzikert, 1071, but spared by Alp Arslan, murdered on orders of Michael VII)*	
1071–78	Michael VII Ducas *(Constantine X's son)*	
1078–81	Nichephorus III *(married widow of Michael VII)*	
1081–1118	Alexius I Comnenus *(nephew of Isaac I)*	
1118–43	John II Comnenus *(son of Alexius I)*	
1143–80	Manuel I Comnenus *(son of John II)*	
1180–83	Alexius II Comnenus *(son of Manuel I)*	
1183–85	Andronicus I Comnenus *(nephew of John II)*	
1185–95	Isaac II *(great-grandson of Alexius I)*	
1195–1203	Alexius III *(brother of Isaac II)*	
1203–04	Isaac II Angelus and Alexius IV *(restored, father and son)*	
1204	Alexius V *(son-in-law of Alexius III)*	
1204–22	Theodore I *(son-in-law of Alexius III)*	
1222–54	John III Ducas *(son-in-law of Theodore I)*	
1254–58	Theodore II *(son of John III)*	
1258–1261	John IV *(son of Theodore II)*	
1259–82	Michael VIII Palaeologus *(restorer of the empire of Constantinople from the Latins)*	
1282–1328	Andronicus II Palaeologus *(son of Michael VIII*	
1328–41	Andronicus III Palaeologus *(grandson of Andronicus II*	
1341–91	John V Palaeologus *(son of Andronicus III*	
1347–54	John VI Cantacuzenus *(father-in-law of John V*	
1376–79	Andronicus IV Palaeologus *(son of John V*	
1390	John VII Palaeologus *(son of Andronicus IV*	
1391–1425	Manuel II Palaeologus *(son of John V, brother of Andronicus IV)*	
1425–48	John VIII Palaeologus *(son of Manuel II)*	
1449–1453	Constantine XI Palaeologus *(son of Manuel II; deposed, possibly killed, by Mehmet II the Conqueror*	

Latin empire of Romania

Latin emperors of Romania (Constantinople)
1204–05	Baldwin I of Flanders
1206–16	Henry of Hainault
1217	Peter of Courtenay
1217–19	Yolanda
1221–28	Robert of Courtenay
1228–61	Baldwin II
[1231–37	John of Brienne

Despotate of Epirus
1204–15	Michael I
1215–24	Theodore

Emperors/despots of Thessalonica
1224–30	Theodore
1230–40	Manuel
1240–44	John
1244–46	Demetrius

Despotate of Epirus
1237–71	Michael II
1271–96	Nicephorus
1296–1318	Thomas
1318–23	Nicholas Orsinir
1323–55	John Orsini
1335–40	Nicephorus II

Sebastocrators of Thessaly
1271–96	John I
1296–1303	Constantine
1303–18	John II

Husaynid beys of Tunisia

1705–35	Al-Husayn I		1882–1902	Ali III
1735–56	Ali I		1902–06	Muhammad IV
1756–59	Muhammad I		1906–22	Muhammad V
1759–82	Ali II		1922–29	Muhammad VI
1782–1814	Hammuda Pasha		1929–42	Ahmad II
1814	'Uthman		1942–43	Muhammad VII
1814–24	Mahmud		1943–57	Muhammad VIII
1824–35	Al-Husayn II		1957	Rashad
1835–37	Mustafa			
1837–55	Ahmad I			
1855–59	Muhammad II			
1859–82	Muhammad III			

(Republic of Tunisia established 20 March 1957)

Karamanlis of Tripolitania

1711–45	Ahmad Bey I
1745–54	Muhammad
1754–95	Ali I
1795–96	Ahmad II
1796–1832	Yusuf *(deposed)*

(Re-establishment of Ottoman direct rule, 1835)

Giray khans of Krim

Ottoman vassals from the late 15th century

1449–56	Hajji Giray I *(1st reign)*	1623–24	Muhammad Giray III *(2nd reign)*	1724–30	Mengli Giray II *(1st reign)*
1456	Haydar Giray	1624	Jani Beg Giray *(2nd reign)*	1730–36	Qaplan Giray I *(3d reign)*
1456–66	Hajji Giray I *(2nd reign)*	1624–27	Muhammad Giray III *(3rd reign)*	1736–37	Fath Giray II
1466–67	Nur Dawlat Giray *(2nd reign)*	1627–35	Jani Beg Giray *(3rd reign)*	1737–40	Mengli Giray II *(2nd reign)*
1467–74	Mengli Giray *(1st reign)*	1635–37	'Inayat Giray	1740–43	Salamat Giray II
1474–75	Nur Dawlat Giray *(2nd reign)*	1637–41	Bahadur Giray	1748–56	Arslan Giray *(1st reign)*
1475–76	Mengli Giray *(2nd reign)*	1641–44	Muhammad Giray IV *(2nd reign)*	1756–58	Halim Giray
1476–78	Nur Dawlat Giray *(3rd reign)*	1644–54	Islam Giray III	1758–64	Qïrïm Giray *(1st reign)*
1478–1514	Mengli Giray *(3rd reign)*	1654–66	Muhammad Giray IV *(2nd reign)*	1764–67	Salim Giray III *(1st reign)*
1514–23	Muhammad Giray I	1666–71	'Adil Giray	1767	Arslan Giray *(2nd reign)*
1523–24	Ghazi Giray I	1671–78	Salim Giray I *(2nd reign)*	1767–68	Maqsud Giray *(1st reign)*
1524–3	Sa'adat Giray I2	1678–83	Murad Giray	1768–69	Qïrïm Giray *(2nd reign)*
1532	Islam Giray I	1683–84	Hajji Giray II	1769	Dawlat Giray IV *(1st reign)*
1532–51	Sahib Giray I	1684–91	Salim Giray I *(2nd reign)*	1769–70	Qaplan Giray II
1551–77	Dawlat Giray I	1691	Sa'adat Giray II	1770–71	Salim Giray III *(2nd reign)*
1577–84	Muhammad Giray II	1691–92	Safa' Giray	1771–72	Maqsud Giray *(2nd reign)*
1584–88	Islam Giray II	1692–99	Salim Giray I *(3rd reign)*	1772–75	Sahib Giray II
1588–96	Ghazi Giray II *(1st reign)*	1699–1702	Dawlat Giray II *(2nd reign)*	1775–77	Dawlat Giray IV *(2nd reign)*
1596	Fath Giray I	1702–04	Salim Giray I *(4th reign)*	1777–83	Shahin Giray *(1st reign)*
1596–1608	Ghazi Giray II *(2nd reign)*	1704–07	Ghazi Giray III	1783	Bahadur Giray II
1608	Toqtamïsh Giray	1707–08	Qaplan Giray I *(2nd reign)*	*(Russian annexation of the Crimea, 1783)*	
1608–10	Salamat Giray I	1708–13	Dawlat Giray II *(2nd reign)*	1783–87	Shahin Giray *(again, as Russian vassal)*
1610	Muhammad Giray III *(1st reign)*	1713–16	Qaplan Giray I *(2nd reign)*		
1610–23	Jani Beg Giray *(1st reign)*	1716–17	Dawlat Giray III		
		1717–24	Sa'adat Giray III		

Mamluk rulers of Egypt

1250	Shajarat al-Durr	1382	Al-Salih Salah al-Din Hajji II	1496–98	Al-Nasir Muhammad IV
1250–57	Al-Mu'izz al-Din Aybak	1382–89	Al-Zahir Sayf al-Din Barquq	1498–1500	Al-Zahir Qansawh
1257–59	Al-Mansur Nur al-Din Ali	1389–90	Al-Salih Salah al-Din Hajji II *(again)*	1500–01	Al-Ashraf Janbulat
1259–1260	Al-Muzaffar Sayf al-Din Qutuz	1390–99	Al-Zahir Sayf al-Din Barquq *(again)*	1501	Al-Adil Sayf al-Din Tuman Bey I
1260–77	Al-Zahir Baibars	1399–1405	Al-Nasir al-Din Faraj *(1st reign)*	1501–1516	Al-Ashraf Qansawh al-Ghawri
1277–79	Al-Sa'id Nasir al-Din Baraka	1405	Al-Mansur Izz al-Din Abd Al-Aziz	1516–17	Al-Ashraf Tuman Bey II *(defeated by Selim I at Raydaniyah; executed)*
1279	Al-Adil Badr al-Din Salamish	1405–1412	Al-Nasir al-Din Faraj *(2nd reign)*		
1279–90	Al-Mansur Sayf al-Din Qalawun	1412	Al-Adil Al-Mustayn *(Abbasid Caliph, proclaimed sultan)*		
1290–93	Al-Ashraf Salah al-Din Khalil	1412–21	Al-Muayad Sayf al-Din Shaykh	## Later rulers of Egypt	
1293–94	Al-Nasir Muhammad *(1st reign)*	1421	Al-Muzaffar Ahmad II	**Egyptian Dynasty of Muhammad Ali**	
1294–96	Al-Adil Zayn al-Din Kitbougha	1421	Al-Zahir Sayf al-Din Tatar	1805–48	Muhammad Ali Paşa *(governor)*
1296–99	Al-Mansour Husam al-Din Lajin	142–22	Al-Salih Nasir al-Din Muhammad III	1848	Ibrahim Paşa *(governor)*
1299–1309	Al-Nasir Muhammad *(2nd reign)*	1422–38	Al-Ashraf Sayf al-Din Barsbay	1848–54	Abbas Hilmi I Paşa *(governor)*
1309–10	Al-Muzaffar al-Din Baibars II	1438	Al-Aziz Jamal al-Din Yusuf	1854–63	Muhammad Sa'id Paşa *(governor)*
1310–41	Al-Nasir Muhammad *(3rd reign)*	1438–53	Al-Zahir Sayf al-Din Jaqmaq	1863–79	Isma'il Paşa *(governor to 1867, then khedive)*
1341	Al-Mansur Sayf al-Din Abu Bakr	1453	Al-Mansour Fakhr al-Din Uthman	1879–92	Muhammad Tawfiq *(khedive)*
1341–42	Al-Ashraf Ala al-Din Kujuk	1453–61	Al-Ashraf Sayf al-Din Inal	1892–1914	Abbas Hilmi II *(deposed)*
1342	Al-Nasir Shihab al-Din Ahmad	1461	Al-Muayad Shihab al-Din Ahmad	1914–17	Husayn Kamil *(Egypt seceded from Ottoman empire 1914; assumed title of sultan in 1917)*
1342–45	Al-Salih Imad al-Din Ismail	1461–67	Al-Zahir Sayf al-Din Khushqadam	1917–36	Ahmad Fu'ad I *(sultan until 1922, then king)*
1345–46	Al-Kamil Sayf al-Din Shaban II	1467	Al-Zahir Sayf al-Din Yalbay	1936–52	Faruq *(deposed by army officers coup)*
1346–47	Al-Muzaffar Sayf al-Din Hajji I	1467–68	Al-Zahir Timurbugha	1952–53	Ahmad Fu'ad II
1347–51	Al-Nasir Nasir al-Din Al-Hasan *(1st reign)*	1468–96	Al-Ashraf Sayf al-Din Qaitbay	*(Egyptian Republic proclaimed, 1953)*	
1351–54	Al-Salih Salah al-Din Salih				
1354–61	Al-Nasir Nasir al-Din Al-Hasan *(2nd reign)*				
1361–63	Al-Mansur Salah al-Din Muhammad				
1363–77	Al-Ashraf Nasir al-Din Shaban II				
1377–82	Al-Mansur Ala al-Din Ali				

INDEX

A
Abaqa Khan 25
Abbas, shah 102
Abbas Hilmi I 149
Abbasids 22, 68, 100
Abd al-Aziz ibn Sa'ud 164
Abd Allah, king 179, 180
Abdul Hamid II, sultan 154-155, 159, 160
Abd'l Mecid, sultan 143
Aden 173
administration, 19th century 140
Adrianople *see* Edirne
Adriatic Sea 54
adultery 138
Aegean Sea 42, 43, 45, 50-51, 68, 73, 83, 86, 89, 92, 111, 119, 151, 162
ahi militia 57
Ahmad Arabshah, poet 71
Ahmad Ibn Mulhim, emir 105
Ahmet I, mosque 128
Ainos (Enez) 88, 92
air force 161, 165-166
akıncı(s) 62, 112-113
'Ala al-Dawlah, Dulkadir prince 98
Alaşehir *see* Philadelphia
Albania/Albanians 52, 54, 56, 78-79, 87, 141, 143, 146, 155, 161-162, 182
Al-Bu Sa'id Omani dynasty 118
Aleppo 71
Alexius I Comnenus, emperor 14
Algiers/Algeria 120, 123, 152-153
al-Giza, battle of 100
Ali Paşa of Janina 150
Alla'al-Din, vizir 62
Al-Malik al-Ashraf Tuman Bey II *see* Tuman Bey II
Alp Arslan 14
Alphonso V, king 83
Altai mountains 9
Amasya 74
America(ns) 146, 152, 157-158
American Civil War 157
Amiens, Peace of 146
Amir Husayn, Mamluk admiral 97
Amir-i Sawahil 50
Anadolu Hisarı 82 *see also* Rumeli Hisarı
Anatolia 14-16, 20, 22, 25, 28-30, 33-35, 38, 42-43, 46-51, 57, 70, 73-77, 82-83, 102-104, 130, 150, 153, 162, 173, 177-178, 182-183
Andrew III, king 52
Andronicus II Palaeologus, emperor 51
Andronicus III Palaeologus, emperor 40-41
Andronicus IV Palaeologus, emperor 41
Angevins 52, 54
Ankara, battle of 71, 75, 81
ANZAC troops 175
Aq Qoyunlu tribe 71, 101
Arabia/Arabs 9, 97, 100, 147, 164-165, 176-181, 182
architecture 31, 68-69, 126, 185
  Seljuq 16
  early Ottoman 34-35
Arghun Khan 25
Armenia(ns) 12, 14, 92, 154, 162, 163, 172, 173, 177, 182
  revolutionaries 174, 178, 189
armies 62-64, 71-72, Mamluk 98,99
  in Syria 103-104, 115
  under Tanzimat 143
  Egyptian, 19th-century 146-149
  Tripolitanian 152
  German influence 161
Arpad dynasty 52

Arslan, Alp 14
Arslan, Qïlïch 14
art 130, 131, 143
Atatürk *see* Mustafa Kemal
Attila the Hun 9
Austria-Hungary 144, 148, 151, 161
Avars, tribe 9
aviation 165-167
ayans local Balkan leaders 150
Aya Sofia, mosque 85
Aydın Oğlu Muhammad Bey 50
Aydın Oğullari (beylik) 29, 31, 40, 50, 74, 75-76, 90
Ayyubids 22, 27
Azerbaijan(is) 101-102, 177
Azov, town 144

B
Baghdad 22, 102
Bahçesaray 95
Balfour, Arthur 179
Balfour Declaration, the 179
Balkan(s) 10, 35, 39, 43, 46, 52-69, 70, 77-80, 83, 90, 113, 141, 150-152, 154-156
  decline of Muslim population 141
  First & Second Balkan Wars 162, 165, 169
bán 52, 53
Banu Shihab, clan 105
Barbarossa, Hayrüddin, Barbary corsair 119-122
Barbary States/Coast 119-122, 152-153
Basra 118
battles:
  al-Giza 100
  Ankara 71-72, 81
  Bulaq 100
  Çaldıran 98, 102
  Dorylaeum 28
  Gran 125
  Hattin 22
  Keresztes 115
  Köse Dağ 23, 28
  Kosova 79
  Koyunhisar (Bapheus) 33, 36
  Kozmin forest 93
  Kyustendil 58
  Lepanto 114
  Maltepe (Pelekanon) 37
  Manzikert 12, 14
  Marj Dabiq 98
  Mohács 108
  Myriokephalon 15
  Nezib 148
  Nicopolis 52, 67, 68
  Pavia 106
  Plocnit 54
  Rashid 146
  Raydaniyah 99
  River Kalka 22
  St Gothard 116
  Sarıkamış 173
  Tavşancıl (Philokrene) 37
  Varna 79
Baydu, Mongol general 23
Bayezit I, sultan 49-51, 64, 67, 68, 70-73, 81-82
Bayezit II, sultan 98
Beethoven, composer 136
bekci watchmen 129
Bektaşi dervishes 46-47, 57, 60
Belgrade 106
  Treaty of 144
Berbers 122
Bessarion 82

Bethune, George 146
Bey, Cavalry Captain Fesa 165
beys 24, 29, 83, 96
beyliks 23, 24, 30, 30-31, 36, 37, 38, 40, 48-49, 50, 51, 74, 75, 90
  Aydın 29, 31, 40, 50-51, 74, 76, 90
  Eretna 48
  Germiyan 29, 49, 57, 74, 77
  Göynük 37
  Karaman 48, 73, 74, 77, 96
  Karası 29, 37, 38, 90
  Menteşe 50, 74, 75
  Ottoman 29, 33
  Saruhan 29, 51, 74
  Teke 49-50, 74, 76
Beqaa Valley 105
Bihać 112
Bilbays 99
binbaşı officer 62
Birkat al-Haj (Pilgrims' Pool) 99
Black Sea 9, 10, 21, 35, 40, 45, 55, 76, 81, 82-83, 86, 92, 94, 95, 116, 119-120, 144-145, 168, 182
Blériot, Louis 165
Bogomil heresy 53, 55, 58, 60
Bonnier, Marc 166
Book of Dede Korkut, The 10
Bosnia/Bosnians 52, 53-54, 106, 112-114, 141, 146, 156, 161
Bosporus 37, 82, 84, 92
  Russia's desire for 145, 175
Brankovic, Prince George of Serbia 79, 83
Breslau, warship 168, 172
Britain/British 140, 145-146, 151, 154, 163-164
  Great War 168-172
  post-war settlements 179-180
Buczacz, Treaty of 116
building regulations, Istanbul 128
Bulaq, battle of 100
Bulgaria/Bulgarians 55, 58, 68, 77, 141, 154, 162, 177
Bursa 33, 34-35, 60
Byron, Lord George, 151
Byzantium/Byzantine 9, 10-11, 12-17, 20-21, 29-30, 31, 33-34, 40-42, 51, 54-58, 81-85, 133-134, 182
  Byzantine civil war 41 (panel), 59
  conversions to Islam 34, 69, 70, 112

C
Cabral, Pedro Alvarez 97
Cairo 68, 95, 97, 177
Çaldıran, battle of 98, 102
Çandarlı family 78
Çandarlı Halil, vizir 78, 82
Candar Oğullari 49, 75
Capodistria, John 151
caravanserais 20, 39
Carinthia 113
Carniola 113
carpet-making 131-132
Caspian Sea 95, 177
Castriota, George *see* Skanderbeg
Catalans, Grand Company of, 33-34, 45, 51, 55 *see also* de Flor, Roger
Cathar heresy 53
Cavit Paşa 168
Çelebi Kâtip, historian 112
Çelebi Mehmet *see* Mehmet I, sultan
Cemal Paşa 168, 174
ceramics 19, 132
çevgen bells 136 *see also* meterhane
çevkâni singers 137 *see also* meterhane

Chalcidice peninsula 86-88
Charles V, HR Emperor 110
Charles VI, king of France 64
Charles Robert I, king 52
Chios, island 43, 59, 73, 88, 111
Chomanoi, tribe *see* Kipchaq Turks
Christianity/Christendom 12, 14, 25, 33, 34, 36, 43, 47, 52, 55, 57, 58, 60, 79, 82, 86-88, 108, 112, 123, 140, 141, 143, 151, 155
  treatment by Timur-i Lenk 70-71
Churchill, Winston 168
Cihannâma (Geography) 113
Cilicia 15, 26, 97
Çobanids 48
cog, ship type 91
Committee of Union and Progress (CUP) 159, 161
Constantine XI, emperor 82, 85
Constantinople 21, 42, 55, 68, 70, 74, 81-85, 86-87, 89, 133
  final days 82-85
Corfu 111
Corinth, Isthmus of 82
Çorlu 55
Cossacks 116, 144
Couman, tribe *see* Kipchaq Turks
craft guild/association 18
crafts 131-133, 143
Crete 111, 115, 141, 151, 156, 162
Crimea 22, 88, 92, 144, 145
Crimean War 143
Croatia/Croatians 52, 113
crusader states 42, 43 *see also* Outremer
crusades: 14, 28, 42, 43, 64-68, 77-79, 83
Cüneyt Bey 74, 76
Cyprus 113, 154, 163
Cyrenaica 153

D
da Gama, Vasco 97
Damascus 71, 103, 105, 177-179
Danishmandid Turks 14-15, 48
Danishmandname 15
Danube, river 27, 68, 70, 106, 140
Dardanelles 29, 38-39, 40, 57, 72, 82, 162, 172, 174-176, 182, 184
  Russia's desire for 145
Dashnak Armenian rebels 159, 163, 173
de Flor, Roger 33, 51
delis, Syrian light cavalry 104
Demetrios, despotate of Morea 83, 88
dervishes 46-47, 58, 60
devşirme recruitment system 103, 115
Despotate of Epirus 54, 56
Despotate of the Morea 56, 82, 83, 88-89
Destan of Umur Paşa 50
d'Hautpoul, General Beaufort 148
Dobruja 10, 55
Dodecanese islands 151, 162, 165
Domani Dağ 33
Don, river 95
Doria, Admiral Andrea 111
d'Oro, Tedisio 44
Doroszenko, Peter 116
Dorylaeum, battle of 28
Dorylaeum, town *see* Eskişehir
Dracula *see* Vlad Tepes
drunkenness, punishment for 138
Druze sect 102, 105 *see also* Ma'an
düdüghü military whistle 137
  see also meterhane
Dulkadir Oğullari 48, 77, 96, 98
Dulkadir, Qaraj Ibn (Dhu'l-Qadr) 48

...ephan 54, 58-59
...name Destan 99, 100

E
Edebali, Shaykh 27, 33, 63
Edessa, Crusader County of 15
Edirne 35, 60, 68-69, 82-83, 123, 124, 132, 134, 162
Edremit, aircraft 167
Egypt 12, 46, 94, 95-97, 119-121, 146-149, 154, 156-158, 163, 166, 181, 182
Empire of Nicaea 21, 32
Empire of Trebizond 21, 40, 56, 71, 77, 83, 93
emperors:
   Alexius I Comnenus 14
   Andronicus III Palaeologus 40
   Andronicus IV Palaeologus 41
   Charles V 110
   Constantine XI 82, 85
   Dusan, Stephan 54, 58-59
   Ferdinand I 108
   John V Palaeologus 39, 41, 56
   John VI Cantacuzenos 39, 40-41, 55
   John VII Palaeologus 81
   John VIII Palaeologus, 82
   Manuel I Comnenus 15
   Manuel II Palaeologus 64, 81-82
   Michael VIII Palaeologus 30
   Peter the Great 144, 145
   Romanus IV 14
   Rudolf II 115
Enveri, poet 90
Enver Paşa 168, 173, 174
Ephesus *see* Selçuk
Epirus 54, 56
Eretna Ibn Ja'far 52
Eretna Oğulları (beylik) 48
ethnic cleansing 141
Ertuğrul 26, 27-28, 33
Ertuğrul, aircraft 166
Erzerum 27, 102, 106, 173
Eskişehir 28, 136
esnaf craft associtaion 18
Euphrates, river 27
Evliya Çelebi, writer 136
Evrenos, Kara Timürtaş Gazi 38, 60
eyâlet (provinces) 49, 87, 116-117

F
fabric(s) *see* textiles
Fadeiell, Rotislav 156
Fakhr al-Din II, emir 105
fakih solicitor 138 *see also* mufti
Faysal, Emir, King of Iraq 177-180
Federated Transcaucasian Republic 177
fellahin Egyptian peasantry 146
Ferdinand I of Austria, HR Emperor 108
Fesa Bey, Cavalry Captain 165
Fethi, Captain 166
fetvas (fatwa, judgement) 138
Fezzan 153
Filibe *see* Plovdiv
First Balkan War 162, 165, 169
First Crusade 14-15, 28
First World War *see* Great war
Finno-Ugrian nomads 10
Foça *see* Phocaea
fornication, punishment for 138
Forum of Theodosius 133
Fourth Crusade 42, 43, 116
France/French 106, 123-124, 140, 145, 146, 153, 154, 157, 165-166, 168
   Great War 169, 172, 175, 176, 178-180
Francis I, king of France 106

Francis II, king of France 140
freebooters *see* pirates/piracy
futuwa 29, 62

G
Gábor, Prince Bethlen 125
Gagik II, king 12
Gallipoli 40, 41, 55, 57-58, 168
   campaign of 174-176
Gattilusi, Dorino I 88
Gattilusi, Palamedes 88
Gazi Evrenos, Kara Timürtaş 38, 60, 65
gazi states 31, 36
gazi warriors 12, 33, 38, 46, 62
General Syrian Congress 178-179
Genghis Khan 10, 22, 24, 27, 94
Genoa/Genoese 22, 41, 43-44, 51, 59, 64, 72-73, 74, 76, 77, 85, 88, 89, 92, 94, 111
Georgia(ns) 48, 145, 162, 177
George of Trebizond 86
Germany/Germans 146, 148, 161, 168
   barbarian tribes 8
Germiyan beylik/Oğulları 29, 49, 74, 76
Ghaznavid Turks 11
ghulat tradition 102
Ghuzz *see* Oğuz
ghulam slaves 28
Giray khans 94, 95
Giromerios, monastery 87
Glück, composer 136
Goeben, warship 168, 172
Gök khaganate 9
Golden Horde 55, 94, 95
Golden Horn 84, 85
Göynük beylik 37
Gran, battle of 125
Grand National Assembly 183, 184
Great Britain *see* Britain
Great War, the 143, 156, 161, 168-180
   armistice and settlements 177-178
Greece/Greeks 42, 43, 54, 56, 68, 87, 89, 111, 151, 154, 162, 182-185
Greek War of Independence 151
Gujarat 118

H
Habsburgs 94, 108-111, 115, 116, 123, 140, 144-145
Haci Bektaş 47, 63
Hafiz Paşa 148
hajj 39, 63, 100, 104
Hakkı, Lieutenant 166
Hamid Oğulları 49
hampas slave-soldiers 152
hans (Khans) *see* caravanserais
harem (Topkapı Sarayı) 134
Hashemites 177-180
Hattin, battle of 22
Haydn, composer 136
Hexamilon Wall, the 82
Hezarfenn, writer 128
Hijaz 96, 100, 117, 164, 177, 178
History of the Prophet and Caliphs 68
HMS *Goliath* 172
Holy Roman Empire 108, 115, 123, 125, 140
Hospitallers 46, 51, 55, 64, 73, 97, 110-111
   fall of Rhodes 110
Hüdavendigar mosque 35
Hülegü Khan 24-25
Hunçak Armenian revolutionaries 163
Hunedoara 77
Hungary/Hungarians 52, 53, 55, 56, 58, 67, 77-79, 80, 89, 93, 116, 123, 125, 144
   see also Austria-Hungary

   Ottoman invasion 108-113 *see also* Imperial Hungary
Huns, tribe 8
Hunyadi, Janos 77-78, 80, 83
Husayn Bey 153

I
Ibn al-Jazari, historian 68
Ibn Battuta 35
Ibn Ja'far, Eretna 48
İbrahim Paşa, son of Muhammad Ali 148-149
İbrahim Paşa, vizir 113
Iconium *see* Konya
Idrisids 177, 181
Ifriqiyah *see* Tunis
ikvan brotherhoods 29
Il-Khans/Khanate 24-25, 26-28, 48-49
illik kafirleri 45
Ilyas, Gürz 113
imaret soup kitchen 17, 69
Imroz, island 88
Imperial Hungary 109, 115
India 97, 118, 131
Indian Ocean 97-98, 100, 117-118, 119
industry 18, 143
Internal Macedonian Revolutionary Organisation (IMRO) 156
iqta fiefs 28 *see also* timar fiefs
Iran 21, 25, 28, 34, 98, 101-102, 162, 173, 182
Iranians, tribe 8, 10
Iraq(is) 102, 141, 143, 179, 180-181, 182
İsa Bey Prandi 39
İsa Ibn Muhammad Bey, mosque 31
İsa son of Bayezit I 73-74 *see also* Musa, Mustafa, Süleyman
Isfandiyar Mubariz al-Din 75
Isfandiyar beylik/Oğulları 49, 75
İshak Paşa 113
Islam, general 14, 16, 17, 19, 24, 33, 95, 96, 114-115
   Shi'a 36, 46, 47, 96, 101-102, 106, 115, 141
   Sunni 36, 46, 96, 102, 105, 106, 115, 141
   pan-Islamic ideology 155
   Balkan migrations 156
   fundamentalists 161, 164
Isma'il Ibn Haydar, shah 97-98, 101
Isma'il Paşa (later *khedive*) 146, 148, 156-157
Israel(is) *see* Jews
Istanbul 21, 86, 92, 126, 128-129, 134, 165, 177, 178, 183
Isthmus of Corinth 82
Istria 113
Italy/Italians 146, 154, 161, 165, 173, 178, 182
   naval dominance of Mediterranean 45
Ivan, Grand Prince of Muscovy 93
Iveron, monastery 87
Izmir (Smyrna) 73, 74, 182

J
Jabal Ahmar (Red Mountain) 99
Jalal al-Din Rumi 46
Jalayrids 48
Jan III Sobieski, king 116, 124-125, 134-135
"Janissary music" 136
Janissary troops 63, 85, 92 (panel), 102, 103, 104, 115, 122, 136, 153
Janos Hunyadi 77-80, 83
Jassy, Peace of 145

Jebei Noyan, Mongol commander 22
Jerusalem 100
jewellery 133
Jews/Jewish 60, 86, 89, 129, 141, 143, 179 *see also* Zionists
Jidda (Jeddah) 100
jihad 33, 122
Jingling Johnnie 136
Jochi, son of Ghengis Khan 22, 94
John V Palaeologus, emperor 39, 40, 41, 56
John VI Cantacuzenos, emperor 39, 40-41, 55
John VII Palaeologus, emperor 81
John VIII Palaeologus, 82
Jordan(ians) 179-180, 196
Juan-Juan, tribe 9
Judaism 9

K
kaba zurna wind instrument 137
   see also meterhane
Kadiköy (Chalcedon) 129
kadi provincial judge 138
Kalolimne island 37, 89
kapı halkı troops 103
Kapıkulu slave-soldiers 62, 77-78, 83, 85
Karaca Bey, beylerbei 83
Kara Halil Çandarli 62
Karakhanid Turks 11
Karaman beylik 48, 73
Karaman Oğulları (Karamanids) 48, 77, 96
Kara Mustafa Paşa, vizir 123, 125
Kara Timürtaş Gazi Evrenos 38, 39, 60
Karasi beylik 29, 37, 38-39, 90
Kasr-i Shirin, Treaty of 102, 115
Kay Khusraw *see* Keykhüsrev
Kemal, Mustafa (Atatürk) 143, 159, 175, 176, 183
Kenan, Engineer Lieutenant Yusuf 165
Keresztes, battle of 115
Keykhüsrev II, sultan 22-23
khaganates (turkish) 9
Khanate of Krim 94, 95, 116, 124
Khan, Shah Reza 182
Khazars 9
Khwarazm-Shah 22, 24
kings:
   Abd Allah of Iraq 179
   Alphonso V of Aragon 83
   Andrew III 52
   Charles VI of France 64
   Charles Robert I 52
   Faysal 177-180
   Francis I 106
   Francis II 140
   Gagik II 12
   Jan III Sobieski 116, 124, 125
   Leopold I 116
   Louis II of Hungary 108
   Louis the Great 52
   Sigismund of Hungary 52, 64, 65, 67
   Stefan III Cel Mare 93
   Stephan Dusan 54, 58-59
   Stephan Uros II 58
   Stephan Uros III 58
   Wakhtang VI of Georgia 145
   Wladislaw V 77, 79
   Yohannis of Ethiopia 157
Kipchaq Turks, tribe 10, 22, 55
Kizilibaş ('Red Caps') 102
Knights of Malta *see* Hospitallers
Knights of Rhodes *see* Hospitallers
Knights of St John *see* Hospitallers
Koehler, General 141
köke see cog

Konya 14, 46
kös war drum 136, 137 *see also meterhane*
Köse Dağ, battle of 23, 28
Köse Mihal 34, 38
Kosovo, battle of 79, 80
Koyunhisar (Bapheus), battle 33, 36
Kozmin forest, battle of 93
Küçük Kaynarca, Treaty of 144
kul (slave) 18
Kuloğlıs (sons of slaves) 122
Kumans, tribe *see* Kipchaq Turks
Kurds/Kurdistan 102, 106, 154-155, 162, 163, 182
Kütahya 29, 73, 74, 132
Kyustendil, battle of 58

L
labour force 126-127
Ladislaus V, king *see* Wladislaw V
Lake Assad 27
Latins/states 42–44, 45, 81-82, 88
Latin empire 42
Lausanne, Treaty of 184
Lavra Monastery 88 (panel)
law 138-139
Lawrence, T.E. 177, 180
Lazarevic, Prince Stephan of Serbia 64
Lebanon 105, 163, 178
Lemnos, island 83
Leninist revolution 177
Leopold I, king 116
Lepanto, battle of 114
Lesbos, island 88
levents, Ottoman marines 104
Libya 153, 154, 161, 165, 182
London, Treaty of 149
Longo, Giovanni Giustiani 85
Louis II, king of Hungary
Louis the Great, king 52
Lüleburgaz 55

M
Ma'an, Arab Druze clan 105
Macedonia/Macedonians 52, 55, 57, 59, 68, 74, 87, 143, 146, 156, 159
madrasa(s) 17, 126, 138
  Karaman 35
Maghrib (North Africa) 120
mağribis, North African/Berber troops 104
mahal/mahalles (districts) 126, 128, 129
Mahmut II, sultan 148, 151
mahonese associations 44
Malik Shah, sultan 14
Malkara 55
Malkhatun 27, 34, 63
Malkoğlu Bâlibey 112
Malta 110
Maltepe (Pelekanon), battle of 37
Mamluk(s) 26, 27, 46, 68, 71, 77, 94, 95–98, 116, 117, 145
Mangoup (Menkup)
  see Theodore Mangoup
Manuel I Comnenus, emperor 15
Manuel II Palaeologus, emperor 64, 81, 82
Manzikert, battle of 12, 14
Maritsa, river 88, 162, 183
Marj Dabiq, battle of 98
Marlow, Christopher 72
Maronite Christians 105, 163
Mecca 63, 96, 97, 99, 104, 118, 177
Mecidiye warship 172
Medina 96, 97, 99, 104, 118
Mediterranean Sea 21, 110, 119-120, 182
Mehmet I (Çelebi), sultan 74-76, 82
Mehmet II, the Conqueror, sultan 49, 76-79, 82-85, 86, 88, 126, 133

Mehmet IV, sultan 123, 125
Mehmet V, sultan 161, 173, 174, 177
Mehmet VI, sultan 184
Mehmetçik 176
Melami dervishes 46-47
Menteşe Oğulları (beylik) 50, 74, 76
mercenaries 29
Mesopotamia 22, 24, 25, 28, 106, 115, 130, 163, 178
Mesudiya warship 172
metalwork 133
mehterbaşı ağa band conductor 136
meterhane military band 135-137
  composition of 136-137
Mevelevi dervishes 46
Michael VIII Palaeologus, emperor 30
Mihaloğlu, family 34
millet communities 138, 141
Mir Ali, admiral 118
Mistra 89
Mohács, battle of 108
Moldavia/Moldavians 52, 80, 88, 93, 125, 145, 150-151
Mongol occupation 18
Mongols, 8-9, 10, 18, 21-23, 24-28, 30, 48-49, 55, 58, 93
  see also Golden Horde
Mongolia 8
Morea, The *see* Despotate of the Morea
mosques 34, 39, 126
  Ahmet I 128
  Aya Sofia 85
  Eski Cami 68
  Hüdavandigar 35
  İsa Ibn Muhammad Bey 31
  Süleymaniyye 126-127
  Üç Serefli Cami 68-69
  Ulu 35
Montenegro 152, 154, 162
Mount Athos 86-87
mouratoi infantry archers 62
Mozart, composer 136
Muavenet Milli torpedo boat 172
mufti solicitor 138 *see also fakih*
Muhammad Ali Paşa 146-150, 151, 156
Muhammad Sa'id Paşa 150
Muhammad Tawfiq, khedive 158
Murat I, sultan 57, 62, 68
Murat II, sultan 68, 76, 77-79, 80, 92
Murat III, sultan 114
Murat IV, sultan 102, 114
Musa, son of Bayezit I 73, 74, 82
  see also İsa, Mustafa, Süleyman
musalah 20
Muscovy 95, 116
müsellem horsemen 62
muslim(s) *see* Islam
Mustafa IV, sultan 148
Mustafa Kemal (Atatürk) 143, 159, 175, 176, 183
Mustafa, son of Bayezit I 73
  see also İsa, Musa, Süleyman
Myriokephalon, battle of 15

N
Napoleon III of France 156
Napoleonic Wars 115, 140-143, 145, 146, 151
Nasi, Duke Joseph of Naxos 89
Nasruddin Hoca 18
navy/navies 45–46, 50, 51, 57, 64, 67, 71, 76, 82-83, 89-92, 151
  Indian Ocean 97-98, 111
  Ottomans in Indian Ocean 116–120
  British influence on Ottomans 161
Naxos, island 89
nekkare ketle drum 136, 137
  see also meterhane
Neo-Mamluk Household System 145

Nestorians 25
Nezib, battle of 148
Nicopolis, battle of 52, 67, 68, 81
Niğde 35
Nile, river 27, 99-100
Niş (Nish) 77, 123
Nizam al-Jadid 147
Nizami Tunisian troops 153
North Africa 111, 115, 120-122, 152-153, 154, 161
Nuri, Lieutenant 166

O
Ögedey, son of Ghengis Khan 23
Oğulları *see also* beyliks
  Aydın 29, 31, 40, 51, 74, 76, 90
  Candar 49, 75
  Dulkadir 48, 77, 96, 98
  Eretna 48
  Germiyan 49
  Hamid 49-50
  Isfandiyar 49, 75
  Karaman 48, 76, 77, 96
  Menteşe 50, 74, 76
  Ramazan 49, 77
  Saruhan 51
  Teke 50
Oğuz Turks 9, 10–11, 12, 27, 48
Ohrid 35, 74
Oman/Omani 118-119
Orhan Bey, emir 33, 35, 39–42, 56–57, 62
Osman Bey 27, 33, 36
Osman Gazi 33, 136
Ottoman beylik 29, 33
Osmanlı, aircraft 166
Ottoman Turks/sultanate, general 9, 11, 52, 55, 70, 71, 74, 96, 135-137, 140
  army organization 62-64
  beginnings of decline 123
  civil war 74, 77
  early conquests 33
  end of Great War 185
  entry into Great war 168
  expansion 35–37, 55–57
  law 138-139
  meritocracy 115
  navy 45, 89-92
  origins 26-27, 33
  pan-Turkish nationalism 161
  Sick Man of Europe 154
Outremer 45

P
Pahlevi dynasty 182
painting *see* art
Palestine 172, 182
Pantokrater, monastery 87
Paris Peace Conference 181, 182
paşas, in Tripoli 152; in Egypt 158
Paulician heresy 53
Pavia, battle of 106
Peace of Amiens 146
Peace of Jassy 145
Peace of Svishtov 145
Péc 58
Pechenegs, tribe 10
Peleponnese 82
Persia *see* Iran
Persian Gulf 97
Peter the Great, czar 144, 145
Philadelphia (Alaşehir) 51
Philippopolis *see* Plovdiv
Philoteou, monastery 87
Piccolomini, Aeneas Sylvius (Pope Pius II) 89
pirates/piracy 43, 45, 50-51, 90, 111, 120, 121, 152
Piri Reis, seaman/cartographer 119

Pitcher, Donald, historian 33
Piyale Paşa 111
Phocaea (Foça) 51
Plethon 82
Plocnit, battle of 54
Plovdiv (Philippopolis) 55
Podolia (Ukraine) 116
Poland/Poles 52, 77, 92, 93, 95, 116, 124, 125, 147
Polovtsi, tribe *see* Kipchaq Turks
'Porte', the 135, 140, 146, 150
  authority in Sahara 153
  neutrality in Great War 168
Portugal/Portuguese 96, 97-98, 106, 116-118, 120
pottery *see* ceramics
pronoai fiefs 61 *see also timar* fiefs
Prousa *see* Brusa
punishments 138-139

Q
qadirğa, war galley 90, 91
qayïq, ship type 90, 91
Qala'at Jabar 27
Qansawh al-Ghawri, Mamluk sultan 98
Qaraj Ibn Dulkadir 48
Qara Qoyunlu tribe 71, 76
Qarluk tribal confederation 11
Qayï, clan 27
Qïlïch Arslan, sultan 14
Qutalmïsh, Süleyman Ibn 14

R
railroad(s) 163, 164
Ramazan Bey 49
Ramazan Oğulları 49
Rashid, battle of 146
Raydaniyah 99
Raydaniyah, battle of 99
Red Sea 97-98, 99, 108, 100, 116-117, 149, 173
rivers:
  Danube 27, 68, 70, 106, 140
  Don 95
  Euphrates 27, 28
  Maritsa 88, 162, 183
  Nile 27, 99-100
  Sangarios (Sakarya) 33, 35
  Syr Darya 11
  Tigris 27
  Volga 95
Republic of Turkey 184
Rhodes 110, 151, 161
River Kalka, battle of 22
Robe of the Prophet Muhammad 135
Roger de Flor 33, 51
Romania 10, 151, 154
Romanus IV, emperor 14
Rudolf II, HR Emperor 115
Rum, Seljuq sultanate 14-23, 24-25, 26–28, 29-30, 46, 48-49, 136
Rumelia (Rumeli, Rum Ili) 57, 61, 68-69, 74, 77, 83, 113, 123
Rumeli Hisarı 82 *see also* Anadolu Hisarı
Russia/Russians 10, 22, 69, 88, 94, 95, 102, 116, 123, 140, 144-145, 148, 150, 156, 161, 183
  Great War 168-169, 173-178

S
Sadık, Lieutenant 166
Safavids (Safaviyya) 96, 97, 101-102, 106, 111, 115, 124
St Catherine, monastery 87
St Gothard, battle of 116
St Irene, church of 134
Saladin 21
Salonica/Salonika *see* Thessaloniki
Samanids 11

sancak bey military governor 138
sancak(s) 62, 92 (panel), 139
Sangarios (Sakarya), river 33, 35
Santa Sophia 85 *see also* Aya Sofia
Sanussi reformist movement 153, 161, 173
Sarıkamış, battle of 173
Saruhan beylik/Oğullari 51, 74
Sassanian Persians 9
Sa'ud, Abd al-Aziz ibn 164
Saudi Arabia 164
Saudis 181
Sauramtes, tribe *see* Kipchaq Turks
scutum bosniensem 53
Sea of Azov 116
Sea of Marmara 35–37, 51, 83, 89, 126, 172
sekbans, Ottoman military dog handlers 104
Second Balkan War 162, 165
Selçuk 31
Selim I, sultan and caliph 98-100, 102, 105
Selim II the Sot, sultan 114-115
Selim III, sultan 148
Seljuq sultanate of Rum *see* Rum
Seljuq, Turkish leader 11
Seljuq Turks (general) 9, 10-11, 12
Selman Reis, Ottoman admiral 119
Serbia/Serbians 53-55, 58-60, 74, 77, 79, 80, 83, 87, 106, 151, 154, 162
Şeriat law 36, 138
Sèvres, Treaty of 182
Shaykh Edebali 27, 33, 63
Sharia *see* Şeriat
Sharif Husayn 177 *see also* Hashemites
Sharifian Arab Revolt 177
Shervashidze, Prince 23
Shi'a(s) 36, 46, 47, 96, 101-102, 106, 115, 141
Sigismund of Hungary, king 52, 64, 67
silahtar troops 63, 64
Sinan, architect 126
Sinan Paşa, seaman 121
sipahi cavalry 63, 70, 103, 116, 122
Sivas, siege of 70
Skanderbeg (George Castriota, Iskander Bey) 55, 79
slaves/slavery 18, 46, 82, 94, 146
Slavs 55
Smyrna *see* Izmir
Socotra, island 97
Sofia 77
Sokullu Mehmet Paşa, vizir 111
Spain/Spanish 147
Sphrantzes, George 83
Stack, Sir Lee 181
Stavronikita, monastery 87
Stefan III Cel Mare, king 93
Stephan Dusan, emperor 54, 58-59
Stephan Lazarevic, prince of Serbia 64
Stephan Tvrtko 54
Stephan Uros II, king 58
Stephan Uros III, king 58
Stoker, Bram 80
Styria 113
Suakin 100, 118
subaşi officer 62, 138
Sübodei, Mongol commander 22
Sudak (Soldaia) 22
Sudan 146-149, 154, 157, 163, 181
Südde-i Seadat 135
Suez Canal 99, 156, 173, 181
Sufis *see* dervishes
Süleyman II the Magnificent, sultan 106-111, 112, 114, 118, 126
Süleyman Ibn Qutalmïsh 14
Süleymaniyye, mosque 126, 127
Süleyman Paşa, admiral 118, 119

Süleyman Paşa (Captain Séve) 146
Süleymanşah 27
Süleyman, son of Bayezit I 74, 81-82 *see also* İsa, Musa, Mustafa
Süleyman, son of Orhan Bey 40-41, 56-57
sultans:
  Abdul Hamid II 154-155, 159, 160
  Abd'l Mecid 143
  Abdulaziz 143
  Bayezit I 49-51, 64, 67, 68, 70-73, 81-82
  Bayezit II 98
  Keykhüsrev II 22-23
  Mahmut II 148, 151
  Malik Shah 14
  Mehmet I (Çelebi) 74-76, 82
  Mehmet II (the Conqueror) 49, 77-78, 82-85, 86, 88, 126,133
  Mehmet IV 123, 125
  Mehmet V 161, 173, 174, 177
  Mehmet VI (Vaheddin) 184
  Murat I 57, 62, 68
  Murat II 68, 76, 77-79, 80, 92
  Murat III 114
  Murat IV 102, 114
  Mustafa I 114
  Qansawh al-Ghawri (Mamluk) 98
  Qïlïch Arslan 14
  Selim I, and caliph 98-100, 102, 105
  Selim II the Sot 114-115
  Selim III 148
  Süleyman II the Magnificent 106-111, 114, 117-118, 126
  Tuman Bey II (Mamluk) 98-100
Sunni(s) 36, 46-47, 96, 102, 105, 106, 115, 141
Svishtov, Peace of 145
Syr Darya river 11
Syria 103-104, 162-163, 178-179, 180, 181
Szapolyai, János 108

T

Tabka High Dam 27
Tabriz 106
Talat Paşa 174
Tamerlane *see* Timur-i Lenk
T'ang Chinese 9
Tanzimat reforms 143, 158
Tarnovo 55
Tatar Pazarcik (Pazardzhik) 76
Tavşancıl (Philokrene), battle of 37
taxes/taxation 17
Tedisio d'Oro 44
Teke beylik/Oğullari 50, 76
Tekirdağ (Rhaedestum) 55
tekkes 47
textiles 19
Theodore Mangoup, principality 88, 94
Thessalonica (Thessaloniki, Salonika) 39, 86, 92, 159
Thirty Years War 115
Thököly, Prince Imre 123
Thomas, despotate of Morea 83, 88
Thrace 40, 41, 51 (panel), 55-57, 68, 162, 182, 183
Threshold of Bliss *see* Südde-i Seadat
Tien Shan mountains 11
timar fiefs 28, 61 *see also* iqta fiefs
Timur-i Lenk 49, 50, 70-73, 75
topcı başi artillery commander 146
Topkapı Sarayı (Palace) 133-135
Töregene Khatun 23
trade 19, 20-21, 44, 50, 64, 93, 97, 104, 106
Transoxania 11, 21, 22
Transylvania/Transylvanians 52, 80, 109, 115, 116, 125
Treaty of Belgrade 144
Treaty of Buczacz 116
Treaty of Kasr-i Shirin 102, 115
Treaty of Küçük Kaynarca 144
Treaty of Lausanne 184
Treaty of London 149
Treaty of Sèvres 182
Treaty of Vasvár 116
Trebizond (Trabzon) 21, 40, 48, 56, 71, 77, 83, 93, 182
Tripoli/Tripolitania 121, 146, 152-153
tüfek, handgun 91-92
tüfenkcis, Kurdish musketeers 104
tuğ ensign 61
Tulip Period 131, 133
Tuman Bey II, Mamluk sultan 98-100
Tunis/Tunisia 121, 152-153
Turahan Bey 88
Turcomans 12, 26, 27, 28, 29, 30, 33, 35, 61-62, 73, 102, 130
  see also akinci(s)
Turgut Reis, Barbary corsair 111
Turkey 102
  Republic of 184
Turkish culture 12, 14, 15-17, 25, 30-31, 33, 46, 70, 126, 128, 130-131, 135-137, 165
Turks, general 8-9
T'u-kiu, T'u-chüeh *see* Turks
Tvrtko, Stephan 54
Tzympe 41, 58

U

uç (frontier) 57, 60, 70
Üç Serefli Cami 68-69
ulema legal-religious scholar 138
Uluç 'Ali, Barbary corsair 111, 119-121
Uludağ (Mount Olympus) 35
Ulu Mosque 35
Umur Bey 40, 50, 90, 91
Umur Han family 37
Unholy Alliance 106
United Kingdom of Great Britain *see* Britain
Uros II, King Stephan 58
Uros III, King Stephan 58
Üsküdar (Scutari) 37, 47, 129
Üsküp (Skopje) 59
Uzes, tribe *see* Oğuz

V

vakıf tax system 17, 126
Varna 79, 82
  battle of 79
Vasvár, Treaty of 116
Vedrine, Jules 166
Venice/Venetians 41, 43-45, 50, 64, 72-73, 83, 89-90, 92, 94, 111, 113
Venizelos, Greek Prime Minister 182
Vidin 55, 67, 70
Vienna, sieges of 108, 123-125, 136
Vlachs 55
Vlad Dracul II, voyvoda of Wallachia 80
Vladislav II, voyvoda of Wallachia 80
Vlad Tepes 80, 93
Volga Bulgars 9
Volga, river 95
von Moltke, Helmuth 148
von Sanders, General Liman 175
voyvoda (governor) 77

W

Wahabi Islamic fundamentalists 164
Wakhtang VI, king of Georgia 145
Wallachia/Wallachians 52, 58, 77, 80, 88, 92-94, 125, 150-152
Wasif, poet 142
weapons 62, 84, 90-92, 99-100, 102, 111, 166
Whirling Dervishes *see* Mevlevi
Wilson, President Thomas Woodrow 182
Wladislaw V, king 77, 79
World War I *see* Great War

Y

Ya'qub II 49, 77
Ya'rubid Omani dynasty 118
yasa law 36
yaya foot soldiers 62
Yemen 100, 141, 143, 154, 164, 173, 177, 180
Yeni-Baçhe (New Garden) 128
Yeniçeri troops *see* Janissary
yerlı kullan local Syrian Janissaries 103
yol ağa (road commander) 146
Yohannis, king of Ethiopia 157
Young Turks, the 158-162, 177
yürük warriors 57, 62
Yusuf Ibn Mulhim, emir 105
Yusuf Kenan, Engineer Lieutenant 165

Z

Zaccaria brothers 43
Zaporogian Cossacks 144
Zayla 100, 118
Zionists 179
Zouave regiments 123
Zrinyi, Nicholas 123